JOURNEYS TO OXFORD

Nine Pragmatic Inquiries
Into the Practice of Values in
Business and Education

Journeys to Oxford

Nine Pragmatic Inquiries
Into the Practice of Values in
Business and Education

Talks by F. Byron (Ron) Nahser, Ph.D.

Delivered at the International Conferences
on Social Values in Education and Business (1991–2008)

Oxford Centre for the Study of Values in Education and Business,
Departments of Educational Studies,
University of Oxford

This book is part of the
International Journal of Decision Ethics (IJDE) Monograph Series on
Studies in Decision Science of Management and Economics

Sponsors: University of Oxford, UK; Global Scholarly Publications

General Editor: Samuel M. Natale

IJDE is published by
Global Scholarly Publication, New York, NY

Typeset with pdfLaTeX by
Michael Goerz

ISBN: 1-59267-102-0

Distributed by
Global Scholarly Publications
220 Madison Avenue, Suite 11G
New York, NY 10016
www.gsp-online.org
books@gsp-online.org
Phone: (212) 679-6410 Fax: (212) 679-6424

International Journal of Decision Ethics
Sponsors and Co-Sponsors

Sponsor:

Department of Educational Studies,
University of Oxford, UK

Co-Sponsors:

Department of Humanities and Information Technology,
Russian Academy of Natural Sciences,
Moscow, Russian Federation

Institute of Philosophy,
Chinese Academy of Social Sciences,
Beijing, PRC

Philosophy Department,
Pontificia Universitas Lateranensis,
Rome, Italy

Center for Dialogue Among Civilizations,
Vienna, Austria

Department of History and Philosophy,
State University of New York at Old Westbury
New York, USA

To my companions,

Br. Leo V. Ryan, CSV, *and*

Dr. Samuel M. Natale, (D.Phil Oxon),

who put me on the path of these Oxford Journeys.

Contents

List of Figures   xiii

List of Tables   xvii

Acknowledgements and Dedication   xix

Preface   xxiii

Prologue   xxvii

Introduction   xxxvii
- Background xxxviii
- A Word of Warning about this Journal xl

1   Pouring Old Wine Into New Wineskins…Again!   1
- 1.1   Introduction 1
- 1.2   Fribourg Union's Utopian Ideal 2
- 1.3   Catholic Social Teaching 5
- 1.4   America's Labor Crises 7
- 1.5   Productivity and Quality 10
- 1.6   Conclusion 13

2   Peircean Pragmatism and the Social Values of American Business   15
- 2.1   Introduction 15
- 2.2   The Pragmatism of Charles Sanders Peirce 16
- 2.3   Application of Pragmatism in Contemporary American Business 22
- 2.4   Conclusion 28

3 Learning to Read the Signs: Reclaiming Pragmatism for American Business and Education   **31**

   3.1   Introduction 31

   3.2   Pragmatism 32

   3.3   Dialogue 34

   3.4   The Practice – a Notebook 35

   3.5   Pragmatism and Advertising 38

   3.6   Reclaiming Pragmatism for American Business . . . 42

   3.7   The Monastic Model 44

   3.8   Conversation 45

   3.9   Conclusion 47

4 What's _Really_ Going On: Creating the Need for Philosophical Inquiry, and How to Do It   **49**

   4.1   Engaging Executives on the Corporate Level 50

   4.2   The Need for a Method of Thinking 51

   4.3   Brand Analysis as a Corporate Narrative 55

   4.4   Personal Narrative 55

   4.5   Conclusion 61

5 Pragmatism: Putting Philosophy to Work in Business   **63**

   5.1   Introduction 63

   5.2   The Advertising Business 65

   5.3   Pragmatism: Classic American Philosophy 67

   5.4   Putting _PathFinder_ Pragmatic Inquiry® to Work . . 73

   5.5   Conclusion 80

6 Business as a Calling; The Calling of Business: A Pedagogical Model and Practice   **83**

   6.1   Introduction 83

   6.2   Can We Teach Character in Business Schools? 86

   6.3   Student Challenges 89

6.4   The Corporate Challenge 91

6.5   Pedagogical Model: A Literature Review 97

6.6   Methodology 100

6.7   The Practice Using the Model 102

6.8   Results 108

6.9   Discussion 113

6.10 Recommendations for the Future 115

7   Uncovering the Values Driving Organizational, Career and Personal Strategies: The Case for PathFinder Pragmatic Inquiry   119

7.1   Introduction 119

7.2   The Premise 120

7.3   The Decisions Made 121

7.4   The Purpose of Business 123

7.5   Marketing Relationships – Three Targets 125

7.6   How to Think About Values 127

7.7   Conclusion 129

8   Marketing as Storytelling: Pragmatic Inquiry's Religious Foundations and Practical Applications   131

8.1   Introduction 131

8.2   Challenges Today 132

8.3   Signs 136

8.4   Abduction 137

8.5   Josiah Royce: Peircean Interpreter 139

8.6   Max Scheler: "Relatively Pragmatic." 143

8.7   Decision Making in Marketing 147

8.8   *PathFinder* Pragmatic Inquiry and Decision Making . 150

8.9   Practicing PathFinder Pragmatic Inquiry 153

8.10 Conclusion 157

9   **Where Do Conflicts Begin? An Inquiry into the Need for Inquiry in Management Education**   **159**

9.1   Introduction – Purpose 159

9.2   Conflict as Story 163

9.3   Conflict as Individual Inquiry 165

9.4   Conflict in Education and Business 174

9.5   Sustainable Management 179

9.6   Nature and Our Place In It 183

9.7   Conflict as War 187

9.8   Culture's Role in Conflict Today 188

9.9   Conclusion 190

Epilogue
The Path Ahead: What's *Really* Going on...and What Can I Do about It?   **195**

The Importance of Balance 195

The Purpose of Management Education 197

Context – Out of Balance 198

Continuity – Moving In and Out of Balance 199

Fallibilism – The Way to Learn 204

Begin Again – The Search for Balance 205

Appendix
Presidio World College Educational Philosophy – Our Values   **207**

Competencies Expected of Presidio MBA Graduates 209

Sustainable Management – Definition 211

Notes   **213**

Bibliography   **243**

List of Figures

*Source: Beyond Entrepreneurship, Jim Collins and William Lazier

Figure 4.1
Importance of Values Driving
Strategy, p. 53

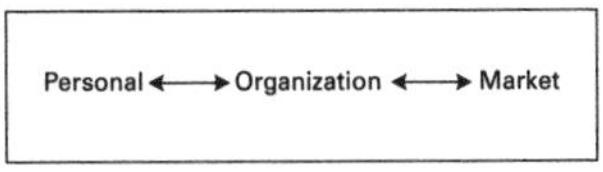

Figure 5.2
PathFinder Pragmatic Inquiry®
Relationships, p. 74

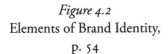

Figure 4.2
Elements of Brand Identity,
p. 54

Figure 5.1 Three Elements of
Strategic Relationships, p. 67

Figure 5.3
Economic Relationship with the
Other – The application of
relationship thinking, p. 82

xiii

Figure 6.1
PathFinder Strategic
Relationships, p. 101

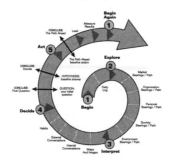

Figure 6.2
Corporantes *PathFinder*
Notebook© Model, p. 102

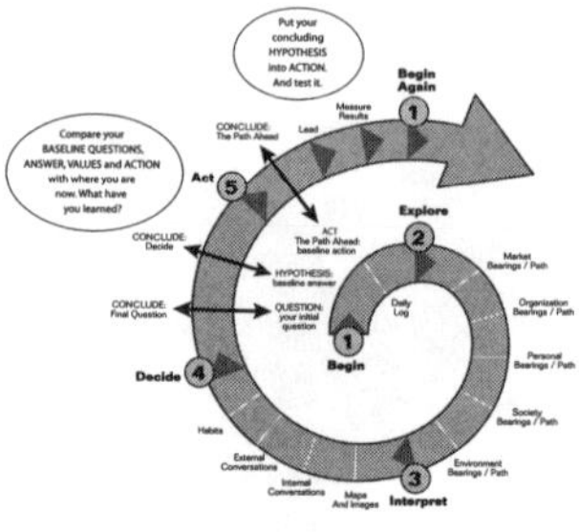

Figure 8.2
Corporantes *PathFinder*
Notebook© Steps, p. 156

Figure 7.1, 8.1
Strategic Relationships,
p. 126, p. 155

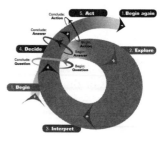

Figure 9.1
The Pragmatic Inquiry® Steps,
p. 168

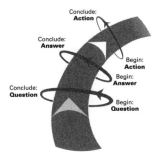

Figure 9.4
Hierarchy of
Job/Career/Calling, p. 180

Figure 9.2
"What Have You Learned?",
p. 169

Figure 9.5
Strategic Relationships, p. 184

Figure 9.3
Presidio School of Management
Curriculum, p. 176

Figure 1
Values-driven Model of Supply
and Demand, p. 201

Note: These figures and diagrams, beginning in 1997, show the movement of the overall project of developing the method of inquiry – the evolution of the language and graphic images to describe the method. The "Brand Identity" chart moved into the "Strategic Relationship" charts which grew to show how these relationships are embedded in the "Society" and then later to point out the obvious that we all exist within the "Environment." Also, it took more time than it should have for me to realize that the *Question* is at the center of the inquiry (Figure 9.5 – *Strategic Relationships*), not *Values* (at the center of all the preceding *Strategic Relationships* figures). That is because the *Question* driving the inquiry tests and ultimately determines the *Values* guiding the answer.

The Pragmatic Inquiry Spiral was developed along the way to explain the movement of the Inquiry. It took on a less mechanical and more organic look (Figure 9.1). We highlight the "learning" step. (Figure 9.2) which leads to what we have found is the most important step: *Begin Again.* And we conclude with the "Values-Driven Marketing Model" (Figure 1) which completes the strategy picture structured around the crux point of customer/organization exchange.

Finally, we have recently renamed the workbook, originally called the "*PathFinder* Notebook," to the "*PathFinder* Lab Journal" to better reflect this testing and learning continuum of inquiry. This core benefit of Pragmatic Inquiry has become clear in reflecting on the *journey* of ideas in developing and giving these talks over the past 17 years.

List of Tables

6.1 A Survey of Student Opinions 116
6.2 Personal Ethics & Corporate Culture, Business Seniors
     vs. Non-Business Seniors   117
6.3 Personal Ethics & Corporate Culture, Before & After . . 118

Acknowledgements and Dedication

My debt to academia is enormous. Many scholars have taken the time to help guide an earnest business executive through decades of struggle with the questions of values, purpose and goals; and their role in business strategy, branding and performance. While I learned an equal amount and different lessons from my business associates over the years (a story I tell in *Learning to Read the Signs*), this book is dedicated to my teachers.

The journeys to England every other year over the past seventeen years have been possible mainly due to the conference organizers in England: members of the Department of Educational Studies, particularly John Wilson (deceased), Richard Pring, Director Emeritus, and Geoffrey Hayward, University Lecturer in Educational Studies.

I would like to thank Jack Ruhe, my long-time colleague and co-author of Chapter 6, our reviewers: James O'Toole, Daryl Koehn (both Oxford graduates and Rhodes Scholars), Wally Olins, Oxford graduate and professor as well as a leading branding expert, and Richard Gray, founder of Presidio World College for their thoughtful reading and remarks. Also Karen Speerstra for her expert, thorough and critical editing. And always to my long-time administrative associates, Florence Agosto and Maeve Kanaley, and to my family for their constant support, led by my wise and caring wife, Mary.

This volume is specifically dedicated to Dr. Samuel M. Natale, (D. Phil. Oxon.) for his patient, hard-working and insightful encouragement who shepherded all the efforts of a wonderful group of scholars and practitioners over the past seventeen years and who long ago took me into his care. I am most grateful for his efforts to bring these papers into this volume. And secondly, to Br. Leo V. Ryan, CSV, my mentor and dear friend for over twenty-five years since he became dean of the Kellstadt Graduate School of Business at DePaul University and brought me in as their first executive-in-residence. I am grateful for his support and for introducing me to Sam many years ago, which began this particular journey.

Sam and Leo are outstanding examples of teachers who pass on the passion for education by igniting the fire in so many. I am honored to be among their legion of students and colleagues.

Finally, while this is a report of my journeys to Oxford University, I wish to acknowledge the many journeys I have made to other distinguished universities – places which, more than other kinds of institutions, draw inquirers together – and the colleagues and students with whom I have worked in the discussions about the practice of corporate strategy, branding, values, purpose and pragmatic inquiry. Some of these encounters were brief; others extending over decades. But each opened up another path to broaden and deepen the inquiry.

In approximate chronological order: Francis Phelan CSC, Oliver Williams CSC, Alasdair MacIntyre, Eugene Halton, Leo Burke, Patrick Murphy, David Hayes and Carolyn Woo, *University of Notre Dame*; Fr. Kenneth Simpson, Lawrence Lavengood, Sidney Levy, Philip Kotler, Michelle Buck, David Besanko, and David Messick, *Northwestern University Kellogg School of Management*; Ronald Miller, *Lake Forest College*; Manuel Velasquez, *University of Santa Clara;* Herman Reuther, Mary Evelyn Jegen SND, Russell Barta, James Kenney, Matthew Fox, and Byron Sherwin, *Mundelein College/Loyola University Chicago*; Wolfgang Schirmacher, *New School for Social Research*: Robert Faulhaber, Fr. Thomas Munson, Stephen Houlgate, William Waters, Manfred Frings, Dennis McCann, Daryl Koehn, David Krell, Laura Hartman, Kenneth Thompson, Scott Kelley and Patricia Werhane, *DePaul University*; Marge Tuite OP, James Hug SJ, and William Thompson SJ, *The Jesuit School of Theology in Chicago*; Charles McCoy and David Krueger, *Center for Ethics and Social Policy*; Ira Progoff, *Dialogue House;* Thomas Duffy, *Institute for Applied Social Logic*; Jack Ruhe, *St. Mary's College*; Willis Harman, Rinaldo Brutoco and George McCown, *World Business Academy;* Michael Ray,

Stanford University GSB; Fr. John Lodge, *University of St. Mary of the Lake/Mundelein Seminary*; James Kuhn, *Columbia University Business School*; Kuniko Miyanaga, *Tama University*; Shuzo Abe, *Yokohama National University*; Kakichi Kadowaki SJ, *Sophia University*; Toshio Matsuoka, *Kanagawa University*; Robert Wargo, *PHP Institute - Matsushita Group*; William Locander, *Jacksonville University*; Michael Stebbins, *Gonzaga University*; Alyssa Groom and Ron Arnett, *Duquesne University*; Vicki Klutts and Donald Parker, *Beta Gamma Sigma*; Drazen Kapusta and Ante Glavas, *Cotrugli Business Academy*; David Banner, *Viterbo University*; Peter Davis, *University of Leicester*; Debra Arvenitz, *Villanova University*; Kenneth Goodpaster and Laura Nash, *Harvard Business School;* James Haefner, *University of Illinois*; David Cooperrider, *Case Western Reserve University*; Anne Carr BVM, Martin Marty, Harry Davis, Linda Ginzel, and Robert Fogel, *University of Chicago*; Robert Bellah, Kellie McElhaney and David Vogel, *University of California, Berkeley*; John Haughey and James Nolan, *Georgetown University*; Molly Burke, *Dominican University*; Gifford and Libba Pinchot and Rick Bunch, *Bainbridge Graduate Institute;* Geoffrey Cox and James Goodrich, *Alliant International University*; Ralph Wolff, *Western Association of Schools and Colleges;* and, most recently, all my colleagues and students at *Presidio School of Management*.

I attempt in this volume to partially repay my enormous debt to these faculty members and students by igniting the fire of inquiry and imagination in others to guide their journeys.

F. Byron (Ron) Nahser, PhD

Provost Emeritus,
Presidio School of Management
The Presidio, San Francisco, CA
and
Managing Director,
Corporantes, Inc.
Evanston, IL

Preface

"We don't receive wisdom; we must discover it for ourselves after a journey that no one can take for us or spare
us."

Marcel Proust

"I criticize by creation – not by finding fault."

Marcus Tullius Cicero

Over twentyfive years ago now, John Wilson and I (then Co-
directors of the Foundation for Education in Religion and Morality) were sitting in the "Rose and Crown" in Oxford after giving a
joint seminar on "Moral and Ethical Education" at the Department
of Educational Studies. At that time we were completing a book and
trying to find a way to institutionalize ongoing reflection in the areas
of moral and ethical education.

Our goal was to invite important thinkers to join us on a biennial
retreat during which we discussed not only the shifting groundwork
in thinking in this domain but real world application of the models
to daily life. In addition, we wanted to marry the theoreticians with
practitioners so that something new might be created. Our dream was
to move from vague or overly static points of view to more appropri-
ately flexible and useful ways of thinking.

Our ultimate goal was to provide an arena for a mutual exchange
of ideas. We were both weary of meetings dedicated to attacks and
counter-attacks where the result was spurious victory for the person
armed with more academic sources.

We sought, let me use that word, *truth*. That is to say, we sought to
avoid the continual carping characteristic of so many academic gatherings and to move toward a more communal approach where we as-
pired to create something new, something the result of our individual
and common journeys.

One of the most significant fruit ("special fruit" as Cardinal New-man would refer to it) that has emerged from these retreats has been Ron Nahser's *Journeys to Oxford*, which is a series of talks given at the conference over many years. The result is this important collection, more accurately entitled: *The Development of a Method of Pragmatic Inquiry to Practice Values in Education and Business.* It is important not only for its rigorous thinking and application but also because it lights a path that reflects one person's journey to integration.

These talks are situated within a context that has been referred to by Robert Perloff as "justly and widely celebrated series of interna-tional conferences on social values in education and business." These meetings, in turn, arose from an environment where there is grow-ing concern as to how one approaches the topic of morality in a post modernist world.

Clearly the debate has gone on for centuries at Oxford (as Richard Pring's *Prologue* makes clear) but it is exacerbated by social movements in England wherein universities have been literally created overnight in cyberspace and where social change found former colleges and vo-cational schools designated as universities without any preparatory transition...where issues of morality and ethics have been consigned to the Philosophy Departments rather than to the vital worlds of busi-ness and education. The same dynamics are impacting the engage-ment of these issues in schools of business around the world.

It is the fundamental presumption of Ron's work that moral ed-ucation should, can and must be applied to business as it has been to areas of faith and morals. This book aims at leaders to enable them to move forward with energy and direction. It empowers them to un-derstand that "[...] wisdom itself springs ultimately from reflection upon experience."[1] It energizes their moral compass.

In these chapters, the reader will find real world methods to a-chieve congruence between *affective* and *cognitive* components in the business executive. These chapters track the development of pragmatic inquiry, which helps business practitioners –and anyone in an organization, charged with developing and implementing strategy – make better, sustainable, moral decisions.

These talks show the path one executive has taken in the search for meaning midst the conflicts and confusion that we all face, especially in business. As you read these talks, consider your own story: how you have made decisions and how your career has developed. Reflect on how your career has been guided in the pursuit and practice of the values and ideas which help each of us approach and engage the seemingly overwhelming problems and challenges we face today.

In the final analysis, the purpose of Pragmatic Inquiry is to help us reflect on our experiences in order to gain the insights and wisdom to make the best business and career decisions, philosophically supported, for the good of all – to foster a just and sustainable world.

In summary, this book provides a roadmap, which teaches a way to uncover the tasks and responsibilities that makes life worth living, (the finding of one's "calling") especially in business and industry.

Samuel M. Natale, D. Phil. (Oxon.)

Director of Research and Funding,
Centre for Social Values in Education and Business
Senior Research Associate,
Department of Educational Studies,
University of Oxford, England
and
School of Business
Adelphi University
Garden City, New York 11530

Prologue

Ron Nahser's *Journeys to Oxford* has given an interesting and valuable plot development to a very old story. That story, exemplified in Oxford over the last two centuries, concerns the struggle for the soul of education, particularly higher education. It might be depicted as a contest between a liberal understanding of education and a much more utilitarian one.

Nahser's embracing of the Pragmatists and particularly of John Dewey and his "pragmatism" is significant here, because Dewey above all scorned the dualisms between mind and body or between academic and vocational – dualisms upon which so much of our educational thinking and practice are built. In overcoming those dualisms, one perhaps needs to think more pragmatically in the truly philosophical meaning of that word, which Nahser develops through the talks which comprise the Journal.

By way of Prologue I want to see that opposition historically, for such an historical perspective might help in the overcoming of it – as indeed Dewey both would and did, seeing the organization of knowledge and ideas as a reflection of broader social and economic patterns. And Nahser, in these talks builds on Dewey's understanding of pragmatism to develop a practice of reflection – Pragmatic Inquiry – to help business executives practice sustainable management, taking into account and basing their decisions on these broader patterns.

It is comparatively recent in British history when universities educated only those who belonged to an intellectual and social elite. Whilst the percentage of young people who entered higher education less than fifty years ago was only 6%, university education was, and could be seen as, liberal in the sense of enabling that small minority to pursue 'intellectual excellence', as described by John Henry Newman in 'The Idea of a University'. He defined it as:

"[...] Liberal. A habit of mind, this form lasts through life of which the attributes are freedom, equitableness, calmness, moderation, and wisdom; or where in a former discourse I have ventured to call a philosophical habit [...]

Will practical objects be obtained, better or worse, by its cultivation? To what then does it lead, where does it end, what does it do, how does it profit, what does it promise, what is the fruit of such a philosophy. I am asked: What is the end of university education, and the Liberal, and Philosophical Knowledge in which I conceive it to impart? Knowledge is capable of being its own end."[1]

And in the pursuit of such intellectual excellence, other exponents of this 'liberal ideal' might well argue with Michael Oakeshott that:

"liberal education is a difficult engagement [...] It is a somewhat unexpected invitation to disentangle oneself from the here and now of current happenings and engagements, to detach oneself from the urgencies of the local and the contemporary, to explore and enjoy a release from having to consider *things* in terms of their contingent features, *beliefs* in terms of their applications to contingent situations and *persons* in terms of their contingent usefulness [...]"[2]

For that reason, universities and schools need to be in places set apart so that the pursuit of intellectual excellence would not be interrupted by the 'busyness' (or 'business') of everyday life.

"In short, 'School' is 'monastic' in respect of being a place apart where excellences may be heard because the din of worldly laxities and partialities is silenced or abated."[3]

But the growth of the industrial society found such a liberal ideal increasingly irrelevant, cut off from, and indeed snobbish about, the development and application of that practical and technical knowledge which fuelled the growing economy – the world of manufacture and production, of overseas markets and entrepreneurship. Indeed, overlapping with Newman's life was that of William Richard Morris (later: Lord Nuffield), who, leaving school at fourteen, started working life repairing bicycles and finished that working life as the pioneer of car manufacturing in Britain – a genius of an engineer and of practical economics (he became one of the richest men in Britain). Despite his being an exemplary engineer, a genius in design and problem solving, he would have been treated with disdain by the liberally-educated dons of Oxford Colleges (until of course he donated so much of his millions to the University and its colleges). Indeed, he was refused membership to the local golf club because he was "in trade" – a problem easily solved by the purchase of the golf club. But he in turn treated them with a certain amount of disdain, refusing (so the legend goes) to employ anyone with a university degree because he thought it made them useless. He had a very different understanding of what it meant to be educated.

Oxford in many ways exemplified this dualism between an understanding of liberal education (exclusive, academic, disdainful of the practical and entrepreneurial) and a much more utilitarian one (also disdainful, but theoretically disconnected from the world of business and everyday life). Its legacy is symbolized by the juxtaposition of the original Morris factory in Longwall Street opposite the ancient Magdalen College and not far from Newman's first college of Trinity, or by the candlelit retreat or little monastery, Littlemore, of Newman and his disciples in Cowley on the outskirts of Oxford, surrounded by the vast factory complex of Morris and then Rover motor cars.

But one needs to be careful in polarizing the positions in such a picture. Voices there were amongst the advocates of liberal education for its relevance, at least to the world of the professions. In his inaugural address in 1867, when installed as Rector of Aberdeen University, John Stuart Mill did indeed argue that universities should not be places of professional education or vocational preparation as,

> "their object is not to make skilful lawyers, or physicians, or engineers, but capable and cultivated human beings."[4]

Universities were places where knowledge was pursued, where the intelligence was perfected, where that culture was acquired which,

> "each generation purposely gives to those who are to be its successors, in order to qualify them for at least keeping up, and if possible for raising, the level of improvement which has been attained."[5]

Education was about "improvement" not about being useful. However, it was also assumed that the educated and the cultivated person would *thereby* be useful. Mill argued that:

> "men are men before they are lawyers and if you make them capable and sensible men, they will make themselves capable and sensible lawyers [...] what professional men should carry away with them from an University is not professional knowledge, but that which should direct the use of their professional knowledge, and bring the light of general culture to illuminate the technicalities of a special pursuit."[6]

Furthermore, looked from the other side of the picture that of manufacture, of making and of producing, there were again voices who called upon the education of those very producers and processes.

Another Oxford William Morris (leader of the *Arts & Craft* movement) printed in 1872 the paper by John Ruskin in which he saw the dehumanizing results of the emerging industrial society.

> "The great cry that rises from all our manufacturing cities, louder than the furnace blast, is all in very deed for this, – that we manufacture everything there except men; we blanch cotton, and strengthen steel, and refine sugar, and shape pottery; but to brighten, to strengthen, to refine, or to form a single living spirit, never enters into our estimate of advantages."7

This 19th century debate is by no means disconnected from the themes of Ron Nahser's *Journeys.* How far can the practical, commercial and business worlds be, themselves part of the liberating educational tradition which was argued for by Newman, Mill and Morris? And how far does that liberal conception of education, which shapes the modern world, need to be broadened to encompass the productive and business activities pursued by the other William Morris, the motor car manufacturer, and his successors? Can we still agree with Edward Copleston, Provost of Oriel College (where Newman was a Fellow) who, in 1810, replied to the criticisms that the Universities of Oxford and Cambridge should reform an outdated system and prepare their students more effectively for the pressures and problems of the 19th Century, by arguing that the

> "purpose of the University is to counter the effects upon the individual of gross materialism [...] not to train directly for any specific profession but rather to develop an elevated tone and flexible habit of mind which would enable them to carry out with zeal and efficiency all the offices, both private and public, of peace and war ."8

That universities are now expected to develop more than "an elevated tone" would seem apparent, at least in England, from recent Government papers. For example, the recent "World Class Skills: the Leitch Review of Skills in England," speaks of the need for employers to become "empowered with the opportunity to exert real leverage and decision making over both the content and the delivery of skills and employment programs" and universities will be expected to be "increasingly responsive to what learning an employer actually want." Business facing " should be a description with which any higher education institution feels comfortable," and indeed one university has declared itself to be the first as business facing in all that it is going to do.

Oakeshott must be turning in his grave.

The variations in the argument about liberal education – between such 19th century luminaries as Newman, Mill, Huxley, Sidgwick and Arnold, all of whom endeavored to define it – were essentially about the degree of social usefulness which should temper the pursuit of intellectual excellence. Consequently, the argument concerned the degree to which the ideal of liberal education needs constantly to be renewed, as new knowledge, and new organizations of knowledge, transform our ideas of "social usefulness." But, whatever the variations, there remained the central significance given to the development of reason and to those studies which enhanced the capacity to know, to understand, to pursue the truth.

Dewey would have found his way through this by questioning first the "false dualisms" between the intellectual excellence and the "intelligent management of everyday life." Far from education taking place apart from the world of business, commerce, community or family, these forms of life were the very ones which, through education, needed to be illuminated – to be intelligent about. Experience is the source of knowledge, but the human organism needs constantly to reshape the understanding of that experience in the light of yet further experience and of the critical appraisal both from oneself and from others. Everything is grist to the mill, a reshaping of how one sees the world. But in so adapting to new experience and in anticipating further experiences and the consequences of one's actions in the world, one is able to draw upon what Dewey referred to as "the wisdom of the race," those bodies of knowledge, those disciplines of enquiry, which have been accumulated over generations but which themselves are but provisional guides, evolving in the light of further experience.

That "experiential continuum" between the sources of intellectual excellence and the everyday experience which each student brings to the academy was central to Dewey's pragmatic philosophy of education. He was equally disdainful of those who separated the "knowledge to be transmitted" from the knowledge of everyday life and of those who saw no relevance in that accumulated knowledge and wisdom to their practical making and doing.

After being some time on the "index of forbidden books," Dewey's writings are once again being read and in the case of this book, transforming the way in which the world of business might, in the words of John Dewey, be managed more intelligently. Education was concerned with the development of the distinctively human qualities – those which make our children more human and thereby able to shape the future and further development. That effort to make everyone more human must, of course, include the perfection of the intellect. After all, what is more distinctively human than the capacity to think and to act intelligently in the management of one's affairs? And what is best that has been thought and said other than what cultivates the intellect in its many different manifestations, practical as well as theoretical? But being human, and becoming more so, is the privilege of everyone, not of an intellectual elite. Each person, whatever his or her individual capacities and talents, is engaged in thinking and doing, in feeling and appreciating, in forming relationships and in shaping the future. All this can be engaged in more or less intelligently, more or less sensitively, more or less imaginatively. But that is possible only if those thoughts, feelings, relationships and aspirations are taken seriously and not contemptuously rejected as of no concern to the tradition of liberal education. And that requires bringing the educational ideal to the vocational interests of young people, educating them through their perception of relevance, helping them to make sense of their social and economic context, enabling them to be intelligent and questioning in their preparation for the world of work.

Philosophy of education needs a more generous notion of what it is to be human than what has too often prevailed or captured in the liberal ideal. Without such a notion, many young people have been dismissed as uneducable. A focus upon intellectual excellence has ignored the wider personal qualities informed by thought, feeling and various forms of awareness, which need nurturing, even if this must be for many in the context of the practical and the useful. The vocational alternative has, however, missed the point entirely by substituting a narrow form of training for a generous concept of education, transforming learning into an acquisition of measurable behaviors, reducing understanding and knowledge to a list of competences, turning educators into technicians. It was precisely the errors of this polarization which Dewey argued so strongly against.[9]

And, inspired by Dewey and the pragmatists, it is precisely to avoid these errors that led to the development of Pragmatic Inquiry, the story of which is told in the nine talks comprising the *Journal*. By showing the development and concluding with an outline of a plan for business learning (an MBA in Sustainable Management) Nahser has made these talks such a valuable contribution to the Oxford Centre's focus on values in education and business over the past seventeen years. And now combined in *Journeys to Oxford*, I trust they will now prove useful to a broader audience interested and engaged in this vital topic of learning and values in education and business and, most importantly, their practice in helping develop leaders who can be considered, in the best understanding, learners.

Richard Pring

Director (ret.),
Oxford University,
Department of Educational Studies,
Emeritus Fellow, Green College

Introduction

"[...] there is no task more crucial than reassessing the modern mode of inquiry."

Willis Harman[1]

Have you ever been seized by a question, concern, issue, or a problem you thought was so important that you felt it was leading you on a journey you had to take? And if you got an invitation to go to some hallowed place like Oxford to inquire about it, might you be tempted to go? I was ...and did. The result of those journeys is this series of lectures.

They tell the story, like a journal, of the development of an idea to understand the role of values in business decisions. The question driving the inquiry: "How do we ignite values and vision – personal and organizational – to drive business performance?"

What you will read is not the answer to that question or some ethical proposition. Rather, these talks trace the development of a method of inquiry to help practitioners determine for themselves, based on the evidence of their own experience, their underlying values, purpose and goals. Or to use an old fashioned word, to better determine their "calling": what work we need to do. Hunter Lovins puts it this way: "what you cannot *not* do." It's what work in the world gives you: meaning and fulfillment. This collection of lecture-essays tells the story of one person's efforts to understand the role which values play in business decisions and then how to put those values into action.

There are three reasons you might be interested in reading about a decade and a half development of the method of inquiry:

1. If you believe that each of us is on a path in life and there are streams of ideas, challenges, quests, projects, and ultimately a "calling" each of us has and needs to uncover in order to meet

these challenges and live our values, then this series of essays might help you reflect on your own and help others to find theirs.

2. If you believe that business and the practice of management can be such a calling or vocation in addressing the larger social and environmental questions we face today, you may find some reinforcement to draw your own conclusions on these vital questions.

3. If you enjoy a story, especially about the journey of a business executive who has been on the murky path of finding/following his calling in the creative and competitive world of marketing, then maybe you may find this an engaging tale of discovery.

The lectures are periodic snapshots or data points, like cairns one sees along mountain paths, in a journey – an arc of inquiry – that led me, over the seventeen years from CEO of The Nahser Agency/Advertising in Chicago, to the founding of Corporantes, Inc., a Values/Strategy/Branding division of the agency in 1994. Ten years later in 2004, I joined Presidio World College as the first Provost and Co-CEO to build their 1 year old MBA in Sustainable Management program. After growing the enrollment; and clarifying and refining the philosophy, curriculum, program and positioning – re-branding the program as Presidio School of Management – in 2008, I was conferred the title of Provost Emeritus.

Background

These Oxford journeys began innocently enough during a dinner conversation in Chicago in 1990 following a presentation at a quarterly "Nahser Agency/DePaul University Business Ethics Visiting Scholar

Series" presentation which our advertising agency co-sponsored and hosted with Br. Leo V. Ryan CVS, dean of DePaul University's Kellstadt Graduate School of Business. Samuel Natale, our distinguished speaker, casually asked toward the end of the evening, "Ron would you like to attend an inaugural Oxford University Department of Educational Studies conference at Cambridge University this summer?" Knowing only that it involved business ethics and conflict in some way, I jumped at the chance to attend such a gathering to discuss a topic near and dear to me in a place I had longed to see. It would also give me the opportunity to follow-up with Sam and learn more about what I had just heard: no stale, lifeless, obscure ethical theories and language, but practical concerns about ethical practice.

Two old friends and scholars (former teacher and student) from Oxford University's Department of Educational Studies, John Wilson and Samuel Natale, published a volume in 1990 sponsored by the Oxford University Trust and the University Press of America entitled "Ethical Contexts for Business Conflicts." The aim of the volume, containing a series of studies, was to clarify "one of the most vexing and ubiquitous problems of contemporary living – ethics and moral education [...] the work of the trust involves ongoing research into the area of moral education." Based on that idea, they co-founded the Center for the Study of Values in Education and Business at Oxford in 1991 and have held a series of conferences every other year since. Sam tells more of that story in his Preface.

While I was eagerly looking forward to my Oxford adventure, as the months rolled on, it increasingly dawned on me just how daunting the task would be to actually deliver a paper of some quality. I had given many talks to all kinds of professional and educational groups, but nothing remotely approaching this academic level. Would it be worth my time to make the long journey? But even more importantly, would I have anything of value to deliver to the distinguished and learned attendees convened at what they are quick to tell you is the "Athens of the North" (John Henry Cardinal Newman)?

My focus at the time was on how to run our advertising agency driven by principles of values – a unique positioning, I was often told, within our highly competitive profession. The first talk, as you will see, is built on the theme of *Rerum Novarum: On the Condition of the Working Class.* The purpose of the conference was to honor the 100th anniversary of this revolutionary encyclical, written by Pope Leo XIII, which launched the great and honored tradition of Catholic Social Teachings. This made the task of preparing the talk easier as these teachings, as I understood them, had long helped ground my basic instinct and interest in social and economic justice. Preparing for this talk also made clear to me the importance of looking on the organization as a system or organism within the larger society. This, as you will see, is a principle insight of sustainable management which figures prominently in the later talks.

As the years and subsequent conferences rolled on, my project and the talks centered more around a method of inquiry which was a way for practitioners to determine the values, purpose and goals which would drive their decisions. And this led to the deep concern with the way business and organizations determine how and why they will serve the needs of society sustainably, and how business schools help future leaders learn the practices of Sustainable Management, and the values driving them.

A Word of Warning about this Journal

You will see some repetition. Initially, it was not our intent to gather and publish these lectures together. One conference talk simply rolled into the next and the ideas built. These conferences were great opportunities for me to stop, at least once every two years, and collect my thoughts, reflect on the experiences and draw conclusions. Therefore, I was delighted and then immediately quite concerned to be asked, at the conclusion of my talk at the 8th OXSVEB in 2006 (Chapter 9), to bring them together into a progressive story of inquiry. My concern: *Would they hold up as a story, much less an engaging and instructive one?*

Since I couldn't expect some overworked regular conference attendee to remember from one conference to the next what I had said at the previous conference (in preparation for each conference, I had to re-read my talks to remember!), you will notice that some of the same background on pragmatism is covered at the start. Often, I couldn't think of a better way to express an idea, and I also wanted each talk to stand on its own. While there has been editing to delete obvious repetition, the intent is for you to see the movement of the overall project of developing the method of inquiry – and particularly the evolution of the language and graphic images to describe the method.

That said, I also confess that the only claim to originality is in the "packaging" of the ancient and current practice of moral reasoning (e.g. "Old Wine into New Wineskins" – Chapter 1) to answer the perennial questions concerning:

- What gives meaning, purpose and direction to our lives?

- How do we make decisions in business? What drives our strategies - that overly popular word to describe any organization operation?

- How do we educate managers – citizens – to make wise career and business decisions?

- What do we pay attention to? What are the most pressing problems today which call us to responsibility and action?

- What is the legacy which we wish to leave to future generations?

Some Background

When I gave the first talk in 1991, I had been teaching a course entitled "Marketing in a Changing Social Environment" at DePaul University as Executive in Residence for eleven years. Because several learned philosophers sat in on my classes and sternly informed me that I was really "teaching inquiry…and not well," I had begun the doctoral studies in Philosophy where I became engaged with the theory and practice of Pragmatism, Classic American Philosophy. In 1993, when I was struggling with writing my dissertation and feeling a bit overwhelmed, I felt the need to get away. Somewhere quiet yet inspiring, far from the daily press of the advertising business. Then I heard a "call": What better place to write than in Oxford? So I readily accepted an invitation to be Visiting Writer in Residence at Worcester College and spent a hard-working, monk-like summer completing the draft. In the middle of my residence, I walked across town to St. Catherine's College and gave my initial talk on Pragmatism at the second OXSVEB Conference.

This led to completing my dissertation titled *Learning to Read the Signs.* So, in addition to being the suspect CEO of an advertising agency, I arrived in 1995 for the third Conference as a newly minted PhD delivering a talk by the same name. (At the ripe age of 55; I was told I was known as a "late-bloomer" in the academic trade. You saw earlier in the "Acknowledgements and Dedication" the enormous debt of gratitude I owe to the many scholars who helped me along the way.)

I tell you this because it proves again the old adage that if you want to learn something, try teaching and writing it. The reason, of course, is that this forces you to articulate what you *think* you know and have it be challenged by a group of cynical, open-minded, and eager students, skeptical professional colleagues and learned scholars and finally a challenging dissertation committee. And perhaps it leads to talks at a distinguished center of learning once in a while.

As you will see in the chapters that follow, I have been applying Pragmatism (for many years unknowingly) to my work in our advertising and communications business for the past forty years. At the agency, we evolved over time a particular Branding Strategy which we call "*Own Who You Are*®" and have further developed Pragmatism into a practical method of Inquiry. The overall project has been to reclaim the practice of pragmatism for business.

Through these essays, I will present the broad scope of the promise of Pragmatic Inquiry®, as I have experienced and developed it with the help of thousands of executives, students and colleagues. Through these experiences, the hope is that you, the reader, will be able to apply the method to your own issues.

I conclude with a talk from the 8th Conference on "Ethical Conflict and the 'Sleep of Reason'" and an "Epilogue" from the 9th Conference. These gave me the opportunity to directly apply the Pragmatic Inquiry to business education and to one of the most pressing problems we face today: Sustainability, and how we might educate business leaders to practice Sustainable Management.

Journeys to Oxford fittingly begins with the Preface by Sam Natale, the co-founder of the Oxford University Centre for the Study of Values in Education and Business. The purpose of the conference sponsored by the Centre has specifically been to bring the responsibilities and tasks of education and business together.

The Prologue which follows the Preface is based on conversations over the years during the conferences (once held on his motorbike as we traveled around Oxford seeing the Newman/Morris sites) with Richard Pring, the Director Emeritus of the Department of Educational Studies at Oxford University and Fellow at Green College. Richard, the Co-Chairman of the Conference in recent years, has embraced the daunting challenge of bringing the two worlds of academia and business together: the two separate worlds traditionally called "education" and "training." He exemplified these two points by contrasting the beliefs and practices of two of Oxford's famous and very different citizens: John Henry Cardinal Newman and the automobile magnet, William Richard Morris. You will see that Richard Pring brings the two worlds together with the sturdy bridge of "learning."

Finally, I hope the readings give some insight and aid into the most basic and worthwhile work any of us can do: the pursuit of our own calling – the work we must do to help foster a just and sustainable world...and lead a meaningful life.

Chapter 1

Pouring Old Wine Into New Wineskins...Again!
A Commentary on Rerum Novarum: On the Condition of the Working Class

1st International Conference
on Social Values in Education and Business
Cambridge University – July, 1991

"The corporation is a legal fiction with no pants to kick
or soul to damn, and, by God, it ought to have both."

Judge Roy Bean

1.1   Introduction

It may come as a surprise to most contemporary American business managers that the discussions and concepts of the Fribourg Union, a now obscure group of Catholic European noblemen, industrialists, and clergy who met regularly in the late 19th century in Germany, may hold the key to restoring today's lagging business structures. On this occasion in which we honor the 100th anniversary of *Rerum Novarum* and its comments on work and the working class, the necessity for modern business practitioners, such as myself, to return to the Catholic Social Teachings tradition is keenly felt as we confront new and very different shifts in business conditions and thinking. The spirit of the origins of Catholic Social Teaching serves as the "old wine" which we now will endeavor to pour into today's "new wineskins." Jesus warns us not to put new wine in old wineskins, but

1

rather to put new wine in new wineskins. He says nothing about old wine in new wineskins or addressing an old story with a new development. (Richard Pring also suggests this approach in the Prologue as he recounts the last two centuries in Oxford.)

1.2 Fribourg Union's Utopian Ideal

At last, the social conditions may be right in the United States, to put into practice the Fribourg Union utopian ideal of the "Regime Corporatif," or "corporatively organized society," giving freedom, dignity and creativity to the individual within the structure of a business community.

If the prophetic voices of the Fribourg Union – The Catholic Union of Social and Economic Studies – resurface now, along with the 100th anniversary celebration of beginning of Catholic Social Teaching, then their insights can help provide an essential understanding and deeper insight into the purpose of business and offer an ideal vision for restoring the corporative system within the socio-economic realm.

Here, as I understand it, is the connection between *Rerum Novarum* and the Fribourg Union.

The endeavors of the Fribourg Union were largely responsible for the awakening of the movement known as "Social Catholicism" in the late 19th century. The Fribourg Union was composed of prominent European business executives, politicians, theologians, and clergy who met yearly in Fribourg, Switzerland from 1834 to 1891. These men were not like Dickens' well-meaning but outmoded business owner, Mr. Fezziwig in *A Christmas Carol*, but rather extraordinarily forward thinkers, far ahead of their time. In theory, neither capitalism, which appealed to owners, nor Socialism, which appealed to workers, created an organically structured community. A third vision was needed to foster the foundation of this creative community.

The leaders of the Fribourg Union were granted a papal audience with Leo XIII in 1888 to review their studies and resolutions: "an important event, which has so to speak consecrated the official existence of the Union by the Supreme authority."[1] The Pontiff basically confirmed many positions of the Fribourg Union, specifically relating to capitalism, private property, worker dignity, the just wage, and charity. This audience ultimately culminated in the 1891 Encyclical, "On the Condition of the Working Classes". However Pope Leo XIII did not incorporate in *Rerum Novarum* the ideal of the "Regime Corporatif" that provided the main thrust and primary legacy of the Fribourg Union. The Fribourg Union proposed to establish the corporative system on the foundation of a reformed socio-economic order.

To precisely understand the meaning of the term *Regime Corporatif*, one must contrast it with the perception of society as held by the Social Catholics and clearly expressed by the Union in 1886:

> "Society is disorganized [...] it is no longer a living being in which each organism, autonomous to a certain point, plays a role and exercises a function; it is a mechanism composed of gears more or less ingeniously assembled, obeying an almighty force; in brief, it is an automaton, and offers but the appearances and the illusion of an animated body."[2]

This definition of an anonymous and impersonal society is as true today as when it was written, for this state of society, unfortunately, still exists today. The utopian vision of the Fribourg Union was one of a living organism composed of distinct individual "social cells", that create and interact, not out of self-interest but out of concern for the common good.

On October 12, 1886 the Fribourg Union defined the corporative system as

> "the mode of social organization which rests on the grouping of men according to their common interests and their common social functions and which results, necessarily, in the public and distinct representation of these different organisms."[3]

Such a perfect corporation follows

> "the providential law according to which in the human order the structure must always be organic."[4]

It is interesting to note that the word *corporation* is derived from the Latin for body (*corpus*), and is defined as "a body of society, entitled to act as a single person [...] made up of many persons."[5]

The members of the Fribourg Union were also practical men of business who studied industrial relations closely to assess how their ideas could be implemented on the factory floor. One central idea was to bring workers and management together, emphasizing worker leadership positions in dispute settlement. Louis Milcent believed that the free enterprise system had a major stumbling block; it fostered competition rather than cooperation, true not only within a factory, but also for one factory pitted against another within an industry. The first step was to have cooperation within the factory and in the second step, to bring all of the members of one industry together in a cooperative system. Milcent and the other members realized that these steps would prove very difficult to implement, but they foresaw the time when both workers and management could work together within an industry. The local corporation was essential to "coordinate the necessary relationships of individuals of the same profession, to regulate their particular rivalries and to define their common interests."[6]

1.3 Catholic Social Teaching

As one who makes his living in corporate business, I pay tribute to the tradition of Catholic Social Teaching. The correlation of work and man's relationship with God has preoccupied Catholic Social Teaching, shifting from the medieval hierarchical view of devotion to God first and social mundane activities further down the ladder to the roots of the Fribourg Union and *Rerum Novarum* and continuing today. Pope Leo XIII said,

> "If we hearken to natural reason and the Christian philosophy, gainful occupations are not a mark of shame to man, but rather of respect, as they provide him with an honorable means of supporting life."[7]

Pope Leo clearly addressed the raging debate on socialism by emphasizing the rightness of private property and the just wage. However, there is a larger issue at stake in the meaning and structure of work. This broader importance of work was put forth by John Paul II in *Laborem Exercens*.

> "It is rather, in order to highlight perhaps more than has been done before, the fact that human work is a key, probably the *essential key*, to the whole social question, if we try to see that question really from the point of view of man's good."[8]

Further, the American Bishops sought to heal the division between Faith and Work. At the National Conference of Catholic Bishops held in Washington, D.C. in 1986, it was declared:

> "Followers of Christ must avoid a tragic separation between Faith and everyday life. They can neither shrink

nor shirk their earthly duties nor, as the Vatican Council II declared, 'Immerse themselves in earthly activities as if they were utterly foreign to religion, and religion were nothing more than a fulfillment of acts of worship and the observance of a few moral obligations.' The road to holiness for most of us lies in our secular vocations […] we cannot separate what we believe from how we act in the marketplace and the broader community, for this is where we make our primary contribution to the pursuit of economic justice."[9]

Leo XIII and subsequent Catholic Social Thinkers forcefully challenged the widely accepted "machine-model of production" in which each individual is considered an interchangeable part in the production of the product, whether goods or service. At its deepest level, this business model has been based on *exchange*, principally between the employer and the worker. Pope Leo does address this problem in *Rerum Novarum*:

"The great mistake made in regard to the matter now under consideration is to take up with the notion that class is naturally hostile to class, and that the wealthy and the workingmen are intended by nature to live in mutual conflict. So irrational and so false is this view, that the direct contrary is the truth […] So in a state is it ordained by nature that these two classes should dwell in harmony and agreement, and should, as it were *groove* (italics mine) into one another, so as to maintain the balance of the body politic."[10]

This notion of the two classes in harmony and *to groove* together, as the poetic term appears in the original translation, are the core goals which American business attempts to achieve today as we face increasing international competition which has exposed shortcomings in efficiency and quality.

1.4   America's Labor Crises

Our own labor history in America is fraught with crisis. At approximately the same time that *Rerum Novarum* was issued, internationally reported labor disputes occurred in Chicago. As a native Chicago businessman whose family has been in business in this city for over 100 years, I feel that these events need to be retold. At the end of the 19th century, over 250,000 Catholics resided in Chicago and only 100,000 Protestant communicants. In the summer of 1886, the most critical labor crisis occurred – the Haymarket Riot – in which a bombing incident killed several policemen and strikers. The next Sunday, the pulpits of Chicago rang with diatribes against labor. The working men in general were denounced as communists who should be hunted down like mad dogs. Militia were called to block all gatherings of labor. One Minister commented that labor was a commodity whose wages were set by the laws of trade. Others preached that the strikes were wrong by their nature and that the workers should turn to God for support, rather than take matters into their own hands.

Yet, the thought of Cardinal Manning of England, who conferred with the Fribourg Union, was noted with great approval by future Illinois governor, John Altgeld. The *Chicago Times* on January 15, 1888 published this quote of Cardinal Manning:

> "My answer that the obligation to feed the hungry springs from the natural right of every man to life and to the food necessary to the sustenance of life. So strict is this natural right that it prevails over all positive laws of

property. Necessity has no law and a starving man has a
right to his neighbor's bread."[11]

Chicago had its infamous sweatshops, where workers would take
pieces of textiles back to their tenements and stitch them together
with leg-operated sewing machines. They were paid on a piece-rate
basis, driven to the lowest subsistence levels by the laws of supply
and demand. There was little incentive for owners to increase their
costs to provide suitable working conditions. The deep moral incon-
sistency of this position is most clearly illustrated by an often quoted
example in which the head of one of the largest clothing firms in the
world supported a local Chicago hospital through substantial charita-
ble contributions. In the winter, many clothing workers, *Sweaters* as
they were called, poured into the hospital suffering from disease and
malnutrition. When it was pointed out to the factory owner that he
could solve two problems at once by giving proper working conditions to the Sweaters, he responded: "So far we have found leg power
and the Sweater cheaper."[12] The Fribourg Union opposed the idea
that an employer would extract the worker's labor at the lowest price
and then give extra income to charity to care for the poor that the employer had, in effect, created: "It is not enough to alleviate the misery
of the poor by your gifts, but that you must go beyond charity to
justice."[13]

The model for creating ideal worker conditions was patterned after the famous Pullman Town, established just south of Chicago. The
unrest and high-handed treatment by Mr. Pullman led to the Pullman Strike of 1893. In response, Jane Addams wrote an open letter to George Pullman entitled "Industrial Amelioration." Decrying
the lack of freedom for Pullman Town workers, she concluded her
brilliant essay by stating clearly and passionately the need to listen
to others:

"A man who takes the betterment of humanity for his aim and end, must also take into account the daily experiences of humanity for the constant correction of his process. He must not only test and guide his achievement by human experience, but he must succeed or fail in proportion as he has incorporated that experience with his own. Otherwise his own achievements become his stumbling block and he comes to believe in his own goodness as something outside of himself. He makes an exception of himself and thinks he is different from the rank and file of his fellows. He forgets that it is necessary to know of the lives of our contemporaries, not only to believe in their integrity, which is after all but the first beginnings of social morality, but in order to attain to any metal of a moral integrity for ourselves, or any such hope for society."[14]

In many ways, physical labor conditions today are much improved. American businesses have, of course, made remarkable progress in giving the workers more rights and protection under the Law as was called for in *Rerum Novarum*. American businesses realize we are in a period now being called a "paradigm shift." While this idea is often misunderstood and clouded by such emotionally-laden references to Postmodernism, New Age, etc., the shift is based on a very simple premise: we have shifted from an economy based on agriculture, to industry, to information. In the Information Age, the dominant technology is no longer the plow or the machine but the computer. The most basic strategic resource is no longer land or capital, but knowledge. The organizational form is no longer the family, nor the corporation, but a network. And the basic production unit is no longer mass production but the individual working within the team.

1.5   Productivity and Quality

In the face of this shift, the issue to be confronted is one of worker freedom within the tight corporate bureaucracy prevailing in American business today without chaotic repercussions or poor product quality. Pope John Paul II calls for the demand of quality in the most recent Encyclical, *Centesimus Annus*: "The quality of the goods to be produced and consumed, the quality of the services to be enjoyed, the quality of the environment, and of life in general."[15] Indeed American business is searching for ways to increase quality as our quality level is not up to the standards of the Japanese, in particular. In the last decade, productivity, as expressed by Gross Domestic Product per Person Employed (GPN) has increased by 35% in Japan and 9% in the U.S. The Japanese clearly understand that maximum worker productivity and quality is not extracted by a return to inhumane working conditions, but rather enhanced by treating workers with more dignity and respect. Within Japanese corporations, over 80% of the workers have a say in decision-making, while in the U.S., less than 12% of workers have a similar say.[16] What the Japanese have done so well in their *Kerietsu*, or trading companies, is to share basic technology and knowledge among competing units within a huge conglomerate. The main focus is not on worker production as in the late 19th century, but rather on releasing the knowledge of individual workers to serve the whole company and, indeed, the entire industry.

This is the legacy of the Fribourg Union and its concept, "organic model of industry." We see that American capitalism needs to have a more human face. A major change in thinking is required in which the creative nature of humankind is emphasized rather than our "fallen nature."

We are brought again to the need for management and labor "to groove into one another," to recapture this central idea of the organic theory of the corporation, the "Regime Corporatif." In business, we are approaching the term *Community* as a way of talking about people working together for the good of the whole. The term *Family* was mentioned by the Fribourg Union, but this must be carefully watched, as too often this notion has been put into practice as "Father (i.e., boss) knows best." Within the corporation, we are really coming to a balanced, interactive and creative relationship among people of all levels in which information is exchanged: a more organic model of business.

This vision has been implemented with most impressive results best summed up in the words of John J. Hudiburg, former Chairman of Florida Power and Light:

> "Let's face it. Most companies operate under the premise that the average employee is lazy, poorly educated, and in need of strict supervision by a better educated, more experienced supervisor. I am sure that most of you manage your employees this way, using discipline to make sure they do their work. In retrospect, I certainly did. The most important element of a successful, total-quality, management program (a concept which is sweeping American business, drawn from the Japanese experience) is choosing your philosophy about managing people. If you leave today with only one idea, this is the most important one: Your TQM program will fail if you do not develop a new management paradigm that is based on job satisfaction."[17]

The most popular American business books and periodicals today are calling for corporations to "involve everybody in everything," to break open bureaucracy, and to turn corporations into learning societies featuring openness, teams, vulnerability and dialogue. One popular author, Peter M. Senge, goes so far as to call for a *metanoia*.

Senge even lays some of the blame for the state of American business on the loss of conversion to the Catholic Church. He states: "In
the Catholic corpus, the word *metanoia* was eventually translated as
'repent,' hardly an appealing or positive concept today."[18]

Major American universities are coming to this idea of the organic
model of business as well. The University of Chicago Graduate School
of Business, home of the Nobel Economist Milton Friedman, recently
held a precedent-setting, three-day conference co-sponsored with the
M. Scott Peck Group called "Foundation for Community Encouragement" to expose executives to the power and benefits of a sharing
community. Philip Kotler, world-renowned marketing professor at
Northwestern University Kellogg Graduate School of Management,
recently voted the number one business school in the country, is now
shifting from his previous definition of marketing as exchange:

> "Marketing started out as an analysis of how commodi-
> ties are produced and distributed through an economic
> system. Subsequently we became interested in the dis-
> tribution channels themselves and in the functions that
> markets performed. At a point, of course, all these things
> got combined. But, each time the field's focus shifted.
> What I think we are witnessing is a moving away from
> a focus on exchange and a narrow sense of transaction,
> and toward a focus on building value laden relationships,
> and marketing networks."[19]

Harvard University also searched to create a module of ethics.
Thomas R. Piper heads the effort and remarked:

> "MBA education seems to have failed in its most impor-
> tant responsibility: to generate excitement about careers
> and the opportunity for making a difference [...] the

expansion of job opportunities and investment banking brought employer pressure for more extensive skills and analysis and we staffed up for teaching those. Without realizing it, we gradually reduced our attention to issues of responsibility and purpose."[20]

Stanford University Graduate School of Business Professor Michael Ray has introduced a course entitled "New Paradigm Business".

American business must realize its potential, and this brings me back to Genesis, so often quoted by John Paul II. Creation is seen as the primary activity and responsibility of humankind. Economist John Maynard Keynes said:

"The next step forward must come, not from political agitation or premature experiments but from thought. We need, by an effort of the mind, to elucidate our own feelings. In the field of action reformers will not be successful until they can steadily pursue a clear and definite object with their intellects and their feelings in tune [...] We need a new set of convictions, which spring naturally from a candid examination of our own inner feelings in relation to the outside facts."[21]

1.6 Conclusion

Now is the time to bring reason to American business and search for a vision and purpose that will bring together the creative efforts of the workers. We have come full circle to the legacy of the Fribourg Union's organic model of business, "Regime Corporatif." Just as the Fribourg Union endeavored to pour the old wine of the medieval spirit into new wineskins, today we are pouring old wine into new wineskins again.

In conclusion, Pope Leo XIII states in *Rerum Novarum*:

> "In the case of decaying societies it is most correctly pre-
> scribed that, if they wish to be regenerated, they must
> be recalled to their origins. For the perfection of all as-
> sociations is this, namely, to work for and to attain the
> purpose for which they were formed, so that all social
> actions should be inspired by the same principle which
> brought the society itself into being. Wherefore, turn-
> ing away from the original purpose is corruption, while
> going back to this purpose is recovery. And just as we
> affirm this as unquestionably true of the entire body of
> the commonwealth, in the like manner we affirm it of
> that order of citizens who sustain life by labor and who
> constitute the vast majority of society."[22]

Pope Leo recognized that energy and effectiveness of workers is so important that "it is incontestable that the wealth of nations origi- nates from no other source than from the labor of workers."[23] As it is through secular vocations that most of us make our primary contri- bution to the pursuit of economic justice and creation, what is truly at issue at the deepest level of reality is our relationship with God. We must be open to the constant dialogue with God at the deepest level and, therefore, we may be more open to dialogue with others. Modern American business practitioners can and must return to the utopian model of the Fribourg Union and address the basic issues of worker creativity, communication and cooperation not only to recover, but also to prosper.

Chapter 2

Peircean Pragmatism and the Social Values of American Business

2nd International Conference
on Social Values in Education and Business
University of Oxford – July, 1993

"The behavior of the community is largely dominated by the business mind. A great society is one in which their men [and women] of business think greatly of their function."

Alfred North Whitehead[1]

2.1   Introduction

Is business properly serving or filling its role in society? Today, in the late twentieth century, can business again be thought of as a vocation? Can business regain its heart? American business today knows that change is necessary but as yet does not see how profound this change must be.

I participate in this conference as an American advertising executive and a doctoral student at DePaul University in Chicago specializing in the pragmatism of the nineteenth-century American philosopher Charles Sanders Peirce. One of the goals in my dissertation is to reclaim Peirce's concept of pragmatism for use in helping business make better decisions so they can, as Whitehead urged, "think greatly of their function." This is an endeavor deeply permeated with values and social implications. It is also deeply fraught with potential for misunderstanding, thanks to the fact that what we conventionally mean by "pragmatism" is very different from what Peirce originally meant. In this chapter I want to clarify Peirce's pragmatism, illustrate how we are applying it to our business, and show how this applies our society, as well as for business. Pragmatism can foster the process of dialogue and being in relationship, as well as to help create learning organizations built on dialogue between people. Peirce's philosophy offers deeper solutions to the individual-collective tension that plagues our industries and society as a whole. The basic questions running through this chapter are:

- What is the use of philosophy?

- How does it come alive for business people to live it?

- Does it hold the key to rediscovering the great function business must perform for society?

2.2   The Pragmatism of Charles Sanders Peirce

It may come as a surprise that the way out of many of our current business dilemmas might just lie in our being more pragmatic. Therefore my goal has been to reclaim pragmatism for the American business practitioner. When I studied Peirce and I came to recognize the true meaning of pragmatism, I realized that I was like the Frenchman who found out at the age of 60 that he had been speaking prose all of his life. I found out at the age of 53 that I had been practicing pragmatism all of my life. I realize, as I studied philosophy, I have been a pragmatist – not only in my conversations with experienced philosophers, but also in deciding on courses of actions with my fellow practitioners in business.

This notion itself is Peircean. Peirce addressed this split, very much a perennial feature of philosophy, between theory and practice. Practitioners rarely think about wider issues as they decide on actions. We business people have a narrow perspective because we focus mainly on our product categories and on competitive action. Theorists, on the other hand, rarely get involved in mainstream American business practices that face the pressures and demands of the marketplace.

I realize that contemporary American business people lack the patience for sustained philosophical argument and like to process information very quickly. Business people are doers and prefer a philosophy based on action; our world changes quickly and we have short attention spans. That is precisely why we need to rediscover and reclaim the pragmatism of Charles Sanders Peirce and see it in a new and useful way.

Peirce's followers – Josiah Royce, William James, and John Dewey – also had ideas that have great relevance today. These American philosophers were concerned with how Americans approach problems and, particularly, how we emphasize individual action based on individual opinion. It was on the work of Peirce that the well-known philosophers James and Dewey, as they themselves acknowledged, built their methods of thought.

When we call ourselves "pragmatic," we usually mean that we are not hampered by an ideology; rather, we do whatever it takes to get the job done. This, however, is an amputation of what Peirce really meant. The "Machine Model" of business that has dominated business thought: fix the problem by replacing people, jobs, cogs, getting the machine to work, etc., is too narrow and, in the opinion of many business observers, this "philosophy" has led us to the short-term-reactive business performance which characterizes much of American business today.

Pragmatism is a method of inquiry; it is neither "action unencumbered by principle" nor a "fixed system of ultimate answers and great truths."[2] Peirce founded it; Royce saw religious aspects of it; James misunderstood it; and Dewey furthered the idea of pragmatism in his writings, namely, in *Logic: The Theory of Inquiry* and *A Common Faith*. Few at the time – and for many years later – beyond James, Royce, and Dewey recognized the importance of Peirce's ideas.

The story of the creation of pragmatism is a dramatic tale of misinterpretation and frustration, and can be traced back to William James's kidnapping of Peirce's original philosophy. James, a widely known, distinguished Harvard psychologist and philosopher, had an intellectual respectability far exceeding Peirce. James first introduced pragmatism to the American public in a speech made at the University of California, Berkeley, on 26 August 1898.

> "This is the principle of Charles Sanders Peirce, the principle of pragmatism. I think myself it should be expressed more broadly than Mr. Peirce expresses it. The ultimate test for what a truth means is indeed the conduct it dictates or inspires."[3]

James felt that your beliefs didn't mean anything if you didn't act on them: beliefs are really rules for actions, and you become what you habitually do. By bringing pragmatism to the attention of the nation, William James is responsible for pragmatism coming to be defined as "practicalism."[4] James asserted that holding beliefs must have consequences, or "cash-value,"[5] because beliefs are irrelevant if they don't make a difference in your actions. James's view of pragmatism as putting your beliefs into actions overshadowed the richer and more powerful definition of Peirce and, ultimately, can be blamed for the narrow focus and the reactiveness of contemporary business. James's interpretation missed the core idea of the communal nature of inquiry, leaving only the action of the individual based entirely on individual experience. Pragmatism then became a philosophical approach congenial to the American spirit and our cultural belief system, and was reduced to "doing what works."

Even 160 years ago the problems associated with this orientation were recognized, most notably by Alexis de Tocqueville. De Tocqueville maintained that Americans are not given to philosophizing as a people; we are people of action. "Less attention, I suppose is paid to philosophy in the United States than in any other country in the civilized world."[6] He then went on to state what is, in my opinion, still the best description of our method of philosophical inquiry:

> "To seek by themselves and in themselves for the only reason for things, looking at results without getting entangled in the means toward them and looking through forms to the basis of things – such are the principle characteristics of what I would call the American philosophical method. To carry the argument further and to select the chief among these various features, and the one which includes almost all of the others within itself, I should say that in most mental operations each American relies on individual effort and judgment."[7]

The history of America has been build on "rugged individualism." Tocqueville defined individualism as a "calm and considered feeling which disposes each citizen to isolate himself from the mass of his fellows and withdraw into the circle of family and friends. With this little society formed to his taste, he gladly leaves the greater society to look after itself."[8] This sets us off on a trail leading to isolation, and eventually to egoism: A passionate and exaggerated love of self which leads man to think of all things in terms of himself. We cling to our dualism: me vs. you. And we ask, "What's in it for me?"

So, what did Peirce really intend pragmatism to mean? It is ironic that he had to bear the frustration of decades and decades of failure to be understood for what he really meant. Pragmatism does have an action element; instead it relies on inquiry and learning. James's essays are collected in the volume *The Will to Believe*, and dedicated to Peirce. While Peirce thanked James for this dedication, he later said the following "I thought your *Will to Believe* was a very exaggerated utterance such as injures a serious man very much."[9]

C.S. Peirce coined the term "pragmatism" from the Greek word for *deed* or *act*. Peircean pragmatism makes three fundamental claims:

1. The scientific method is best.

2. The scientific quest provides further development of concrete reasonableness.

3. The scientific method is a social and self-correcting communal process promoted by smoothly function habits and beliefs that are upset by doubt.

Peirce applied the scientific method of inquiry to philosophy and logic, as well as to the hard sciences. The collective, shared pursuit of the truth is central to Peirce; we must, he said, be open one to the other. A key component is the constant interaction, interpretation, and awareness of larger perspective. The pragmatic method of inquiry begins with a doubt or a surprising fact which leads to the formulation of a hypothesis. Then the pragmatist tests the hypothesis by interpreting the signs, trends, facts, of what is seen. This is a process closer to scientific reasoning: "If thus and so is true, then, of course, the result is this." Pragmatism, then, is a way of handling predictability by a scientific process. Pragmatism itself is not predictable; it is not action and reaction. It is a constant pursuit of the truth. Peirce stated: "Yet my attitude was always that of a dweller in a laboratory, eager only to learn what I did not yet know [...]"[10] He felt that passionate aspirations are devotion to the truth and that a sense of wonder should color all of our work.

Peirce was one of the first to realize what we are now coming to recognize as a culture: that interpretation is the key to knowledge, and knowledge is based on relationships between people. Interpreting strikes at the roots of individualism, perception, community, and sharing of a connection between people. Peirce investigated how groups of people go about knowing or discovering something. He proposed the view that a person does not exist in isolation but in a social circle. He picked up Tocqueville's idea of Americans as confined within their own view of things. Peirce felt that this limited creativity because it hindered the sustaining of two conflicting ideas. Creative insight, according to Peirce, occurs when someone compares facts with ideas or theories, then finds a new third idea which mediates, illuminates and interprets their relationship. Peirce's scientific community is composed of different people looking at evidence and trying to determine what is going on. Peirce describes the scientific method as a cable, not a chain, for this makes it stronger and more powerful. The cable image also reflects the spiral nature of truth, in which all hangs together and also goes to deeper levels. Peirce's way out of individualism is through the idea of a community of inquirers, the scientific community. In his essay, "The Doctrine of Chance," Peirce came to the startling conclusion that "to be logical men should not be selfish."[11] Peirce uses the example of the soldier rushing the wall in battle even though he knows the odds are great that he might be killed. The soldier, however, has given his life to a larger cause. He sees himself as part of a larger effort or story, a central idea we will develop later in this chapter.

Josiah Royce, one of the three noted, yet least known, of the Peircean followers, referred to a community of interpreters as the "Beloved Community." Royce focused the greater part of his writings on the religious aspects of pragmatism and used the example of the Pauline community of Believers which came together to tell the story, as they had experienced it, of Jesus' life and works.

John Dewey brought pragmatism as a philosophy into twentieth-century American life. Dewey captured the pragmatic method this way:

> "The mind of man is being habituated to a new method and ideal: there is but one sure road of access to truth, the road of patient, cooperative inquiry operating by means of observation, experiment, record and controlled reflection. It is constituted by a method of changing beliefs by means of tested inquiry as well as arriving at them."[12]

2.3   Application of Pragmatism in Contemporary American Business

"Patient, cooperative inquiry," like "sustained philosophical argument" noted earlier, are not words which characterize the short-term, reactive decision-making mode of American Business today, and, as I have shown, Americans have deep cultural biases which keep us from embracing Peircean pragmatism. Our aim, reclaiming Peircean pragmatism for American business, is to help move business away from this short-term, reactive mode which is proving increasingly inadequate. Business people are focused on quarterly profits, bottom lines, and a limited, narrow view of competition.

Today the leading American business schools are attempting to broaden the focus. Yet, on a recent visit to the Harvard Business School, where I was a guest in the class of my friend Professor Ken Goodpaster, I saw how deeply ingrained this focus on profit is. I went to observe Ken's ethics class in Harvard's famous case method of instruction. Ken's students were conducting an analysis of the case of Wisconsin-based Warner Brake and Gear Company. The case dealt with union-management relations and the question of how management should handle a situation which could have long-range impact on the company: Should they take labor into their confidence and tell them all the facts, or should they not enter into discussions fully trusting the labor group? There was a lot of history of bad faith between the two.

The students quickly looked at the evidence from the point of view of maximizing return to shareholders and came up with a decision that would manipulate the workers and not enter into a full trusting relationship with them. Ken persisted in asking if there might be other decisions or other motives that management should look to. Despite his continued hammering away, none came forward in the next hour and a half.

After class, in talking with several students, we asked if they had thought of the action of management doing the right thing and just telling the union the full story. The three students stopped and one thought about it for a moment and finally said: "Why would they do that? No one in our society does something for that reason. We only do things to get something. Why, even our religious culture tells us that. We only do good things to get to heaven. Why should business be any different?" I was immediately reminded that Puritan Work Ethic and the Exchange Model is alive and well. Perhaps the case method does, in the words of one professor, "breed a very narrow type of mind."[13]

What might pragmatism have to offer to correct this narrowness of mind? How might our minds become more creative and inclusive? Here is an unusual pathway: my profession of advertising.

Pragmatism and Creativity

In the advertising business individualism hampers getting the best ideas out as one person staunchly defends his or her own idea. Even though it's a creative community, the advertising business has not been known for collective thought, and we have many sayings to show our disdain. "My idea was nibbled to death by ducks." Or, advertising patriarch David Ogilvy's oft-quoted rhyme: "Search the parks in all your cities, you'll find no statues to committees."

Clearly, our American individualism has hampered us in trying to run our businesses in new and more effective ways. Dr. Robert Bellah describes the "emotivist individualism" as follows: "The goal of living is to achieve some combination of occupation and 'life-style' that is economically possible and psychically tolerable, that 'works'."[14] Peirce's pragmatism is well suited to answer the questions raised by Bellah of how you live and act in the day-to-day world of business.

What is offered here is a way of thinking as old and as intuitive as our American culture, but one that has been overlooked and too seldom, if ever, practiced in business. Pragmatism offers a method for corporate inquiry, discovery, interpretation, and, most importantly, action to help American Business reclaim the trust and integrity of everyone in their organization. "In the workplace of the future, the fiercest competition between firms may not be for customers, but for the hearts and minds of employees."[15]

In the advertising business, this is our world and we deal with trends constantly. They keep coming at us. We compiled a study called *What's Really Going On* to help interpret, and even predict, the consumer trends coming at us. We looked at over 6,000 facts, researched books, articles and gathered anecdotal evidence. From this 250 page study aimed at business practitioners, here are a few of the many trends we found:

> Downsizing, rightsizing, re-engineering, new rules, HMOs, HIV, LBO, MTV, Dr. Death, Pro-Life, the homeless, implants, transplants, two-tier societies, offices, the triple-squeeze generation, PUPPIES, SKIPPIES, MOBYs, DOBYs, Biocides, green teens, Zoo

Doo, clothes chic, global cops, urban yoga, aromather-
apy, cosmoseuticals, component life-styles.

These statistics and facts are like the thousands of dots in a pointil-
list's canvas, or the dots which make up the four color picture in a
magazine. Seen up close by themselves they mean nothing and offer
no clues as to what is going on. You need to stand back and gain some
perspective. These facts begin to form patterns into trends. We look
at the bigger picture and, instead of asking: "What is our business
doing in the micro-sense?" we ask: "What is our business doing in
the macro-sense?"

This larger perspective gives business practitioners help in answer-
ing some of their pressing questions:

- How does a business person get out of the short-term, reactive
  rut that most are currently stuck in?

- How do you plan more accurately for the future when things
  are changing so fast?

- How do you spot the larger patterns and forces that are going
  to affect your business?

- How do you stimulate creativity and flexibility and innovation
  in a time when people are scared for their jobs?

- How do you evaluate the performance of your business in a
  way that goes beyond the quarterly profit and loss statements?

Companies are responding to the current business climate with
a commitment to quality, values, and innovative ways of bringing
people together. Corporantes, a research and study effort within The
Nahser Agency (the next step in our family's over 110 years in the
communications business), undertook this lengthy study as a result

of the development of our *Corporantes PathFinder Notebook©*. The *PathFinder* is actually a scientific notebook, and this method of corporate inquiry is based on the pragmatism of Peirce. We have used it in 25 U.S. companies, including the Quaker Oats Company, Bang & Olufsen, and the Harris Bank & Trust Company.

Pragmatism and a Religious Foundation

One of the key elements of the pragmatic method of inquiry is continuity: to see how issues and ideas have developed throughout the history of the corporation. The corporation has its own story: its culture, history, philosophy, mission, and vision. Naturally, this goes beyond the machine model of business. Because interpretation is central to the process, we got away from the traps of *perception*–reacting to whatever we see – and *conception* – hanging on to ways of seeing reality.

The *PathFinder* challenges business people to look at their own methods and beliefs, articulate an hypothesis, and then weigh their hypothesis against the evidence of what is going on in the world around us. The aim is to come, then, to a different and broader point of view as to how the world might work. Then we can see the movement in the life of the corporation and what the possible next steps might be. When we put the life of a corporation in the form of a narrative or story, we gain an extremely important perspective. This larger perspective is one, in my belief, that can only be labeled as "religious." Or as Robert Bellah put it, "Suffice it to say," that I find "spirituality no more incompatible with business practice than is ethics."[16] This finding has led us to what we believe has been a major breakthrough in the application of pragmatism for reclaiming a religious foundation for business and the meaning of work.

In developing a statement of mission and vision for business which grows out of the story of the corporation, we are doing something that places us in the traditions of action based on what was called "virtue" going as far back as the Greeks. "Generally to adopt a stance on the virtues will be to adopt a stance on the narrative character of human life."[17] I take this remarkable insight by Alasdair MacIntyre to mean that, since stories deal with the dangers and opportunities facing everyone, they help define the virtues which guide our behavior. Stories tell us where our lives have been, where we are now, and what we are becoming.

Through the sacredness of the narrative, we are led to interpretation, a reading of the signs of the evidence of the world around us. This narrative view reveals how the corporation is developing and responding to circumstances. Our aid is neither to react simply in a machine-like way, nor to hold to a conception of the world. In fact, the corporation can interact and interpret what's going on in a true Peircean pragmatic sense.

I share with the insightful observers M. Scott Peck, Peter Senge, Alasdair MacIntyre, and Robert Bellah the concern to break out of the traps of dualism and individualism that prevent us from coming together as a community. In *The Fifth Dimension,* Senge proposed the "learning organization" and "systems thinking," which foster real dialogue by suspending certainty in the presence of another. Peck recognizes the need for abandoning the "fixation of belief" as a precondition for community. I share with Bellah a need to develop language and techniques that would permit and sustain substantive moral discourse. And MacIntyre is sensitive to the moral state of business and the loss of virtue that plagues our society.

Pragmatism and Social Values

Luther McKinney, the corporate counsel for the Quaker Oats Company, once reminded me of the original purpose of incorporation for a business. States issued articles of incorporation only because a corporation was deemed to be providing a service to society. In other words, our major corporations got their start originally out of a mindset that was built on social value. They were permitted to exist because they provided a valuable service which promoted the general welfare.

During the l980s, when the cry was "Greed is Good" and everyone was "Looking out for #1," we lost our tradition of social values in business. Peircean pragmatism is helping to restore social values to American business. Business ethics do not equal simply "what works." Peircean pragmatism gets us past this ethical expediency. From individualism we move to a collective method of inquiry. We move past the action/reaction, machine-model mode. Peircean pragmatism gets us out of the dualistic way of thinking by seeing beyond dither-or thinking. Peircean pragmatism requires cooperative, joint effort to determine the truth.

2.4   Conclusion

According to many observers, we are at a hinge point of about a 300 year change, the "Post-Capitalist Society." Today we have an opportunity to again bring together spirituality, social values, and work.[18] The work of our agency (*What's Really Going On* and the *Corporantes PathFinder Notebook*©) is a search for a spiritual basis for business. I began this pursuit because I had questions: What is the role of business today? Can business have a spiritual foundation for action? Is business properly serving its role in society?

Business has an unprecedented opportunity to be a leader in this change because of its position at the center of power and change in our society. We see this in the office buildings have replaced the churches and government offices as the most predominant buildings in our cities. Alfred North Whitehead understood this when he noted: "The business mind dominates our social thinking."[19] How is business suited to shoulder this great responsibility to help foster a better society that is fair and just for all?

Corporations struggle with the search for a philosophy, a purpose, a meaning which can capture the hearts of their employees and also provide the foundation for their marketing strategies. By using Peircean pragmatism, American business people can come to see the points of view of others, which then leads them out of their individualism and helps them realize that their products and marketing have an impact on the mental, spiritual, and physical ecology of our culture.

For example, from my advertising communications background, I see advertisers as the symbol-makers of society: we create symbols which represent goods and services. As such, we are in the role of helping people lead productive, fulfilling lives. In this powerful role advertising must no longer manipulate the consumer. The goal of our agency is to provide creative, productive work that serves the needs of society.

The Nahser Agency and Corporantes, Inc. have benefited from using Peircean pragmatism also in terms of developing ideas for our clients to see how their goods and services help. their consumers to live, prosper and be successful in a changing world. In the internal agency structure our goal is for people to contribute to the fullest level of their talents in developing the work for our clients. As Chairman and Chief Executive Officer, I have responded to the various pressures and trends of business by endeavoring to give our agency, and my career, a virtuous foundation and to make the best business decisions as we compete and work in a rapidly changing world.

On a deeper personal level, the Peircean perspective has helped me to take a long-term view of the continuity of my life, the agency, and the role that we in advertising play in society. I see that I am part of a longer story of people in advertising who have wrestled with the questions of integrity in creating sales messages. I see that I am part of a larger story: that business has become central to the future of our civilization.

Ultimately, we will make one modest change in that great Benedictine rule, "*Labore et orare*," with the addition of one letter. "*Labore est orare*." Thus, we can see that the work we do is holy work. It is a wonderful story, at the base of which is a religious reading of the signs of God's presence and our work as co-creators in the world.

The final answer will be in the continued devotion to the truth we do not yet know. In the inspiring spirit of the Gospel:

"Those who have eyes, let them see; those who have ears, let them hear."

Chapter 3

Learning to Read the Signs: Reclaiming Pragmatism for American Business and Education

3rd International Conference
on Social Values in Education and Business
University of Oxford – July, 1995

"Signs come from without, but get their meaning from
the living psyche [...] Success is achieved when one is
ready to accept the sign at the appropriate moment, integrate it into the particular situation and thus create a
meaningful cosmos."

Walter Burkert, *Creation of the Sacred*

3.1 Introduction

How do you run an advertising agency, or any business organization, that needs to be creative?

As corporations, including our own, are looking for better ways to work together and respond to the changing business and social environment, pragmatism, that unique American contribution to philosophy, can help. It offers a way of interpreting evidence to discover the truth of a situation on which an individual and a group can form plans of action. While helping the business practitioner discover the purpose and direction of their careers in addition to learning business techniques.

In this chapter, after a brief explanation of pragmatism, I will highlight the basic features of the method and then show how it can be practiced.

3.2   Pragmatism

Business practitioners often claim pragmatism as the unofficial philosophy of business. However, when we call ourselves "pragmatic," we usually mean that we are not hampered by an ideology; rather, we do whatever works – whatever it takes to get the job done. The "Machine Model" of business has dominated business thought: fix problems by treating the company as a machine, trying to find the right buttons to push or parts to be moved or replaced to get the machine to optimize profits. This narrow definition of pragmatism, based on a stimulus/response or behaviorist model, has led us to the short-term-reactive business performance which characterizes much of American business today.

This view of pragmatism, however, overlooks the key element of interpretation in the logic of pragmatism developed by Charles Sanders Peirce in the late 19th Century. He saw pragmatism as a method of inquiry, which he carefully distinguished from a "fixed system of ultimate answers and great truths."[1] While Peirce founded pragmatism, Josiah Royce saw religious aspects of it, William James partially misunderstood it, and John Dewey furthered the idea of pragmatism in his writings, namely in *Logic: The Theory of Inquiry* and *A Common Faith*.[2]

Pragmatism deals with the issue of interpretation: how do we see and come to understand what's going on in a particular situation? How do we read the evidence or "signs" as he called them? Josiah Royce, following Peirce, focused on this aspect of interpretation, distinguishing three aspects of philosophy which he felt established the essence of pragmatic thinking: perception is simply what we take in from the outside environment; what we see. Conceptions are our ideas, beliefs, assumptions, and understanding which direct our attention. In the process, we often filter and fit what we see into what we believe. Interpretation is that dynamic mode of thought mediating between conception and perception, and is at the heart of pragmatic logic. Based on this model, Royce went so far as to say: "Interpretation is, once and for all, the main business of philosophy."[3]

Consider what happens when two of these three modes of thought – perception and conception – without the benefit of interpretation, guide business behavior. If a company is very perceptive, they are always making moves to react to the changing marketplace. But, in the process of reacting, the managers are in danger of losing their sense of their purpose, what they believe, their uniqueness, and can erode their core competencies. Currently, newspapers and TV news departments attempt to compete in the entertainment business, weakening their journalistic skills, focus, and purpose. In a business that holds on to a conception, they have a view of the marketplace and whatever is going on out there makes little difference to them because they know their product and what the market needs. For instance, IBM believed: "It was mainframes yesterday, and it is mainframes today, and it will be mainframes tomorrow," missing the trend toward personal computers. Or, as in the case of Schwinn Bicycle, one of our former clients, they continued to market the immensely successful Schwinn Varsity model too long, ignoring the growing popularity of mountain bikes and more technically advanced road bikes.

The most successful companies are those which can move back and forth between the two through the process of interpretation: view the needs of the marketplace, using the skills of perception, and interpret them in view of what the company can uniquely offer based on its beliefs or conception of its product. This process of interpretation lies at the heart of pragmatism, developed by Peirce and furthered by Royce, which holds such great promise in formulating action for business practitioners.

3.3   Dialogue

One useful way that interpretation takes place is through dialogue, a very popular word in business today. Peter Senge, who sees it as being the essential practice of what he calls a learning organization, says that:

> "[…] the purpose of dialogue is to go beyond any one individual's understanding. People are no longer primary in opposition, in dialogue a group explores complex difficult issues from many different points of view. Individuals suspend their assumptions, but they communicate their assumptions freely."[4]

Senge quotes David Bohm, one of dialogue's most articulate advocates: "The purpose of dialogue is to reveal the incoherence of our thought." I think that within business many of us know what a necessary step that is to clear business thinking.

I came to apply the process of dialogue in business through a very unusual way: holistic depth psychology. I explored the issue of keeping a journal of one's life and wanted to do it in a way to help business people discover our values. In the journaling process, you put down dreams and reflections on your notion of your life as a seed, and the seed within that seed is the containment of your life. Your life story, then, is a way to see and understand the development of that seed and plan future directions.

A couple of philosophical pieces that I had been wrestling with started to come together at this point. Peirce saw that, as you examine your life, suddenly it will become apparent that you are responding to a destiny, or a call. This central insight of Peirce's is one of the results of practicing pragmatism: "This activity of thought (pragmatism) by which we are carried, not where we wish, but to a foreordained goal, is like the operation of destiny."[5] Your purpose is then to respond to that call, to be able to read the signs of your life, through pragmatism. Holistic depth psychology is a way for the individual to achieve this response. I saw in working with this process that it could be applied to inquiring about the life of a corporation. Peirce talked about the mind of a corporation:

> "Namely, if this is the case, there should be something like personal consciousness in bodies of men who are in intimate and intensely sympathetic communion."[6]

Like an individual, a corporation seems to have a destiny, a life, a vision. Where is the corporation going? What is its personality or culture? So my associates and I started to draw a parallel between the life of an individual and the life of a corporation and explore these lives through the practice of pragmatism. We gave a name to this exploration: *Corporantes* from the Latin present participle of corpus meaning "forming into a body." We then asked, how might we practice pragmatism?

3.4   The Practice – a Notebook

Following Peirce's model of scientific inquiry, we developed an actual process to practice pragmatism by keeping a journal or notebook investigating the life and destiny of a corporation. It is called the *Corporantes PathFinder Notebook*© (*PathFinder*), the pragmatic method for corporate inquiry, discovery, interpretation and action.

The *PathFinder* process is a flexible collection of exercises to help users look at a situation from several angles or to bring a group to a shared point-of-view. Keeping notes on an ongoing basis as ideas and facts present themselves is an important use of the *PathFinder*. With enough entries in the *PathFinder*, readers will discover their own interpretation and meaning of the evidence or signs they have collected. In addition, the *PathFinder* process can be used to explore specific situations:[7]

- Gain a broader viewpoint on a complex issue from which to assess puzzling facts (perception) which challenge your assumptions (conception).

- Clarify and examine a hunch or gut feeling about a situation.

- Use the process to stretch your visionary capabilities to see or hear what is not currently known to you.

- Challenge current wisdom to probe for more enlightened solutions.

- Explore how your company currently does business and whether that will serve it well in the future. Articulate the obstacles (habits) that stand in the way of change.

- Learn to use effectively the "still, small voice within."

- Learn how pieces of opposing views can help shape a stronger plan while reducing the stress normally encountered when defining your position against others.

Following Peirce, there are three parts to one's exploration: First, to investigate the issue or problem you choose; find out the facts; Second, to form a hypothesis based on your investigations; and finally, to test the hypothesis through action. The power of this process lies in developing the hypothesis. You will know you have formulated a hypothesis when you can make a prediction or define rational expectations about what the outcome of acting upon the belief is likely to be. If you have no such expectations, then you don't have a hypothesis yet. The reality of surprise which leads to doubt is directly tied to harboring such expectations. In other words, how can you be surprised if you have no expectations? Generally, we stop thinking about our proposed action and move to defend it against opposing voices. By classifying your proposed actions as hypotheses, you are willing to stay open to opposing comments or evidence and use this information to learn, refine and strengthen or even reassess and discontinue the action.

If during your investigation you are surprised that your hypothesis is not true, then you may experience what scientists do when new precepts begin to disturb their thoughts. Doubts can challenge the mind toward a new discovery much the way scientists uncover new cures or develop new theories for explaining reality.

Thomas Edison demonstrated this idea during his thousands of unsuccessful attempts to develop electricity. He did not consider these failures, merely ways in which his proposed innovation would *not* work. Undaunted by what others would have called failures, he proceeded toward his intended outcome and got there before others who were much further along in the process than he was when he started his inquiry.

The *PathFinder* is designed to help executives develop the skill of interpretation: to investigate a situation, to discover and articulate both personal and corporate beliefs in light of the investigation, and then to test their beliefs in action. We have been using the *Corporantes PathFinder Notebook©* for the past five years, in about fifty corporate settings in various ways, as well as in academic settings.

Most recently, we used it at the University of South Florida for a Leadership Colloquium. We had forty graduate business students who were wrestling with the ideas and practices of leadership. The premise was to have them explore their own sense of leadership and, using the *PathFinder*, we took them through his kind of a method of pragmatic method of discovery.

We have used it in corporations to help executives wrestle with this idea of what are they seeing out there, what is the context within which their businesses are operating. And what we found to be very powerful is this notion of continuity of their stories:

- Where does *their life* seem to have been?

- Where has the life of the corporation been?

- Where does it seem to be going?

They are then able to put their own lives and the lives of their corporations into a dialogue and a narration, often reflecting on the ethics of the situation. Alasdair MacIntyre has said, "Generally a stance on virtues will be to adopt a stance on the narrative (i.e., story) character of human life." He goes on to say why this is so:

> "[…] each human life will then embody a story whose shape and form will depend on what is counted as harm and danger, success and failure and is opposites are understood and evaluated. To understand these questions, we will also explicitly and implicitly answer the questions as to what the virtues and vices are."[8]

3.5   Pragmatism and Advertising

Remember that all this began as my search for a better way to create advertising. Pragmatism, as a method of inquiry, has special significance for me in advertising. I apply the pragmatic method through the interpretation of signs of activity in the marketplace, and then the creating of symbols or signs which give meaning to products and services to the marketplace through advertising. Our communications task might be more efficient it we treated consumers as machines, but what is the effect of these messages in the larger scheme of things? Is such an approach uplifting for us and for society? Advertising has been maligned by so many critics of contemporary American culture, because advertising "manipulates" people, presenting products and services as ways to fulfill their otherwise unsatisfying and anxious lives.[9] Advertising began as a part of the ancient and honored discipline of rhetoric, or persuasion. Over thousands of years, our job seems to have narrowed to supporting the acquisitive instinct for material goods. But as we enter a new era of limits brought on by social friction and ecological demands, we all need to redefine the role of consumption. Can we create an advertising philosophy by which we can participate in creating the "great society" Whitehead hoped to see, where "men (sic) of business think greatly of their function?"[10]

At The Nahser Agency, we believe a new paradigm is needed for marketing and its arm of persuasion must be based on a different image of what it means to be human.[11] We need a model of marketing built not on a machine-like exchange alone, but on the principle of extended relationships based on dialogue and interpretation with customers and employees, existing within the larger society and natural environment.

Advertising is criticized because it employs powerful psychological ploys to feed on fears and insecurities by treating the individual as the consuming entity who needs advertising and products for self-definition, to be happy, and to feel fulfilled.[12] At our company, we reject such advertising, as it is born out of the machine model – both the kind that tries to find the buttons to push on the consumer/machine, and the kind that accepts the less rigorous legal standard of "truth in advertising" which, by the way, exempts "puffery," allowing for persuasive exaggeration. We believe there is a much larger truth – that people buy and consume products to aid their own personal development, to express and reveal parts of themselves to others and, finally, to contribute in the development of their own lives and the lives of their community.

Our goal then is to create "advertising that tells the truth" about the company and its products and how they affect personal being, to aid people with the narrative of their own lives and the lives of the society in which they live. Our ethical stance, therefore, uses the twin standards of societal context and respect for the individual. We consider the products we sell in terms of how they are consumed and whether they and their advertising, which is the visible sign of the product, help to foster a fuller sense of what it means to be human. Or, if a product imposes an identity on a person, as opposed to helping express and develop that identity, the product diminishes his or her wholeness. We differ with Christopher Lasch who has pointed out that the healthy person would be bad for business: "The anxious person is the ideal consumer."[13]

The branding we help develop at The Nahser Agency and Corporantes, starts from the belief that the consumer is healthy now, rather than presenting the product as medicine to make the sick person well. We also refuse to play on fears or weakness. In principle, we look on the products as a way for the consumer to grow in respectful relationships with others. Therefore, we like to think of the consumer as a customer, which implies "custom" or relationship with dialogue at the base, rather than one of mechanical exchange.

Development and implementation of the *PathFinder* process to determine what's going on has helped me define and demonstrate what it is for me to be a human being and head of our organization as we go about our work of creating and producing advertising and seeing its moral dimension. Ultimately, one must be in dialogue (conversation, as we will call it later) and ensure that the corporate environment in general nurtures development and growth, especially for employees. This rejection of the machine model applies to how we work together in trust.

Stories like the following support our view. One day we were working on creative strategy for Bang & Olufsen, maker of beautiful Danish hi-fi equipment. The creative strategy came to this basic position: "Buy a Bang & Olufsen product and feel good about yourself." When I asked the writer about this strategy, explaining the difference between viewing the consumer as healthy instead of sick, he looked at me for a moment in disbelief and then said somewhat patronizingly, "Ron, ninety-five percent of all creative strategies are based on this idea."

In another instance, I overheard one of our account representatives telling a prospective client not to worry that his product didn't have much of a competitive difference because "so much of advertising is designed to create a difference between parity products."

Our approach turned the usual process of creating advertising on its head.

We challenge the popular format for creating advertising called the "Who-What-What" creative format. Anyone can become an overnight expert in analyzing advertising using this formula:

1. Who is the advertising aimed at?

2. What do they think now?

3. What do we want them to think?

This often leads to the "What Button Do We Push?" method of communication based on the machine model of the consumer.

In the spirit of pragmatism, however, we go on to confirm the truth of what we want them to believe about our product. We ask: *Would people who truly know the product enthusiastically agree with our statements about it?* We then create advertising to draw attention to these central truths about the product experience. The brand – the sign for the product – becomes a believable picture of reality on which trust can be built.

This view of advertising based on relationship has an additional benefit within the agency. A new employee was trying to understand our model of advertising and was still puzzled. After several weeks on the job she recognized that she went home each night feeling that people were not trying to knife here in the back – a most unusual feeling for her compared to her previous experience in the business world. One of our managers explained how we actively try to create an environment where people can feel safe and free to express themselves (dialogue); it's called "putting down your shield."[14] She was used to working in ad agencies where the focus was on exploiting the weaknesses in people to gain advantage. We are convinced that, when employees have a positive environment, a place to work where they feel safe to present their ideas, to work together, the advertising we produce is equally positive and nourishing.

3.6 Reclaiming Pragmatism for American Business

My investigation has convinced me that our contemporary dilemma in American business is not the result of our needing to be more pragmatic (as some have suggested), but of our having practiced the wrong version of pragmatism. The conventional version – "do whatever works" – is not only erroneous but has also gotten us into our present impasse with its short-term, reactive, tactical thinking distorted by the filters of dualism, individualism, ethical blindness and the machine model of business.

A pragmatism reclaimed for its originator, Charles S. Peirce, holds a way out for us. In the *PathFinder* notebook, people discover and tell their stories and exchange their beliefs, based on and discovered through their life experiences. Stories are one of the most powerful forms of reading the signs. Both listeners and storytellers benefit in this process. We benefited from our insights during a painful downsizing last year. Because we were clear on our vision and the qualities of the people needed within the organization, we were able to make better decisions with broad participation and acceptance, even by those asked to leave.

When people deeply listen, they get the chance to discover other people's reality which creates deeper mutual understanding. Through the stories we share, we can also come to a better sense of the virtues that guide, or should guide our behavior.[15] Tellers also benefit by being observers of their own lives and by bringing a sense of meaning and purpose to a corporate life they all share. By telling a story, an individual comes to see what he or she is becoming and where his or her life is heading. We can see more clearly the path, plot or plan for our lives through the stories we share. Through exchanging stories we come to realize our own story is a part of a much larger one so that we are part of and responding to a larger calling. And the means by which we accomplish this thought, which I see as the beginning point of the scientific method, is what Peirce calls *musement*:

> "Enter your skiff of musement, push off into the lake of thought and leave the breath of heaven to swell your sail. With your eyes open, awake to what is about or within you and open conversation with yourself for such is all meditation."[16]

This important idea of *musement*[17] brings the intuitive to what too often is considered a very utilitarian form of logic. This has been particularly important in my work in advertising where we rely so much on intuition, yet need to be guided also by more formal structured thinking so we can work together in developing ad campaigns. By opening my associates up to this form of *musement,* I have found that we can look at our business beyond the more narrowly rational and manipulative model in which we turn the consumer into a machine and try to find the right buttons to push.

3.7   The Monastic Model

The model of dialogue as a central activity for the modern corporation has deep conceptual, practical and legal roots going back to medieval monasteries which began the way in the West of organizing work life. Some critics go so far as to believe that a return to the small communities exemplified by the monasteries offers the solution to today's social problems.

Alasdair MacIntyre, for instance, draws a parallel between our own time which he characterizes as "After Virtue," and the time of the decline of the Roman Empire as we entered the Dark Ages:

> "[…] men and women of good will turned aside from the task of shoring up the Roman imperium and […] what they set themselves to achieve instead, often not recognized fully what they were doing, was the construction of new forms of community within which the moral life could be sustained so that both morality and civility might survive the coming ages of barbarism and darkness."[18]

He believes, as many do, that we are at a similar turning point in our own history. Interpreting signs like those facing business every day convinces me that we are indeed going through massive change. What are we to do? MacIntyre continues,

> "What matters at this stage is the construction of local
> forms of community within which civility and the intel-
> lectual and moral life can be sustained through the Dark
> Ages, which are already upon us [...] We are waiting for
> another – doubtless very different – St. Benedict."[19]

My thesis is that corporations can and must, given their dominant influence, be one type of these communities who guide their actions through pragmatic inquiry. We need to look beneath the turbulence and too-frequent wreckage of expense reduction thinly disguised as re-engineering, to the issues of quality, customer relationships, worker empowerment, team learning, flatter structures and to the broader purposes our corporations are meant to truly fulfill in society.

3.8 Conversation

I have described the practice of pragmatism and how this method of logic and inquiry can help us examine more accurately the evidence of change all around us, and thereby realize a different purpose for business. While I agree with MacIntyre that we are waiting for another St. Benedict, I further believe that the modern "monastic" (*ora et labora*) organizational models will centrally include the corporation. Benedict valued conversation which he called listening with the "ear of your heart" (*aurem cordis tui*). By telling our stories and listening with our heart's ears, our conversations can help the modern corporation interpret, understand and act in ways that can profitably foster a just and compassionate society.

As we have continued to work with the *PathFinder*, (remember that *Corporantes* is the Latin present participle of *Corpus* meaning "forming into a body") we found that as a corporation inquired about some issue of importance, the members through dialogue formed themselves into what Peirce called a "community of inquirers" and

Royce went further calling this a "Beloved Community" on the model of the Pauline early Christian community. Royce developed this community formation in *The Philosophy of Loyalty*. Loyalty, he said, is fostered within a group because people believe in and develop the mission of the corporation. That led us to look at the monastery as a similar group of people inquiring about the best way to live. Benedict even called the monastery a school to learn service to God.

Visit any Benedictine monastery and you will see prominently displayed on everything from walls to napkins the phrase *Ora et Labora*, Pray and Work. While Benedict clearly valued work, he never actually said these words.[20] He had something else in mind, an unusual phrase: *Conversatio morum* – Conversation as a way of life or custom.[21] To say how conversation is deeper than dialogue, consider that conversation also means sexual intercourse. Benedict wanted, in the most graphic manner possible to make the point that we had to be in intimate conversation with God, that "still, small voice" that spoke to the prophet Isaiah.

Before you dismiss the idea of basing business on the deeply spiritual model of the Medieval monastery, remember that Benedict is credited with bringing together practical or technical knowledge with the spiritual, or as Alfred North Whitehead has said: "I recur to the thought of the Benedictines, who saved for mankind the vanishing civilization of the ancient world by linking together knowledge, labour, and moral energy."[22]

Consider two points from *The Rule of Benedict*. First, what does the "still, small voice" mean to you? Some call it intuition, a gut feeling, a hunch. Others call it conscience. You may not choose to call it the voice of God, but we have all experienced it and recognize its creative value. Second, you might recall another time when business embraced a religious idea and developed the wildly successful, if individualistic, Puritan work ethic.

Also consider a re-interpretation of the three monastic vows. *Poverty* we can interpret as a commitment to "voluntary simplicity," to moderating our consumerism, and to living a life of ecological sustainability. It might also lead us away from the inordinate disparities in income in our society and the excessive compensation of our corporate and professional elites. *Chastity* we interpret as an attitude of respect in all our relationships. It involves the renunciation of any kind of sexual exploitation, but more fundamentally it means abstention from that which demeans, lessens or exploits the personhood of self or other. *Obedience* we interpret in accordance with its Latin root as "to be willing to give ear to one another." These three vows lead to the humility, central to Monasticism, which brings a willingness to listen to another.

3.9 Conclusion

We conclude that what pragmatism and the *Corporantes PathFinder Notebook*© offers business practitioners is a method of logic, a way to see what is really going on in the journey of their corporations and in their careers. It is a way to see, think, and to interpret the world and its events. At the core is the dialogue with ourselves which Benedict based monastic life on: "the still, small voice."

One of the oldest biblical dictums of interpretation can guide us. "Those who are deaf, listen; those who are blind, see and understand." Then we will learn the truth on which to form beliefs leading to action.

Chapter 4

What's *Really* Going On: Creating the Need for Philosophical Inquiry, and How to Do It

4th International Conference
on Social Values in Education and Business
University of Oxford – July, 1997

"To live philosophy is to explore one's own temperament and yet, at the same time, to attempt to discover the truth."

Iris Murdoch.[1]

How might business executives and students begin to use the power of philosophical reasoning in better equipping themselves and their corporations to properly determine what is *really* going on and to then take appropriate action?

If it is true that "the gap between philosophy and ordinary life is horrifyingly large,"[2] then the first step is to find ways to engage business people in the philosophical process. I believe the means to do that on both the corporate and on the individual executive levels are readily at hand. While the starting points to engage in philosophical reasoning and questioning for corporate and individual career life are different, they both offer the two aspects of what it is to *live philosophy*: to attempt to discover the truth and to explore one's own temperament. I have called this way of thinking, a philosophical habit – the habit of holding paradoxes of fact and theory, short-term and long term, the general and the concrete.

I will look at the possible, admittedly unusual, avenues to engage executives on the corporate level and business students on the personal/career level. I will then very briefly suggest two methods of inquiry to help the executives and the students in their questioning. My major point is not to explain in detail the methods but to show possible bridges over that "horrifyingly large" gap between philosophy and business life.

4.1   Engaging Executives on the Corporate Level

That we live in a time of rapid change is evident to everyone. You need look no further than the birthday card you might have received recently and on opening it, heard a stirring rendition of "Happy Birthday". The little chip playing the song has more computing power than existed in the entire world in 1950. Nintendo's first hand-held computer game, Game Boy, had more computer capacity than NASA had on board the first Apollo space capsule. And recently, Nintendo crammed a $10,000 workstation into their $200 64-bit box.

Technological change is only one major trend we experience. Every day we are inundated with reports and evidence of the variety and scope of these trends. Business people, of course, are on the forefront of analyzing these changes because they have such enormous impact on the way we conduct our businesses.

To cope with the uncertainty of all these changes, executives are constantly looking for rules or guidelines to follow. Recently, as an example, a new "star to sail by" has appeared on the scene, known as *Economic Value Added* (EVA). Businesses are eagerly adopting it as a measure of shareholder value.[3]

Other consultants have jumped on to this as a new way of helping corporations structure their thinking. However, it follows on the heels of *re-engineering* which swept through the business world wrecking havoc earlier in the decade, which followed Total Quality Management, which followed Management by Objectives, which followed a seemingly endless series of initiatives *du jour*.

But many observers and practitioners realize that, just as in life, there are no certain guidelines for success. What we really need is a *method of thinking* which will help us make sense of the turbulent world around us. In attempting to understand the change of which we are a part, and to help structure the change to our advantage, we are prone to behave in one of two extremes: either we react to every change, unsure exactly what is going on, or we stay with convictions and strategies too long, convinced that we know what is going on.

4.2   The Need for a Method of Thinking

It's easy to collect mountains of data in this information age, but then the tough questions surface: What does the data mean and what insights can be drawn on which to base decisions leading to some concerted action?

Occasionally we can glimpse these individual trends adding up to some larger changes of which we seem to be a part. This conclusion leads to some simple, but important questions:

- How substantial are these changes or are they fads?

- What is the nature of the change?

- Are we going through some sort of transition or change of direction?

- If so, where are we in it and where is it heading?

- Then, what can or should we do about it?

What seems to be necessary is a method of getting a clearer picture of what's really going on in the world and then based on that insight, develop plans of action.

This may be summed up in corporate terms as the need for a company to develop a particular strategy based on a vision, a sense of purpose and goals, and a mission. All these are an expression of the corporations' decisions about the world – the manner in which the corporation "adopts a certain posture, a certain stance towards it."[4]

The question, of course, is how does a company become conscious of the conditions of the world and become aware of what its stance or posture is or should be.

As an advertising practitioner for over thirty years, I have observed that a useful way to approach these deeply philosophical questions is through the unlikely window of what is called *strategic brand analysis*. With all the attention paid to determining what is *really* going on" and what our business response should be, executives are seriously engaged, and desperately looking for any help they can get. We might call this process by its ancient name: *viam sapientiae*, "the way of wisdom." Consider the way strategic brand analysis is conducted and see if it doesn't lead to attempts to answer rather profound questions that can only be called philosophical.

Most businesses recognize that they must base tactical action on a strategy. *Strategy* simply means the way the corporation is to fulfill its vision and reach its goals. Usually overlooked in the drive to action is the need for this even higher understanding of the vision. A way to put strategy in its proper place is to consider the diagram in Fig. 4.1:[5]

I leave it to your imagination how an analysis of corporate purpose, mission, and core values and beliefs leads naturally to philosophical questioning. (Hint: It starts at the source: values.)

The term *brand* is a little more complicated. In an advertising and marketing sense, the brand is the expression of the company and the product's reputation, its attributes, role, relationship with its market,

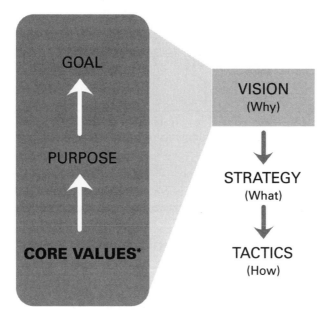

*Source: Beyond Entrepreneurship, Jim Collins and William Lazier

Figure 4.1: Importance of Values Driving Strategy.

and customers. In a seminal booklet on the subject, the central point was made that "in daily practice, the word *brand* stands as a surrogate for the word *reputation*. In fact your brand acts just like a person."[6]

How we come to determine the brand's core identity invariably involves the three elements as shown in Fig. 4.2:[7]

Ultimately, the so-called "core identity" (or timeless essence) of the organization captured in the brand follows from the answers to some tough, introspective questions:

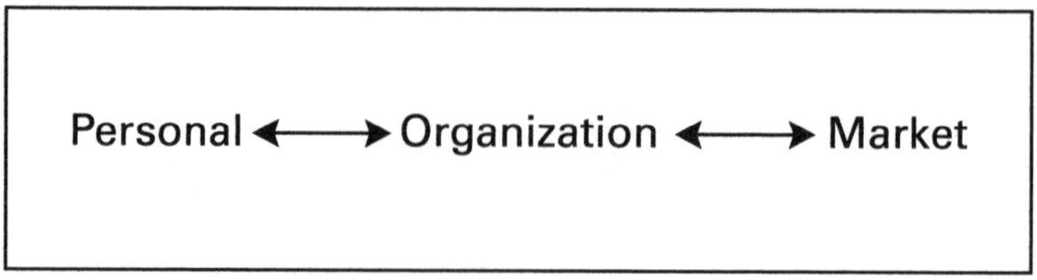

Personal ⟷ Organization ⟷ Market

Figure 4.2: Elements of Brand Identity.

- What are the fundamental beliefs and values that drive the brand?

- What are the competencies of the organization behind the brand?

- What does the organization behind the brand stand for?

- What is the "soul" of the brand?

A leading text on the subject states: "One brand strategist observed that if you get the values and culture of the organization right, the brand identity takes care of itself."[8]

Again, as any student of philosophy will quickly see, strategic brand analysis offers the opportunity to raise deep, philosophical questions leading to such questions as: Who are we? and What is our purpose? The answers define the company's *soul.*

The work in branding can then be seen as a way of thinking of the corporation as a person; a provocative model that helps us analyze our selves as well as the corporation's relation to the outer world. This approach can properly be called philosophical if we follow Iris Murdoch's definition: "To live philosophy is to explore one's own temperament (core identity or brand) and yet, at the same time, to attempt to discover the truth (what's really going on)."[9]

4.3 Brand Analysis as a Corporate Narrative

Once a corporation can see itself as a person and its brand or reputation expressing its stance or a posture toward the world, – it is an easy matter to see what its role actually is in society. The practice of pragmatism – as a method of inquiry between induction (following every trend) and deduction (sticking with a strategy) – offers the useful posture of investigation, hypothesis, and action. The nature of pragmatism, though simple in application, requires initial courage to question the assumptions that lie below the present stance toward the market.[10]

4.4 Personal Narrative

It takes a lot of philosophical effort to bridge the enormous gap between the relevance of philosophy and our everyday concerns. It is usually done under the rubric of business ethics.

While the corporate narrative helps managers to understand their organization's unfolding potential and its stance toward the world as expressed by their brand, each person within an organization must also look to see what is expressed through their individual business lives. One way to engage students in philosophical questioning is exemplified in a class conducted with Oliver Williams CSC at the University of Notre Dame College of Business Administration for MBA students in the Fall of 1997, entitled *Ethical Dimension of Leadership*.

The purpose of the course is presented in this introductory statement in the syllabus:

> "If the manager is technically competent and at the same time guided by a value system that reflects the nature and destiny of the person, his or her efforts will benefit and enhance the lives of others. Such a career is ideal for the

most creative, intelligent, and resourceful people in our society."

The question is: How does one engage students and put them in touch with this notion of "nature and destiny of the person"? One way is to assess the assumptions that lie beneath the person's stance towards the world. We can readily do this by looking at what kind of a life has been and is being led: what one remembers and what one counts as danger, success, friends, and enemies will show the stance the person has taken.

The course is, on the surface, based around the Note Dame students who were brought into close contact with four executives-in-residence who worked with them for several days at a time. The executives presented material which they thought was important to challenge the students' thinking on important questions concerning behavior in a business career and they addressed the following issues:

- How do you ethically run a company?

- What is success?

- What is the good life?

- How are we to live?

- On what basis – on what principles – do we make decisions?

Our method of pragmatic inquiry goes further by bringing in the perspective of holistic depth psychology in the sense that each person's life may be seen as a seed or an acorn. Each life has potential which we are seeking to find and develop. This potential (or *calling*, to use a more religious perspective) can be seen by considering the events of our lives and where we seem to be heading.

The students received a *PathFinder* Notebook in which to listen for and write down the themes that shape the narrative of the executives' lives. This narration offers them a framework that engages and allows them to reflect on their own narratives.

We posed ten key broad-ranging questions to the students. They are designed to engage and stretch the students' thinking, to help them discern themes, patterns, and clues to the executives' narratives, and thereby, to their own:

1. How would you describe the strategies and values of the corporations in which the executives work?

   What were the key strategies of their companies (e.g., core competencies and strategic intent upon which business policy is built), and how did they help formulate them and how did they change?

2. What is the basis of the executive's business success , their core competencies? In addition to the techniques learned in business schools: Finance, Marketing, etc., what else do they seem to have?

3. What are the executives' professional beliefs and how do we verify this?

   - What was their initial hypothesis of the purpose of business and how did this drive their behavior?

   - Has this view of the purpose of business changed or expanded over the years?

   - What now do they see is the purpose of business and how does it guide their action?

   - What actions and other evidence do we have from the presentations that demonstrate beliefs driving actions?

4. What are their personal beliefs?

- What do they hold important, value, and pay attention to?

- How were these beliefs formed?

- How are their personal and professional beliefs different?

- How have their personal beliefs affected their companies?

- How have principles of their religious beliefs guided their behavior?

- Did they or do they now have some sense of calling or vocation?

- Do they feel that there was a certain flow or destiny to their career that, looking back now, makes their careers into a compelling, engaging story.

- Have they come to different perspectives? And, if so, how?

- What are the key points of tension that require a constant evaluation and balance (e.g. profit and values, friendship and results, work and family, etc.)?

5. Describe how the executives think:

- What did they learn? And how did they learn it?

- What questions have become most important to them?

- What are the key points of tension that require a constant evaluation and balance e.g. profit and values, friendship and results, work and family, etc.?)

- Looking back now, what can they see from their student days that they learned or the beliefs that have served them best?

- What have they had to discard or modify since and how did they discover it?

- What doubts do they still have about their role in business?

- What would they tell others to look out for?

- What were the seeds back then that have now blossomed to be an important part of their character?

- What questions do they want to challenge the students with?

- How do they investigate the facts, survey situations, and then formulate courses of action based on their set of beliefs.

- How do they use and develop their knowledge?

Note: Since one goal of the course was to determine and improve the managerial thinking process in a time of rapid change, we needed to learn to manage information and come to insight that is critical to a successful business.

6. How would you describe the intuitive or creative side of their management thinking?

- How important was this in their careers?

- Do they have a method for this type of thinking?

Note: Creativity is often described as taking existing ideas and facts and putting them together in new combinations or in seeing patterns before others do – reading the clues in a situation or in the marketplace. This is often an individual effort but discovered by listening to different voices. What examples of this kind of creative activity do you see in their careers?

7. The role of chance and synchronicity.

- When did events seem to unfold as in a "flow" or the executives were driven by events beyond their control?

- How did chance events seem to change direction in their careers?

- How did fortuitous events, "good luck", unexpected co-incidences and turns seem to play a role in their careers? (As in "life is what happens to you while you plan to do something else".)

- Do you have the feeling that they are part of a story with their lives unfolding and that often they just needed to be alert to clues of where they should go next?

8. What crises did they face?

- What was determined as a crisis?

- What was the nature of the crisis and how did their values determine whether it was a crisis or not? (One person's crisis is another person's non-event.)

- What did they do about it?

- Did they have to compromise?

9. Relationships

- Who were their mentors?

- What did they learn from them?

- Who were their associates within the company?

- How important was forming networks in relationships for success in business – the ability to work with others?

- On what basis did they determine and form relationships with the all-important customer?

10. Results.

- What results were most satisfying to them?

- What beliefs drove those results?

- How did their beliefs help form the key strategies of their companies? Or were their beliefs actually a hindrance or constraint on action?

- How did they convey these beliefs to their management and help provide a passion to the organization's efforts?

In summary, we asked the students to determine what it takes to be successful in business, what is success, and what should be a professional, and philosophical, stance towards engaging the world and their career. They also learned that a compelling way to determine that stance was to observe over time what is measured as success and failure, danger, risk, and what is learned as these definitions change.

4.5 Conclusion

My purpose has been to show ways to engage business practitioners and students in philosophical inquiry. The engagements aim to help students and practitioners discover for themselves and their corporations what is *really* going on in the world and within themselves. Therefore, they can determine their stances towards the world. By doing that, they will fulfill the promise of philosophical inquiry and, as Murdoch said, attempt to discover the truth.

Chapter 5

Pragmatism:
Putting Philosophy to Work in Business

5th International Conference
on Social Values in Education and Business
University of Oxford – July, 1999

"Love is the extremely difficult realization that something other than oneself is real."

Iris Murdoch, *The Sublime and the Good*

5.1 Introduction

If you wander over to the Business Section of any modern mega-bookstore, you will be surprised to find, in the midst of the more traditional and widely acclaimed books such as *Competitive Strategy*, *Built to Last* and *Competing for the Future* – such provocative titles usually reserved for the Self-help or Spirituality sections: *The Heart Aroused*, *The Feminine in Business*, *If Jesus Were the CEO*, *Awakening the Corporate Soul: Four Paths to Unleash the Power of People at Work*, and even a fast-selling *Chicken Soup for the Soul at Work*. Actually, there are hundreds of similar titles pouring out of such publishers as Butterworth Heinemann, Barrett-Koehler, and HarperCollins who sense a major market opportunity in business people's search for something more meaningful in their work lives. With business and economic models dictating and dominating the patterns of thought in our culture today, this focus on and search for business and larger purpose and meaning should not be so surprising after all.

The result of this search is cropping up in unusual places, such as Victoria's Secret, which states a corporate philosophy inside their provocative catalog. Jaguar Corporation has a philosophy. If you check, your local dry cleaner will most likely give you a copy of their Mission Statement. And recently, while visiting Seattle, I walked into the Pike's Place Brewery, and, after a casual look at that most American of products – the six-pack of beer – I was shocked and pleased to see these words begin the copy on the side of the carton: "Microbrew is a philosophy." [1] Clearly, philosophy has come of age. Now the question is: How do we put it to work?

This chapter will make the case that all the searching for deeper meaning in business will be greatly enhanced by the application of that unique, and often maligned and misunderstood philosophy: pragmatism. Pragmatism means far more then the usual "do whatever works" or "action unguided by principle." Since philosophy may be characterized as "love or pursuit of the truth" or the "pursuit of the truth," we can assume there is a reality out there – a truth, an *other*, with which I must be in touch and understand, and perhaps even love. Pragmatism, as I will be using the term, is the method of inquiry which helps determine a belief or truth in terms of the consequences which result from embracing that belief or truth. As William James asked: "What is the cash value of the idea?" Business people find this turn of the phrase to describe pragmatism particularly engaging. John Dewey would say something like: "If this is what we believe, then this is the action we should take." Pragmatism, therefore, involves an *other*.

I will examine how this pragmatic philosophy, or what I am calling *PathFinder Pragmatic Inquiry®* (*PathFinder*), with its three key elements, emphasizes the narrative quality of the inquiry and can be put into actual practice. How ironic that, midst all the philosophical wrangling about the actual meaning of pragmatism, few philosophers actually address how to practice this most practical philosophy.

At first glance, it may seem unusual for the CEO of an advertising agency to have stumbled onto the importance of pragmatic inquiry, the major elements involved in it, and finally its application for practitioners in business and educational settings. However, it makes all the sense in the world, as you will see, because advertising, as a part of marketing, focuses so intently on a very particular "other" – the customer.

5.2 The Advertising Business

Let me begin by stating how I came to understand the importance of the "other," the central figure in this chapter. Admittedly, it is a long journey from advertising to philosophy, but practiced at its best, advertising is one of the richest areas for the application of philosophical thought and especially pragmatic inquiry. Behind the ubiquitous presence of the advertising veil, lies the powerful (and some would say seductive) pursuit of meaning. Advertising is designed to define and support a brand, the sum total of the meaning of the product or service – its philosophy. The activity of branding is coming to be seen as the critical component of business strategy, since the purpose of business is to create and serve a customer. In earlier days, marketing was looked on as structuring a one-time exchange between the buyer and the seller. Marketing worked with Four Ps: product, price, place and promotion – and adjusted these elements to come up with an optimum exchange. Today, marketing's role has been raised to a much higher level. It is responsible for the *relationship* with the customer to determine their needs and then respond with a flow of ideas and products for the long-term benefit of the relationship over time. This change of view can also be seen as the familiar move from the mechanical view of nature, which is highly structured and to be manipulated like a machine, to the organic or biological view of nature

as a living entity with a wide range of choices, responses, relationships, and interdependencies. The company must consider the needs
of the "other," whether for love or profit, and then make the necessary
choices and investments to deliver what the market needs.

Therefore, the discipline of Strategy, increasingly driven by marketing considerations, focuses on investment choices that create the
points of product differentiation providing the corporation with a
"sustainable competitive advantage". (See Chapter 3). One leading
strategist has gone so far as to say that the fundamental role and purpose of strategy is to "induce your competitors not to invest in those
products, markets, and services where you expect to invest the most
resources"[2]

Advertising tells the story of the meaning which results from the
company's investments in terms of filling the customer's needs. This
meaning is summarized in the Brand Philosophy which always includes the statements of:

- Target audience;

- The role the product plays in the target audience's lives – what
  problems it solves;

- The brand promise – the benefit;

- The reason to believe the promise – the product's "sustainable
  competitive advantage".

We have also found that the rigors of the strategic marketing and
branding analysis work equally well on the individual level as well as
on the product or corporate level. As they inquire about the marketing
strategies in the corporation, executives come to see what investments
they, as individuals, need to make to further the corporation's plan.
And individuals outside a corporation who are contemplating their

careers in terms of what industry, profession, organization, or corporation they wish to join, face exactly the same questions and search for meaning in how they plan to invest their time and talent. This has been especially effective with business school students.[3]

The three elements of strategic relationships in *PathFinder Pragmatic Inquiry*® may be shown as in Fig. 5.1.

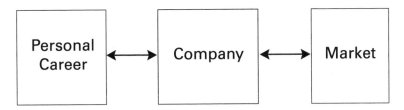

Figure 5.1: Three Elements of Strategic Relationships.

We now turn to consider the general promise of Pragmatic Inquiry and three key activities which *PathFinder Pragmatic Inquiry*® (PPI) helps foster. We conclude by describing a structure and method for practicing *PathFinder* – putting pragmatic philosophy to work – with *Corporantes PathFinder Notebook*©.

5.3 Pragmatism: Classic American Philosophy

Because pragmatism has now been widely recognized as America's only contribution to the history of Philosophy, it has been designated as Classic American Philosophy. It even has its own canon of all-stars: Charles Sanders Peirce, Josiah Royce, William James, John Dewey, George Santayana, and Alfred North Whitehead.[4]

Pragmatism holds great promise for the type of strategic investment inquiry suggested above. The founder of Classic American Philosophy, Charles Sanders Peirce, states the case quite dramatically:

"A certain maxim of Logic which I have called pragmatism has recommended itself to me for diverse reasons and on sundry considerations. Having taken it as my guide in most of my thought, I find that as the years of my knowledge of it lengthen, my sense of the importance of it presses upon me more and more. If it is only true, it is certainly a wonderfully efficient instrument. It is not to philosophy only that it is applicable. I have found it of signal service in every branch of science that I have studied. My want of skill in practical affairs does not prevent me from perceiving the advantage of being well imbued with pragmatism in the conduct of life."[5]

Allowing for the fact that Peirce was trying to impress his audience at Harvard, his alma mater which had rejected him, this is high praise for a simple insight that ideas and beliefs are the action and consequences which result *from* those visions and beliefs.[6] While simple, it has profound implications for pursuing the truth. Yet, this original meaning has traveled quickly down the slippery slope to the much maligned "do whatever works" stance. This is far from the original intent of these earnest members of the canon who urged the most rigorous and challenging thinking and feeling in order to arrive at the best beliefs to guide actions.

Peirce has said that the truth was approached in the movement between ideas and the reality in the form of constant testing. His basic model was Scientific Inquiry in which you establish a hypothesis and then go out to test it, continually modifying your hypothesis, based on the evidence. He called this *abduction* in distinction from *induction* (constantly collecting facts and evidence) and *deduction* (applying a conclusion, law, or truth).

The word *pragmatism* therefore, needs a dramatic redefinition. Several elements of pragmatism help correct and expand the truncated definition and which guides PPI. I will suggest three:

- Interpretation.

- Intuition.

- Reflection on experience.

There are many other features and aspects to this rich philosophy, but, since the framework for this discussion is to help individuals and corporations determine the investment they need to make for future action in developing a relationship with the *other*, these three strike me as the most helpful. They offer strong medicine to remedy the traditional narrowness and traps of business thinking usually characterized as:

- Short-term.

- Overly rational.

- Internally focused.

- Individualistic.

- Command and Control.

- Repetitive – rote – habitual.

- Stimulus-response – reactive.

- Non-reflective.

Now that we have some general background on business strategy and levels of inquiry which corporations and individuals have to go through to determine their choices of investments, we will turn to three elements of pragmatism that help structure and facilitate the application of pragmatism to practical inquiries.

Interpretation

Since the meaning of pragmatism today has degenerated into a simple "do whatever works (for me)," we need to remember that the major breakthrough of pragmatic thinking established the relationship between one's ideas and the "other" in the outside world. Modern thought, for example, can be characterized as either falling to one extreme of individual, subjective interpretation or to the other extreme of worship of objective science.

Peirce's successor, Josiah Royce, noted these two extremes as two categories of knowledge – perception and conception – which he saw as dominating the greater part of the history of philosophy. Perceptions are what we see; the signs or evidence around us which we take in through our senses. Conceptions are ideas, especially our beliefs, which filter what we see. Royce took from Peirce the realization that there is a third category of knowledge, different from perception and conception, called interpretation. It brings perception and conception together and compares them. In Royce's words, interpretation "surveys from above. It is an attainment of a larger unity of consciousness."[7] Reality must then be understood as a *sign* which needs to be interpreted, not as a thing in itself. It is to be known, understood, and judged true by the activities that keep it going as a sign. Royce's insight overcomes the centuries-old debate between realism – something out there – versus nominalism – the construction of reality in our own minds. The pragmatists say it is both; it is the constant interaction between the two that make up the pursuit of truth.

Intuition

We have now seen how pragmatism corrects the individual's subjective orientation at one end of the spectrum and focuses on the movement between the individual and the outer reality of the *other*. Pragmatism's emphasis on intuition also corrects the orientation to fact and the rational at the other end of the spectrum. The following quote states the problem:

> "The status of intuition has declined over the last century, perhaps with the increasing emphasis on formal logic and explicit data and assumptions of science."[8]

Valuing intuition has been especially important in my work in advertising where ideas need to incubate. Plato says much the thing in the *Phaedrus* #270 where Socrates says: "Every great art must be supplanted by leisurely discussion, by stargazing, if you will, about the nature of things."

William James put it quite poetically:

> "Dive back into the flux itself if you wish to know reality, that flux which Platonism in its strange belief that only the immutable is excellent, has always spurned; turn your face towards sensation, the flesh-bound thing which rationalism has always loaded with abuse."[9]

We now apply intuition and interpretation to the flux of our experience, the center of *PathFinder Pragmatic Inquiry*®.

Reflection on experience

Many people today claim that the scarcest commodity is time to reflect.

Pierce, the founder of pragmatism, attributed this not to a lack of time but to a more fundamental problem:

"Few persons care to study logic because everyone can see themselves to be proficient enough in the art of reasoning already. I observed that this satisfaction is limited to one's own ratiocination and does not extend to that of other men [...][10] But it is doubt or uncertainty that begins the process: The irritation of doubt causes a struggle to attain a state of belief. I shall term this struggle, inquiry [...]"[11]

John Dewey embraced that idea. Dewey, who focused on the logic of inquiry, said "all learning is a continuous process of reconstruction of experience."[12] Looking at experience in this way, we need to ask what assumptions were behind the experiences, challenge these assumptions, and look for clues as to how we might develop and change these assumptions and beliefs. Keeping in mind that pragmatism states that beliefs are seen in light of their consequences, then this idea has considerable importance in pursuing the truth and modifying beliefs for future action.

This focus on consequences and action leads naturally to the idea that truth is not told once but is always in the making. This relationship with an *other*, as told through the experiences forming into a plot, tells a great deal about the set of beliefs and assumptions that guide the storyteller as well as the people in the story. Their beliefs have been driving the action.[13] The simple reason for this is that only by knowing the underlying beliefs and direction of the story can we determine such things as success, failure, danger, alliances, and practice of virtues.

This brings us to the central feature of pragmatic inquiry, the practice of Pragmatism leads people to reflect on their own experiences and see what assumptions and beliefs are behind them. It also shows them the clues they can get as to where the narrative of their lives might go based on their vision and beliefs in connection with the *other*.

A good place to conclude this discussion of the three basic elements of the *PathFinder* is to relate the definition of philosophy by Alfred North Whitehead, the last member of the canon of Classic American Philosophers. He gave an address at the Harvard Business School in 1934 entitled: "On Foresight." In that talk, he encouraged the students to be looking ahead, constantly testing the environment, and going from the general to the specific, all of which he felt were indications of philosophical thought. He concluded his statement with this definition of philosophy:

> "Philosophy is an attempt to clarify those fundamental beliefs that finally determine the emphasis of attention that lies at the base of character."[14]

Whitehead's emphasis on character becomes clear as we reflect on our experience because the fundamental beliefs that one holds determine the action which exhibits one's character. And it starts with what we pay attention to!

Having examined pragmatism and the three major elements which have guided the development of the *PathFinder Pragmatic Inquiry®*, we will now consider how pragmatism has been put to work through the *Corporantes PathFinder Notebook©*.

5.4 Putting *PathFinder* Pragmatic Inquiry® to Work

As I mentioned before, we ask the inquirers to consider the three elements of relationship with the *other*. The inquiry process can begin at any point and then move to the other two.

Below is the basic relationship triangle. Before people begin an inquiry, they identify the three elements.

The inquiry process can begin at any point and move to the other two, depending on the audience and their questions:

Members of a corporate group – or senior executives individually – who need to inquire about their vision and strategy issues in general, or who face a particular issue concerning their relationship with the marketplace should ask:

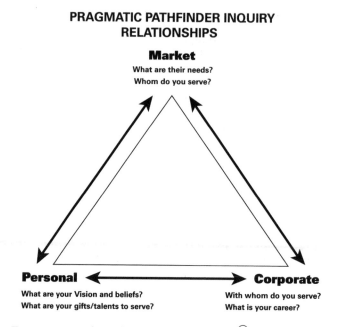

Figure 5.2: PathFinder Pragmatic Inquiry® Relationships.

- What direction should we go?

- What beliefs and assumptions are driving action?

- What investments should we make?

(Order of Investigation: Corporate – Market – Personal)
Senior executives who want to reflect on their individual leadership issues, dilemmas, personal beliefs, etc. and their impact on their corporation need to ask:

- What is my relationship with the corporation and what needs to be done?

- What are the beliefs guiding my leadership decision?

- What personal beliefs inform my business beliefs?

(Order of Investigation: Personal – Corporate – Market)
Students beginning their careers, executives contemplating a career change, and senior executives reflecting on their legacy. might ask the following:

- What field do I want to go into?

- Whom do I want to serve – what market or audience?

- What is the vision and belief driving my career motivation and choices?

(Order of Investigation: Market – Personal – Corporate)
When the work is done in a group, we find that the use of "interpretation" is particularly important. Each person has a different view of the reality the corporation faces. It is helpful to imagine everyone being part of a cable where each strand is important as opposed to a chain where the line of reasoning is only as strong as the weakest link. We always remind participants in a group that everyone has a piece of the truth.

At the Personal level, we have used PPI in helping individual executives and leaders of corporations determine the direction of their careers and how they can articulate their leadership beliefs and structure the Vision, Purpose, and Strategy statements of their corporations. Students of business schools have a particular need to reflect on their careers. They too often have moved into career decisions, either guided by outside influences or by narrow monetary interests, but not by a clear grasp of Vision, Beliefs, and Values to drive their decisions.

The *Corporantes PathFinder Notebook©* ("*PathFinder*") provides a method of inquiry, discovery, interpretation, and action. It offers a flexible framework of exercises to help individuals or groups look at a situation, problem or idea from several angles to get a better picture of reality.

A brief explanation of the name, *PathFinder Pragmatic Inquiry*®, practiced using the *Corporantes PathFinder Notebook*©, and how they developed might be of help. After considering the key elements of pragmatic inquiry and working with students and executives in hundreds of setting for over twenty years, we developed a notebook called *PathFinder*, It helps readers with the narrative aspects of their inquiry. Likewise, *Corporantes* or "forming into a body" suggests ways people might inquire together. Inquiry begins with a question. In business, this is easy because generally there is some crisis which prompts the inquiry. It requires a stance of uncertainty. Students, especially MBAs who are seeking a pot of gold at the end of their rainbow, are less eager to seem uncertain, especially in job interviews. It is important, at the beginning of the inquiry process, to state their preliminary beliefs, assumptions and answers which then frees their minds to explore other alternatives. The exercises are then organized in three steps of logical thought: Investigate, Hypothesize and Act! Here is an outline of the inquiry:

- BEGIN!

    - Visions and Beliefs
      What are our beliefs now?
      As we move forward, what question, issue, doubt, problem, situation, do we face?
      What is our preliminary answer now?

  - The Path Ahead

    Why is the question or issue important? What actionable steps will we be able to take when we get an answer? (This will sharpen the question and make it actionable.)

    What actions do you now think should be taken?

- INVESTIGATE!

  - Corporate Bearings

    Where is the corporation and its products and services now?

  - Corporate Path

    Retrace how the corporation and products have developed.

    What has been learned?

    Recount decisions made and not made.

    Where do we want to head in the future?

  - Market Bearings

    What are our thoughts regarding where the market situation, the customer, the industry, and this society are now?

  - Market Path

    Retrace important events and decisions and how the market, competitors, distribution, etc., have developed and where they seem to be headed in the future.

  - Personal Bearings

    In terms of your individual career or your career within the corporation right now, what are your thoughts regarding your personal situation?

- Personal Path

  Retrace your experience with the issue or problem that the corporation faces. Or, if you are contemplating your career, reflect on the path you have been on and where it seems to be heading.

- Path Notes

  Record facts, data, insights, experiences, hunches, and observations.

- HYPOTHESIZE!

  - Conversations

    Explore the inner voice as well as what you think others might say.

  - Maps and Images

    Engage in various drawing exercises in what the situation looks like, what it should look like and what action plan should look like.

  - Habits

    Explore known and unknown habits, strategies, or tactics, which lead or limit our progress. On what assumptions are they based? What needs to change?

  - Listening and Learning

    Compare your ideas with others, ask questions and get their opinion.

- ACT!

  - Vision and Beliefs

    Create a Vision (purpose, mission, values, and beliefs) for your corporation and for your involvement with that corporation, or for your own career.

– The Path Ahead

Put your Vision and Beliefs to the test in action. What actions will the corporation take and what actions will you take?

PathFinder inquirers work much like a healthcare practitioner works with clients. They survey the symptoms, collect test information from many sources, probe for causes, form an hypothesis, take action in recommending a healthful regiment, and monitor the results.

Treating the corporation and one's career as living entities with talent, character, a service to provide, and a path to follow is central to this inquiry. As in any exploration, we urge inquirers to be open to surprises, capture vague impressions, feelings and memories, and look for patterns and connections. We ask them to be willing to entertain new explanations and ideas they don't now believe in. We invite them to use their intuition, their right brains as well as their more rational left brains.

We encourage participants to keep notes as ideas, facts, and impressions present themselves. With enough entries in the CPN, Inquirers discover their own interpretation of the evidence they have collected. This offers them a way to:

- Explore and interpret the reality in which they operate.

- Respond to the reality.

- Improve their habits and thought.

- Think more intuitively.

- Understand their unique, sustainable role, individually and as a corporation, to serve the needs of society.

- Think together as a group and make the best use of different perspectives and talents.

The result is a simple statement of logic: If this is what we have discovered and believe in, then this is the action we need to take.

5.5 Conclusion

Many business thinkers are looking at and taking seriously the importance of moving from the mechanical point of discovery to a biological or organic point of view. Under the mechanical theory, scientific inquiry was to determine the truth of how something actually operated. This gave rise to the spectacular success of science and mathematics to explain the great Newtonian machine of the universe. As we move from that machine model to the more organic model, we need to develop different models and the best ones come to us from biology. Consider a cell or organism, and how it needs to relate to its environment. It is constantly *absorbing* data and *interpreting* it to determine a better way to engage the environment and survive and thrive. This model rings true with business people who are constantly in contact with the marketplace and need to take in information and modify their behavior.

A second model, in addition to the organic model, is an arts-based model in which observers begin to see this process of relationship and movement as the unfolding of a drama. Arts-based management studies are springing up and seizing the imagination of the theory laden and passion starved executive. For instance, the Cranfield School of Business outside of London is using drama, such as Shakespeare's *Henry V* or *Julius Caesar*, as the theme for students to study lessons of management.

A third model, first suggested by Fr. Oliver Williams and John Houck of the University of Notre Dame, is story writing and story telling. They have focused on "character traits that endure over time, [that] display what it means to be a Christian in the business world. Christian beliefs give shape to a person's lifetime story".[15] Other people's stories will be shaped by different beliefs. But the point is the evidence of beliefs will be revealed through the story.

The *PathFinder* combines these approaches since students write their own dramas and learn the lessons from their own experience. The story of business and people's individual careers needs the awakening to the extremely difficult realization that something other than oneself is real. That to me is the major connection between business strategy and deeper questions of business purpose. This connection can best be shown by the diagram in Fig. 5.3.[16]

This spiral diagram is an attempt to show the constant movement of an *other* manifesting itself in this world. It begins with a transcendent spark, which we embody in a spirit, or a soul, or life force. This is then expressed in our psyche, our temperament, personality, inclinations. The psyche then finds expression in a career which, along with others, forms an organization to serve some market need.[17] This market exists within a larger society which lives by prevailing ideas and beliefs. Then images emerge at the so-called global consciousness level, which is not nearly as vague a concept as one might think. Major examples include the movement from the machine age to the information age, the awareness of the ecological crisis and interdependence of the planet, rise in the respect for the feminine, concern for rights in ethnic conflicts, and third world labor issues building to the wider issue of global, political, and economic justice. Others go so far as to see this global consciousness as an expression of the emerging of a Divine Consciousness.

Whether *PathFinder Pragmatic Inquiry®* as practiced using the *Corporantes PathFinder Notebook©* can awaken the realization of "love" or not, as we all search for relationships with others, is a story which each one of us tells through the evidence and activities of our own lives.

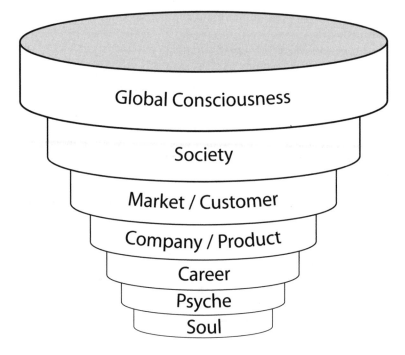

Figure 5.3: Economic Relationship with the *Other* – The application of relationship thinking.

Chapter 6

Business as a Calling;
The Calling of Business:
A Pedagogical Model and Practice

5th International Conference
on Social Values in Business and Education, [1]
Oxford University, July, 1999

"Vocation [...] The place God calls you to is the place where your deep gladness and the world's deep hunger meet.

Frederick Buechner[2]

6.1 Introduction

This chapter, written in collaboration with Professor John (Jack) A. Ruhe, Ph.D. at St. Mary College in South Bend, Indiana, presents the story of our efforts to improve the character trait development of his business students, especially those traits relevant to ethical decision-making (e.g., *courage – critical and questioning attitude toward authority* and *compassion*). We chronicle, here, the development of a new course, "Personal Ethics & Corporate Culture," and how we monitored the impact of changes made to the course since 1994 with the survey instrument of Michael Maccoby in *The Gamesman*.

We present evidence, first, that character traits can be diminished in business programs, and then that teaching ethics courses can help foster the development of character. This issue is important today as society increasingly looks to universities to help stem the increasing

violation of laws and values in business through ethics courses of instruction. This has resulted in a dramatic increase in the numbers
of business ethics courses being taught. Because ethics are values-
laden and the generally held belief is that values are developed from
childhood, one must ask the question, as people have since Aristotle, whether ethics courses can help in this development of character.
Limited research, if any, has examined the effectiveness of the ethic
instruction on the time-honored effort of character development of
students. This research examines the effectiveness of a popular ethics
course by contrasting pre and post class student perceptions of character trait importance and examining the elements of students reflecting
on their experiences (through narrative) which might explain the differences. We find that students' perceptions of the character traits of
openness, compassion and *courage* change significantly, while the traits
of *learning, confidence* and *independence* remain stable. How? By
putting students in touch with real life situations and goals: their own.

The most significant improvement was the addition of *PathFinder
Pragmatic Inquiry*® that helped students find answers to such questions as vocational choice – finding their "calling" and to identify
the values and vision on which their choices are based. Also, student ratings on the Maccoby character trait survey showed perceived
higher value and higher reinforcement in their business studies after
we added the *Corporantes PathFinder Notebook*© to the course.

Current business magazines have focused on the disillusionment
that many in business have faced in their recent corporate lives as a result of the failure of DotComs, LBOs, IPOs, the stock market, corporate malfeasance, etc. With lost confidence in leaders and institutions,
the current difficult economic climate serves as a form of reckoning.
People are searching for what really matters when it comes to work
and are asking: "What should I do with my life?"[3] After interviewing
over 900 people, Bronson found that most people had good instincts
about where they belong but made poor choices and wasted produc-

tive years on the wrong work.[4] He indicates that most career choices are made on impulse and whim with little investigation. People may seek happiness but ignore what Seligman[5] contends is the lasting satisfaction that comes from rising to the challenges of work, love, and raising children. He asserts that this work orientation is a "calling" that is a passionate commitment to work for its own sake, regardless of the money or status it brings. Sanders[6] contends we can attain a great sense of meaning and satisfaction if we assume that" love is the most powerful force in business".

These popular examples, particularly Bronson and Sanders, are unknowing restatements of deep philosophical insights drawn from pragmatic philosophy as well as theology. Here are two sources. Pragmatic philosophy is based on a method of inquiry to test hypotheses in pursuit of the truth, which leads to action. The heart of pragmatic inquiry as a philosophy as defined by Alfred North Whitehead[7] would help Bronson's subjects think about what they "should" do: "Philosophy is an attempt to clarify those fundamental beliefs which finally determine the emphasis of attention that lies at the base of character." Bernard Lonergan[8] articulates a parallel method of theological inquiry which concludes with Sanders' "love as the most powerful force in business" when he proposes:

- be attentive

- be intelligent

- be reasonable

- be responsible

- be in love

Both Lonergan and the pragmatists place central importance on action guided by fundamental beliefs or what we call values and vision.

But the central question is: "How do we uncover what it is we are called to do?" It is our contention that pragmatic inquiry, by reflecting on the evidence of our experience, is designed to uncover the operational values and vision on which vocational decisions can be based. We will state at the start our definition of a value:

> A value is any belief, principle or virtue held so deeply (consciously or unconsciously) that it drives behavior, decisions and actions.

6.2   Can We Teach Character in Business Schools?

Maybe, but our evidence indicates that it can also be un-taught!

There can be little doubt that American colleges and universities are, and have been, deeply concerned with shaping the values, attitudes, and beliefs of their students. Morrill[9], Sloan,[10] And Pascarellan and Terenzini[11] found that most faculty, administrators, parents, legislators, alumni, and students themselves agree that higher educational institutions should be involved in shaping values. The question is whether some institutions are more effective than others in preparing their students in values or character development.

For over twenty years at St. Mary's College we have used the Maccoby Head and Heart survey of character traits instrument .[12] The survey lists nineteen character traits, which are evidence of values according to the above definition. (See Table 6.1) Students are asked to rate each trait as to its perceived importance in achieving business career success. After rating the importance of each trait for career success, the students also identify which of the traits they consider to have been stimulated or reinforced during the course of their past studies.

Maccoby contends that the valuing of character traits are behavioral inclinations in general that can be classified as head traits (thinking qualities related to conceptualizations) or heart traits (feeling qualities related to consciousness). His survey instrument includes nine head traits and ten heart traits. Maccoby argues that head and heart traits should be balanced for one to be sensitive to ethical implications in business decisions. He further argues that comparatively low valuing of heart traits is symptomatic of careerists who constantly ignore *idealistic, compassionate,* and *courageous (critical of authority)* impulses that might jeopardize their careers.

Emotions behind heart traits can help resolve certain ethical dilemmas. Research by Kochunny and Rogers:[13] Ruhe and Drevs[14]; Stevens;[15] (and Kreitner and Reif[16] suggests that business schools do a good job of emphasizing and developing analytical skills (head traits) but a poor job in developing qualities of the heart associated with ethical behavior. Allen et. al.,[17] found an increase in perceived importance of heart traits related to ethical inclination such as *honesty, compassion, and generosity* in the same six universities over a fifteen-year period. Ruhe et al.,[18] contend that differences in Maccoby's trait importance seemed related to reinforcement differences in school types.

We tested a group of Saint Mary's students as first year students (1987) and then again when they were seniors (1991) using the Maccoby instrument. As freshmen, all students rated the character traits nearly the same, both in value to their careers and in their perceptions of the extent to which the traits had been reinforced in their past studies. However as seniors, *business* students, compared to *non-business* students, perceived lower value and lower reinforcement in their business studies of nine of the ten heart traits. (See Table 2.)

This research jolted us. We were especially concerned that the survey indicated that traditional business studies tended to suppress the character traits most important to ethical decision-making: *critical questioning of authority* and *compassion.* We decided to develop and require a new course, "Personal Ethics & Corporate Culture," as well as to try to integrate ethics throughout the business curriculum.

The new class required students to write a paper discussing their career choices and the reasons for their choices. We expected the students to choose based on a Personal Strategic Audit evaluating their personal strengths and weaknesses and external opportunities and threats (SWOT analysis). However, in their papers most students wrote only "sterile" outlines that focused on "facts" derived from the audit, with little examination of the broader question of their "calling or vocation." What was missing in the papers was a context within which to determine meaning and direction. We wanted to challenge students to look on their careers as a deeper study of choices and decisions based on their values and vocation within a larger societal context.

As we realized that traditional business studies do not prepare students for an "in-depth inquiry" of who they are and what they love to do, we began to look for a process (instead of self-help books) that would help. To this end, the *PathFinder* material proved most helpful. People who thrive, focus on the question of who they really are, based on what they value, which leads them to work they truly love to do. Although this is not a new idea, it may be the one most disrespected in the corporate world. Too many people look for exciting and challenging work but see no need to consider what is meaningful, significant, and fulfilling. It is equally as important to find an environment that reinforces one's set of values and beliefs and uses the gifts one has to offer. This discovery of meaning and direction occurs as we write the stories of our lives and the stories of our potential places of work.

Progoff[19] contends that we can find where our life wants to go with the use of intensive journaling. The *PathFinder Notebook*© builds on Progoff's journal concept to help individuals and organizations attain a sustainable, competitive advantage in the marketplace by developing their unique potential, what Progoff calls an individual's "seed." We must treat what we know about ourselves, and our choices based on that knowledge, as assumptions to be challenged. Among other activities, *PathFinder* inquiry involves reflection on how our values and beliefs play out in our experiences.

The students' career choices are informed when they interpret the evidence of their own experience from multiple perspectives and uncover their values, core purpose and goals. They then can choose careers that enable them to live their values and put their talents to work in service to others.

As we challenge our assumptions, we examine the evidence of our experience (e.g., life choices and business decisions) and may find that the values and goals driving our stories are different than what we had assumed, and therefore the meaning of the story is different than we had assumed.

6.3   Student Challenges

For many college students the choice of a vocation in business is a foreboding one. Students are faced with increased globalization that spreads even higher-skilled jobs across the world; competition from others not only across the world, but from others more skilled and experienced who have suffered downsizings; an uncertain and listless economy limited by terrorism and war; and corporate scandals. Many prospective business students are wondering: Why should I major in business with all these problems? Those with strong Christian values might be even more critical of a business career choice.

Corporate Scandals

For those students who considered business schools as a meal ticket to their future, business as a vocation does not appear to be all that promising. Corporate scandals have tarnished the image of many corporate icons and brought down such mighty corporate high-flying and well-respected corporations as Enron, Xerox, Arthur Andersen, Nortel, BroadComc, AOL, Global Crossings, Adelphia, and Im-Clone, HealthSouth, as well as many DotCom companies whose CEOs milked their investors while they enjoyed perks. In many of these companies (and in many others) executives were cheating their stockholders, employees, and customers as they manipulated their boards to provide higher salaries, perks, and stock options. Many then inflated corporate revenues by accounting tricks and cozy relationships with Wall Street that pumped up a stock to encourage others to buy, while they sold their stock before it dropped. Dash, et al. reported that hundreds of greedy executives at America's worst performing companies sold $66 billion worth of stock while encouraging complicity of Wall Street analysts to promote others to buy.[20]

For a time it seemed as if every day a new scandal burst into public view: Bankrupt Kmart's cooking of the books; Adelphia's founding family using corporate funds to subsidize their hockey team; Edison Schools' booking of revenues they never saw; Dynergy's use of special entities like Enron; and the use of other accounting tricks by firms such as Tyco, Qwest, HealthSouth, Reliant Resources, CMS Energy, and HCA hospital chain.[21] Entire industries such as mutual funds and insurance are under investigation currently.

Some analysts suggest that many more accounting irregularities were yet to be reported because company auditors were co-opted. Even blue-ribbon companies such as Boeing face investigation. These unethical practices, especially in corporate accounting, resulted in many firms declaring bankruptcy or restating their financial statements. The result created a loss of trust by investors, employees, *and* college students. Horror stories of persons caught in immoral organizations that force them to do distressing things abound in today's headlines and popular fiction. Too often personal values are compromised by a business climate that condones unethical acts.[22] However, we do find stories of courageous women in such companies as Enron, WorldCom, and the FBI who challenged the system and spoke out about their discomfort.[23]

6.4 The Corporate Challenge

The challenge for corporations is to be ethical (make strategic decisions based on their values, which include ethical considerations) and socially responsible as they provide jobs, products, services, and a reasonable return to shareholders and standard of living for employees. Kotler states: "[…] the organization's task is to determine the needs, wants and interests of the target markets and to achieve the desired results more effectively and efficiently than competitors, in a way that preserves or enhances the consumer's or society's well-being."[24] However, recent scandals, as well as those in previous decades, have tainted the reputation of corporate America, and some students avoid business careers and their possible contamination. To offset this problem, many corporations are promoting their set of values and goals to help attract, motivate, and retain quality people. Unfortunately, many of these *proclaimed* values are not internalized within a firm and applicants have difficulty in discerning the "truth." A company's Values and Visions should be used to drive performance, not hang on a wall to provide ethical guidelines.

Current conventional wisdom suggests that college students, in determining whether they should apply for employment, should reflect on the values of an organization and an industry to avoid being ethically challenged.[25] Scott contends that organizational values and "values fit" should be studied because they affect important individual and such organizational outcomes as productivity,[26] job satisfaction,[27] commitment,[28] and job tenure.[29] "Values fit" has been shown to be relevant to application decisions.[30] Obviously, students need a process to examine the fit between the moral values of organizations and their own individual values.

Opportunities in Time of Ethical Disgrace

What are students to make of these problems? What does the Christian tradition have to say about a person's possible future in business? After twenty-five more years of corporate misdeeds, can we be optimistic amidst the growing problems? Is it possible to be a success in business and still remain a faithful Christian? Williams and Houck[31] contend that a career in business can be a challenging and exciting vocation for persons of talent and integrity. They argue that in many corporate scandals decent people were just doing their jobs, but later found themselves doing things that they otherwise might not have even considered, had their "roles" not seemed to demand it. But how can college students prepare to avoid getting caught up in such corporate cultures? How can they consider business as a vocation given all the threats presented above from the Marketplace and a specific corporation? Unfortunately, little has been done in business pedagogy to enable students to recognize and evaluate the values of organizations (and how they might fit with their own values) and find a vocation in business. A recent poll by the Aspen Institute at twelve top business schools revealed that only 20% thought that their schools were seriously preparing them to deal with fraud or ethical dilemmas. Few were concerned with 'values-fit.'

University Responses

Although some academics are critical of vocational preparation as a valid and important goal of higher education, Colby[32] contends that vocational preparation need not compete with or be disconnected from other goals such as integrating a concern for ethical and socially responsible occupational practices that place student understanding of their occupation in a larger social and intellectual context for deeper meaning. In other words, she contends "higher education can help turn occupations into callings, and they will be better for it." Treating one's life's work as a calling should now be accepted as a legitimate agenda for higher education. Unfortunately, that purpose of education has fallen by the wayside. As late as 1967, developing a meaningful philosophy of life was a major concern of 83% of all college freshmen, but that focus dropped to only 40% in recent years. There is hope because as students mature, the concern for a philosophy of life increases to approximately 60% for seniors graduating in 1999 and 2001 (UCLA, 2003).

Unfortunately, too many students and their parents still consider career preparation as the primary purpose of their undergraduate studies, even at small liberal arts schools. The business disciplines are believed to be the quickest, safest route to highly paid employment. Also lamentable is that moral and civic responsibilities are considered distinct from their business studies. However, work is central to the lives of most adults (especially college-educated women) and, therefore, is a place for seeking meaning and an opportunity to contribute to the welfare of others in the community.[33] Developing a fully integrated life is one of the most challenging psychological tasks of adulthood. For these reasons, educational programs should seek to integrate ethical and socially responsible occupational practices with an understanding of occupation in a larger social and intellectual context for deeper meaning. Universities began from a spiritual base where one's work was considered as a calling and accepted as a legitimate agenda for higher education.[34] For example, at Northwestern University, home of the Kellogg School of Management, the undergraduate college was started as a feeder for Garrett Methodist Seminary.

Equally unfortunate, many business schools tend to limit their focus to what the market wants instead of finding the proper "fit" for an individual in the world of work. To some extent higher education has been responding to market pressures that concentrate on preparing students for American industry by giving them the skills needed to compete economically. This corporate model of education places greater importance on the values, assumptions, language, and administrative policies of the business world and ignores a focus on character development. Colby believes that higher education's move toward a corporate and individualistic approach is risky because it may subordinate concern for many important learning outcomes and public purposes. For example, colleges may even foster a hidden curriculum that rewards faculty for pursuing their own professional prestige rather than caring for others. This encourages competitive climates where one student's (or professor's) success contributes to another's failure. However, when faculty are honest, fair, and caring with their students and have integrity in their scholarship, they teach important moral lessons.

Pattillo and Mackenzie[35] in a report for the Danforth Commission on U.S. colleges identified that the most valuable contribution an institution (of higher learning) can make to the lives of its students is a reasoned framework of belief that gives meaning to human existence, a faith that has something to say about the inescapable realities of life. While a college cannot "give" a student faith, it can at least help inform the student about the principal alternatives and help him/her acquire the intellectual tools and a disposition to consider maturely fundamental questions. Unfortunately, they found relatively little of this kind of deeper inquiry and synthesis going on in their in-depth study of fifty church-sponsored colleges and universities. The organization of the curriculum educates students away from a willingness to look at broad questions, and the tempo of college life militates against reflective thinking. They concluded that these weaknesses are common to American higher education across the board.

Hauerwas argues that many of today's Christian universities tend to reinforce the dominant morality of our culture that is corrupt and corrupting. He argues that these students lack the virtues necessary for sustaining the life of the mind, because "in the name of objectivity we refrain from trying to shape the lives of our students in a manner that might change their image of what they are or should be."[36] This omission was noted in a study by Leatherman[37] of administrators of thirty-three Catholic colleges who were concerned that their institutions were not actually teaching the values that make Catholic colleges unique.

More recent studies by Naughton and Bausch[38] of thirty-one Catholic undergraduate business programs indicated that ethics was one of four areas of distinctiveness compared to public business schools. Inclusion of core values is typically encouraged, anticipated, and rewarded at religious schools. Religious schools also tend to attract a more homogeneous faculty who share (or at least support) the values of the sponsoring organization. Students generally attend a private religious school because they understand and accept the culture and values of the institution, and they anticipate that these beliefs will be reinforced. Therefore, one might expect the faculty at religious schools would welcome ethical instruction within their courses.

Parker Palmer also advocates exploration of "the spiritual dimension of teaching, learning, and living," wherein occurs the "ancient and abiding human quest for connectedness with something larger and more trustworthy than our egos."[39] Frederick Buechner sees the discernment this way: "We search, on our journeys, for a self to be, for others to love, and for work to do."[40] McGee and Delbecq[41] contend that leaders in the business community are requesting opportunities to examine the spiritual connections to their vocations. Even though the terms *vocation* and *calling* may be alien to many leaders, current research suggests that a moral and spiritual dimension plays a part in CEO success.[42] They, as well as McGee and Delbecq, contend that contemplative practice is essential to maintaining commitment of leaders to their calling.

This contemplative practice along with self-knowledge is important in the discernment of an ongoing commitment to a calling that is derived from the belief that vocation is first and foremost a calling from within.[43] For the Christian, vocation can be seen as a continual process of discovery of the particular image of God in which one is created. Vocation can come from listening to an "inner voice" through contemplative practice. Palmer suggests that vocation comes from "listening to my life telling me who I am. I must listen for truths and values at the heart of my identity, not the standards by which I must live – but the standards by which I cannot help but live if I am living my own life."

Critics, such as Colby, from outside and within the academy are calling for a revitalization of the public purposes of higher education, including educating for students' moral and civic development Because higher education has such a powerful influence in shaping individuals' relationships with each other and their communities, its influence must be constructive rather than corrosive. Colby argues that students' values, moral and civic assumptions, and identities are shaped in college and, therefore, faculty and administrators should be more intentional about this. Hutcheon[44] argues that post-secondary education provides a second chance in socializing young people into a society. Documenting and sharing the students' efforts with others will allow for public scrutiny of these programs. We hope sharing this paper will encourage other faculty to consider this or other models for vocation development among their students.

6.5   Pedagogical Model: A Literature Review

The Role of Stories

As Palmer argued, our *PathFinder* model does involve listening to the story our lives are telling us who we are. Why does everyone love a good story and how is story related to theological reflection? TeSelle[45] contends that the answers to these questions are related. Most of us love a good story because we like the basic narrative quality of human experience, especially if we can relate to it and it rings true to human life. Elwood[46] concurs that it is critical to reflect on the story of our lives – and on the stories in our lives, especially the role of God in our lives. We may recognize our own problematic journey in the stories of others' experiences and struggles. For Christians we can see in the story of Jesus his own struggle of moving forward and discerning his calling by God. "The most basic call we have from God is to be lovingly conscious of our life as it is given to us in the here and now."[47]

TeSelle believes the bold business of theology starts with the ordinary and everyday, with personal life, with corporate stories, with "our times" in their political and social agony. It is exactly where Jesus' parables start. But to understand Jesus' parables, Daniel Berrigan insisted we must become skilled at reading the text of the events of our own lives – and order our lives accordingly. Although McCann contends that most American theologians have overlooked the role of narrative in interpreting religious and moral experiences, he presents examples of how readers might see God's hand even in narratives of Wall Street.[48]

MacIntyre argued that man is essentially a story-telling animal. He contends that the key question is not "What am I to do?" but "Of what story or stories do I find myself a part?" He says that "Generally a stance on the virtues will be to adapt a stance on the narrative character of life." That is because, through story, we understand and define what success and failure, danger, harm, allies, and enemies mean.[49] Even management professors such as Downs and King[50] argue for making greater use of stories in the classroom. They suggest that stories in management education can be valuable, because:

1. People remember narratives;

2. Stories make concepts stand out from the clutter;

3. Stories enhance understanding;

4. Stories motivate us to understand 'reality';

5. Stories motivate us to "know thyself" hence each other; and

6. Stories convey moral wisdom.

Ready[51] agrees and suggests that storytelling is emerging as the preferred approach for teaching leadership effectiveness in many companies today. He contends that top management must recapture leadership development from outsourced consultants who offer out-of-context, ill-conceived leadership programs. For stories to be effective Ready suggests that they must:

1. Be told by respected individuals;

2. Have drama to grab attention centering on making tough choices;

3. Have high learning value to produce changes in behavior;

4. Be level-appropriate to the managers or students; and

5. Be context-specific or linked to cultural or strategic context.

Being autobiographical increases the level of trust. An autobiography is the story of a life, and the best autobiographies are written as stories that order events around a central focus. Pascal[52] argues that the reader as well as the writer of a good autobiography should be able to see oneself, the self inside and the world which created the writer and say, "Aha! There it is!" In the autobiography, we move from the known to the unknown; through the mystery (story) of self-discovery and through the myriad details of the known, we attempt to discover the mystery of God's calling.[53] The stories of others also help us in our own self-knowledge.

An autobiography can become an effective story rather than merely a series of jottings and notes because, like a parable, it is a metaphor of the self. The story has a purpose; the revelation of the self is realized only in and through the details of an actual historical self. Both the writer and the reader identify with the process, the voyage of discovery.[54] A good autobiography contains four components: "concern with self, the importance of a dominant point of view, the harmony between outward events and inward growth, and the similarity between the kind of 'knowing' we call aesthetic and that which comes from the writing and reading of an autobiography."[55] Nash[56] proposes that personal narratives reveal a self-understanding of why we are here, who we are, what our purpose is, and why certain causes are worth sacrificing for. By asking the right questions, we are able to develop new forms of understanding and interpretation. Meyer[57] contends that narratives are the essential means humans use to perceive and communicate about the world. By revealing values, these narratives suggest how people should act within society.

The story of each and every Christian is formed by the story of another, Jesus of Nazareth. The Christian story is always in the service of that prior story – a Christian autobiography is always vocational.[58] Saint Paul apparently found his own story useful for his vocation as a preacher. He not only uses himself, but he thinks in and through himself. TeSelle also considers journals as pictures of a journey if the journaling process involves a reflection and analysis of self. Narrative mode is uniquely important in Christianity. Christians can confess their faith wherever they are, and without their Bibles, just by telling a story or a series of stories.[59] Walker (2002) found that moral exemplars when assessed were found to have: a) integrative narratives of the self, b) dispositional traits, and c) contextualized concerns such as developmental tasks and personal strivings.

6.6   Methodology

Instrument

The following section describes how students can learn to write, read, and retell the text of their personal stories in a journaling process. Students learn to apply the method of inquiry – discovery, interpretation, and action – to solve critical questions such as "What should I be doing with my life?"

This flexible framework of exercises in the *PathFinder Notebook* has been used with students and executives for more than twenty years in hundreds of settings to help users, individually or as a group, look at a situation, problem, or idea from several angles to get a better picture of reality. While students use it for their Personal Strategic Plan and Leadership Development, executives have also found it useful for uncovering foundational values, developing compelling visions and organization strategies as well as for understanding their realities. More than a dozen colleges and universities, thousands of students, as well as over 100 profit and non-profit organizations and hundreds of executives have used PathFinder process successfully.

Their strategic inquiry begins with a question at the base of a triangle of relationships: a person, a market, and an organization or corporation (or an industry or profession) all existing within a broader society.

Figure 6.1: *PathFinder* Strategic Relationships

During an Inquiry we look at our question, issue, or challenge from our personal perspective and those of the market, our current or possible organization, and the larger society. The Inquiry then proceeds along a Spiral Path using a notebook, with five major headings (Begin, Explore, Interpret, Decide, and Act), that provides leading questions for investigation, reflection, and journaling. (Later in the example, we will discuss how we seek God's perspective in finding our calling.) As we reflect on what values, beliefs, principles, or virtues are driving our behavior, decisions, and actions, we ask ourselves: "Whom do I want to serve – what market or audience? What organization do I want to serve?" Next, we look at the question within the context of our role in society. From that data, we begin to interpret meaning and to form assumptions that are further tested.

6.7   The Practice Using the Model

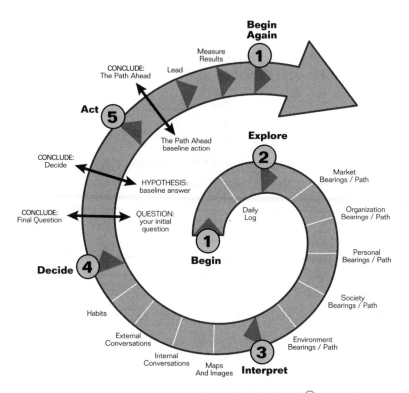

Figure 6.2: Corporantes *PathFinder* Notebook© Model

Students *begin* with a Question concerning their career choice and writing out their preliminary answer which establishes a baseline assumption to be tested. Then they *explore* their personal beliefs, values, and gifts and reflect in their journals on how those beliefs and values have impacted their lives up to now, the path they have been on and where the path seems to be heading. By responding to questions in the Notebook, they then *explore* the Market in terms of serving the needs of customers, as well as the challenge of competition, and how the market has developed and where it seems to be headed. Next they *explore* how they can serve society, specifically or in general. (Concurrently, students are involved in a required Service Learning Activity of volunteering in the local community to better understand the broader market.) Finally, the organization/corporation/profession/industry is *explored* in terms of how it serves the market, where it seems to be headed, and where the students would like it to head. Also concurrently, student teams spend most of the semester *exploring* the Ethical Climates of local or regional organizations or the proclaimed and real values of actual corporations or organizations to evaluate their Family Friendly benefits.

Each bit of information in terms of facts, evidence, and impressions researched and collected is recorded in the journal. However, the information is viewed as assumptions that will help formulate *hypotheses* that are continually modified, based on evidence that leads to possible answers to their Question. This is process as "abduction" or pursuing "the truth we do not yet know" as the students reflect on their experiences. We see abduction illustrated in the film, *Erin Brockovich*, when the heroine questioned why medical bills were part of a real estate file.

Next, students are asked to sketch out the question in the form of some image or map. Often this *interpretation* results in finding an answer in the picture. After examining the Maps & Images for ideas, students are asked to explore for other points of views from an imaginary conversation with a person they think can help them with their question. Many students select God, the Holy Spirit, a saintly, deceased parent or grandparent, a former boss, for example, as they seek an "inner voice." Next, they compare their ideas with opinions from others such as parents, roommates, friends, professors, etc. Grabner[60] contends that we will be able to discern the movement of God as he works in our present moment by being imbued by the Spirit through our silent listening, and through listening to others.

The next step is to identify and *interpret* known and unknown habits, strategies or tactics which lead or limit their progress. On what assumptions and values are these based and what needs to change? Finally, students conclude by reviewing and reflecting on all collected data to see what answers come to them, and what values, beliefs, knowledge, assumptions, and purpose become clear. This information forms another *hypothesis* that they put to the test in *action*. For most it leads to a Path Ahead that they might take. For others it means they have refined their Question and can begin their discovery process again.

The *PathFinder* originally was developed as a method for corporate decision-making inquiry, to determine and articulate the values and vision of the Nahser Advertising Company. These values and vision, the company's brand, not only guided and inspired, but also drove business performance. We soon learned that Progress in business ethics depends on developing organizational cultures (on which reputation is grounded and which drives business decisions) and that both institutionalized ethical norms and responded to religious and spiritual concerns that moved individuals to espouse them. The conventional version of pragmatism ("do whatever works") contributes to the ethical blindness, short-term thinking, individualism, and machine model of business that limit businesses today because of their lack of focus on Market and Society, that is, service to others. Instead, Pragmatic Inquiry® provides a way for people to discover and tell the stories of their values and beliefs, based on reflection of the evidence of their experience. Learning begins when we face a situation that leads us to question or doubt what we know. Although we can state what we know as a baseline answer, we should treat that as a hypothesis to be tested. We then are asked to rethink our experiences, our plans, and what we know as we search for new ideas and explanations of who we are. We are, in effect, reinterpreting the meaning of our experiences and forming new belief patterns. John Dewey embraced this idea as the heart of learning. He focused on pragmatism as the logic or theory of inquiry, said "all learning is the continuous process of reconstruction of experience".[61] Reflecting on and reinterpreting these experiences is the foundation of any successful Inquiry.

Procedure

For the past six years over three hundred business students at Saint Mary's College have been required to complete a sophomore level business course entitled, Personal Ethics & Corporate Culture. During the first week of class the students begin an Inquiry and for the next twelve weeks cover each notebook section with in-class time to write and share their journal reflections.

Although students may complete the course later in their business program, we have developed a unique model for a business ethics course that focuses on ethics as a reflection on values rather than merely learning principles of philosophical schools that, according to Stark, do not connect with many managers[62] Therefore, this course develops the capacity of our students to inquire and reflect not only on their own values and life experiences but also on the real values practiced in organizations as well as how they can find their vocation in business.

The seventy-five minute classes are taught over the course of thirty sessions to provide time to develop and discuss their stories, case studies and presentations. The students are required to write three individual papers and two team papers. The first individual paper, "Personal Values & Goals," evaluates the ability to identify and reflect from their journals on the sources, implications, and potential conflicts of their values in five goal areas (Spiritual, Career, Learning, Relationships, and Leisure). The second paper, "Service Learning," evaluates reflec-

tions on how students might be involved in the lives of others less for-
tunate through Community Service. The third paper, "A Final Reflection," documents their search for "truth" around the original question
developed at the beginning of the semester (usually a career/vocational
question). Critical skill analysis and learning are major objectives.

The two Team assignments are both papers and presentations
dealing with analyses of case studies. A first-person research report
analyzes a local or regional organization in terms of its ethical climate. They also evaluate, as a team, a value-oriented case from the
case book.

The first, a "Family-Friendly Analysis," is used to analyze organizations nominated as family-friendly with work/life balance policies and practices. The students analyze an organization's proclaimed
values by *reading* mission and policy statements, *listening* to CEOs
(or other top officials) present their understanding of values, *observing* how people are treated in an organization, and finally asking a
number of questions to current and former employers as well as to
customers and other stakeholders regarding the application of those
values. (These questions, especially suited for prospective working
moms, deal not only with family-value issues but also with ethical issues that help students develop skills necessary for finding their proper
organizational culture "fit".) Each team of students develops an analytical paper comparing the proclaimed with the real family values
practiced in the organization. The executive summaries of these papers are then used by a distinguished panel of judges to select organizations for recognition from the list nominated and evaluated at an
Annual Family Friendly Benefits Award Luncheon. The "Ethical Climate Analysis" paper is completed by the teams as a way of helping
students distinguish differences between Proclaimed Values and Real
Values perceived by current and former employees. These assignments
help students to differentiate between organizations and industries as
possible vocation possibilities.

Ethical Climate Analysis

The major team paper, an "Ethical Climate Analysis," evaluates a team's ability to apply the *PathFinder* process to investigate the ethical climate of an organization's culture. Students are expected to compare the differences between proclaimed values and real ethical practices of a chosen corporation using the abduction process discussed earlier. The process includes using proclaimed values as hypotheses and testing them against reality by observing and listening to the signs or indications of actual practices and by asking various stakeholders (employees, former employees, customers, suppliers, community leaders and residents) about ethical practices in order to arrive at new theories until new facts are gathered. To encourage students to doubt corporate documents and stay open to the possibility that they might be misinterpreting the signs, drafts of papers are required that provide opportunities for instructor guidance. Also, alumnae speakers and others are invited to tell their stories of being "taken in" by their employers and to suggest critical questioning of their prospective employers. They also offer insights and dilemmas regarding ethics. Students view parts of the movies including *The Firm* and *Erin Brockovich*, and the video, *The Enron Story*, to gain further insights for detecting unethical practices. We also present models for analyzing organizational values and ethical case studies.

In today's challenging ethical corporate environments, we feel students must understand the values of an organization *before* they apply for employment. There are too many horror stories of persons caught in immoral organizations that pressure them into unethical behaviors.[63] Unfortunately, there is lack of empirical research that enables students to recognize and evaluate the values of organizations. It is important for students to seek a "values fit" which is much easier when they have identified and reflected on their values in the *PathFinder* process.

Students are assigned three textbooks: G. F. Cavanagh's *American Values with International Perspectives, 1998;* F. Byron Nahser's *Learning to Read the Signs.* 1997; and Pffeifer and Forsberg's *Ethics on the Job: Cases & Strategies,* 1998. These books often stimulate reflection in the *PathFinder* notebook. Cavanagh's book is used as a foundation for discussion and quizzes on values content as well as the specific paper assignments (Values & Goals, Service Learning, and Ethical Climate Analysis). Other readings from Catholic social tradition and assignments come from Kirk Hanson's *Christian Values in the Workplace* which helps students understand how Scriptural values are applied by the American Bishops' *Pastoral on Economics.* While reading and discussing Cavanagh and Nahser's books, the students are expected to write at least weekly in their *PathFinder Notebook* as content is developed. Students share examples of their journal reflections to stimulate other students' commitment to the journaling process. This active inquiry process is then applied in the students' investigation of their own personal questions as they examine the areas of Personal (visions, beliefs, gifts, and motivations), the Market (who do they serve and what are the needs), and the corporation (with whom do they serve).

6.8   Results

Although the *PathFinder* process has been tested on several different groups of graduate and executive students at DePaul, Stanford, Notre Dame, Northwestern's Kellogg School of Management, Duquesne and South Florida universities, this group of undergraduate students during five Spring semesters was especially challenging with a mixture of sophomores, juniors, and seniors from business and the liberal arts. (Ironically, the seniors in business who had jobs were the ones most likely not to question their decisions and thus limited their investigations. This suggests that the sophomore year is a good time for students to learn this method of inquiry.

To assist the students with their final papers, we told them that their success would be evaluated in three ways: 1) the *depth and quality* of the final reflection paper (8-10 pages) that examines what insights they *learned* about themselves, their religion, and the corporate cultures they investigated; 2) the notebook process, and 3) the ACTION they identified based on the insights for their vocations/careers;

Student satisfaction with the process and the Reflection Paper was rated on a scale of 1 (low) to 6 (high). More than 90% felt very satisfied (5-6) with the process. (Only six percent felt the Inquiry was not valuable to them; most of them were seniors.)

A review of the final papers demonstrates:

- Greater insight to vocations (their purpose or calling);

- Significant self-awareness;

- Greater sensitivity to others – especially in the community; and

- Greater sensitivity to organizations and their cultures

A few student comments regarding Inquiry are:

- The *PathFinder* was an excellent way to present your feeling, values, goals, and dreams making it easier to produce decisions that have dramatic impacts on your life;

- I feel the *PathFinder* has helped me put my thoughts on paper and helped me understand what I am being called to in life.

- Although I had my doubts in the beginning, the *PathFinder* turned out to be a wonderful tool of discovery. This has been an awesome semester of enlightenment.

- The *PathFinder* helped me logically identify questions about all aspects of my life and to think clearly through every detail of the situation. I plan on using this notebook to help guide me in making the correct decisions in the future.

- It has been truly helpful in crystallizing my values for me and giving me a sense of where my future lies. I hope to be able to continue reflecting on my personal experiences and focusing where my talents and gifts are needed most.

- It helped get our thoughts together and map our futures;

- It helped me read the "signs" and get back on track to a path that I temporarily lost. The process of evaluating the signs in your life and the direction that I am being 'called to' is an ongoing one that I will need to continuously step back and take the time to see the big picture in order to know what my next step will be.

- It made me realize how confused I was about my future;

- After changing my focus from what the career can do for me to what I can offer society, I am no longer ashamed to admit I have a disability, one that will help me communicate with both the hearing and hearing-impaired.

- The repeated self-evaluation will help me to have a solid balance that will integrate my spiritual life and my job.

- The *PathFinder* brought about a sense of stability when really I was making radical transformations that will forever affect my life.

- I plan on keeping my *PathFinder* intact and using it again after a year of working. In that year I most likely will have more pertinent questions and need the personal query guide.

- At the end of my work in the *PathFinder*, I was still looking for a concrete answer. However, I realized that working in the journal gave me another path to follow pursuing my answer.

- I am ever so thankful for being introduced to such a wonderful, self-discovery experience. You learn from what life deals you.

- Keeping a journal and later reflecting on your writings helps you see how far you have come and how far you still have to go.

- I was not thrilled in having to write in a journal. I felt I didn't have any questions that are important, but I've come to realize that every question I have is important. My future and what will happen to me are especially important questions worth thinking about.

- It was a great method in helping me grow; I enjoyed the chance to reflect on my beliefs, wants, and life direction;

- A neat way to deal with our lives; It helped me concentrate on what I want out of life;

- It helped me answer a lot of questions I had never thought about;

- I think everyone had a burning question and it was helpful to journal about it; It would be helpful to share our progress in small groups.

- I never expected to learn so much from an ethics course. I have learned a lot about myself, more than I thought I would ever attain from a class.

- I really wish I had this course earlier in my college career because it really gave me direction and insight into what I really want in life.

On the Maccoby scale, the addition of *PathFinder Pragmatic Inquiry*® seems to have resulted in the students' perceived higher reinforcement of the character traits of *compassion* and *critical questioning* of authority with improvement in the traits of *independence, satisfaction in creating something new, cooperativeness,* and *self-confidence.* This higher reinforcement was reflected in higher importance of the heart traits of *compassion, critical questioning of authority, idealism,* and *generosity* as well as the head traits of *satisfaction in creating something new* and *open-mindedness.* These results continued to be consistent in pre- and post tests for the two classes in the Springs of 2001 and 2002. While we cannot attribute causality of these changes to the introduction of *PathFinder Pragmatic Inquiry*®, it appears that since its introduction in 1998, students perceive greater reinforcement and subsequent valuing with the changes made. Over the past twenty years the Maccoby scale has seemed quite reliable with few other changes in ratings noted among its 19 character traits. Personal observations of student behavior at another university also suggest strong validity.

Since the prime rationale for developing the Personal Ethics & Corporate Culture course was the comparatively weak character development of business majors in 1991, we have continued to monitor each addition to the course by the Maccoby survey. (See Table 6.1 for the survey.) Early use of the survey indicated that traditional business studies tend to suppress the character traits most important to ethical decision-making (*critical questioning of authority* and *compassion*).

6.9 Discussion

The prime purpose of this model is for the students to see the presence of God (Divine, Grace, Spirit, Calling, Destiny, Purpose, Vocation, etc.) in the narrative of their lives and how they can find a better fit with their values for their organizational future. The premise for this focus is the reality that women traditionally have been seen as the developers of values in our families but now their values are being challenged as they enter the workforce in increasing numbers. To avoid having their values changed by unethical or unsuitable organizations, we help them discover their own values, loves, and goals as well as help them learn how to investigate the *real* values, mission, and goals of their prospective employers so they can find the proper alignment with their own Christian values. Students need to ask whether it would be a better "vocational fit" to work in a business that is extremely hierarchical, structured, inflexible, and where there is little room for initiative or would it be better to be in a company with a "lateral" structure, where creativity and flexibility are encouraged but ambiguity is rampant.[64] For women students with expectations for a family, this analysis seems to be especially critical. Peck also identifies other questions regarding whether to seek a vocation for money, security, interesting work, or benefit to society.

Students at Saint Mary's College, Notre Dame, Indiana, learned to assess organizational and individual values through a combination of journal reflections, community service projects, alumnae guest speakers, team research, scholarly study, case studies, simulations, role playing, problem-solving sessions, and personal interactions among students, alumnae, faculty, and various business connections about what business is like and the challenges they might face in corporate America and even in specific firms.

An added expectation of the Personal Ethics & Corporate Culture class at Saint Mary's is to reinforce character traits or heart values that

Maccoby considers essential to avoid a *careerism* based solely on one's own career planning and personal fulfillment. The careerist tends to ignore idealist, compassionate, and courageous impulses that might jeopardize his or her career. To evaluate the course's reinforcement we give a pre- and post-test of Maccoby's Head and Heart survey instrument of character traits. So far, we have found higher perceived reinforcement of *idealism* and higher valuing of *critical attitude of authority*. These are in line with our expectations.

Recent research by Ruhe, et al.[65] suggests major differences of heart reinforcement and perceived importance between college business seniors in coed and single-sex institutions. They found that business seniors in the women's college valued thirteen of the nineteen character traits more highly than their female counterparts in three coed religious universities. These character traits included: *honesty, compassion, generosity, openness, independence, idealism, loyalty, friendliness, sense of humor, cooperation, open-mindedness, pleasure in learning something new,* and *flexibility.* Most of these heart traits were also perceived to have been reinforced in their studies. Compared to their counterparts in three coed public universities, females in the three coed religious schools valued more highly only *critical attitude toward authority, ability to take initiative,* and *sense of humor.* It seems that women in coed schools (religious or public) tend to take on the character traits of men. Of the nineteen character traits, males in religious coed schools valued only *generosity* more than their public counterparts, while their counterparts were higher on *open-mindedness* and *pleasure in learning something new.*

As professors, we personally, can adopt the Pragmatic Philosophy and Theology that underpin Sanders' view of love if we help others to grow to become the people God is calling them to be. As a result, we are being loving/compassionate and, therefore, we grow.

6.10   Recommendations for the Future

- Incorporate journaling at an earlier (sophomore) stage. (Prior to 1998 a Personal Ethics class was offered as an elective course primarily for seniors, but we found that the course was offered too late in fulfilling a need to develop an understanding of their vocation. Most students were already too committed to a particular career field and did not want any dissonance.)

- Bring alumni (alumnae) to share wisdom of career choice and possibly serve as mentors.

- Encourage students to analyze their organizational experiences.

- Require in-depth ethical climate analysis of corporate cultures applying the same inquiry method.

- Continue use of the Maccoby instrument for pre- and post-evaluation of the results of these efforts that could be used for accountability.

- Finally, try to reflect our "love" in the way we help our students develop. Perhaps then business can become a loving vocation based on the character traits of compassion and critical questioning of authority.

Maccoby argued that our values are shaped and achieved by our organizations. Since 1980 this instrument has been used by various authors in *Journal of Business Ethics, Journal of Business Education, International Journal of Value-Based Management, SAM, Advanced Management Journal, Journal of Contemporary Business Issues,* etc. and found to have high reliability and validity in various university settings.

Table 6.1: A Survey of Student Opinions

University: _____   Major: _____   Sex: ___ M ___ F

Please indicate the extent to which you believe the following traits of character help one achieve success in a career.

		Very	Importance Somewhat	Not
1.	Generosity	—	—	—
2.	Satisfaction in creating something new	—	—	—
3.	Sense of humor	—	—	—
4.	Idealism	—	—	—
5.	Ability to take the initiative	—	—	—
6.	Compassion	—	—	—
7.	Openness, spontaneity	—	—	—
8.	Flexibility	—	—	—
9.	Pleasure in learning something new	—	—	—
10.	Coolness under stress	—	—	—
11.	Self-confidence	—	—	—
12.	Open-mindedness	—	—	—
13.	Critical and questioning attitude towards authority	—	—	—
14.	Friendliness	—	—	—
15.	Loyalty to fellow students	—	—	—
16.	Honesty	—	—	—
17.	Independence (vs. dependence)	—	—	—
18.	Cooperativeness	—	—	—
19.	Pride in performance	—	—	—

Now please *circle the numbers* of those traits which you consider have been stimulated or reinforced during the course of your studies in the past.

(Adopted from Michael Maccoby, *The Gamesman*, Simon & Schuster, New York. 1976.)

Table 6.2: Personal Ethics & Corporate Culture, Business Seniors vs. Non-Business Seniors

Personal Ethics & Corporate Culture, Saint Mary's College
Perceived Value of Importance & Reinforcement of Character Traits
Business Seniors vs. Non-Business Seniors
1991
(Note: Scores were virtually identical for both groups as freshmen in 1987)

Character Traits (Heart Traits in Italics)	Perceived as Very Important (%)		Perceived as Reinforced (%)	
	Business Seniors (N=58)	Non-Business Seniors (N=180)	Business Seniors (N=58)	Non-Business Seniors (N=180)
Generosity	33	39	12	18 *
Satisfaction in Creating Something New	53	70 *	21	44 ***
Sense of Humor	57	69	14	33 **
Idealism	31	39	7	18 *
Ability to take the Initiative	97	93	62	62
Compassion	36	54 **	16	26
Openness, Spontaneity	62	68	24	36
Flexibility	93	89	83	46
Pleasure in Learning Something New	74	78	45	44
Coolness under Stress	86	93	40	31
Self-Confidence	98	98	78	67
Open-Mindedness	84	89	33	58 ***
Courage – Critical & Questioning Attitude toward Authority	26	41 *	22	37 *
Friendliness	64	75	22	39
Loyalty to Colleagues	59	61	34	33
Honesty	90	90	53	58
Independence	52	75 ***	47	61 ***
Cooperativeness	86	90	55	48
Pride in Performance	88	93	53	64

Probable Statistics: * p<.05   ** p<.01   *** p<.001

Table 6.3: Personal Ethics & Corporate Culture, Before & After

Personal Ethics & Corporate Culture, Saint Mary's College
Perceived Value of Importance & Reinforcement of Character Traits
Before and After
PathFinder Pragmatic Inquiry®
Spring 2002

Character Traits (Heart Traits in Italics)	Perceived as Very Important (%)			Perceived as Reinforced (%)		
	First Day of Class (N=41)	Last Day of Class (N=29)		First Day of Class (N=41)	Last Day of Class (N=29)	
Generosity	56	66		12	31	*
Satisfaction in Creating Something New	63	72		24	38	*
Sense of Humor	56	45		37	14	
Idealism	71	41	*	2	14	*
Ability to take the Initiative	95	97		73	72	
Compassion	66	86	*	20	55	**
Openness, Spontaneity	62	69		32	34	
Flexibility	93	86		59	62	
Pleasure in Learning Something New	57	79		44	52	
Coolness under Stress	73	72		22	45	
Self-Confidence	98	97		61	93	*
Open-Mindedness	93	90		70	59	
Courage – Critical & Questioning Attitude toward Authority	22	55	**	24	62	***
Friendliness	68	66		37	38	
Loyalty to Colleagues	85	72		46	55	
Honesty	98	97		73	76	
Independence	61	59		39	52	+
Cooperativeness	80	90	*	63	72	
Pride in Performance	83	69		41	66	

Probable Statistics: * p<.05   ** p<.01   *** p<.001   + p<.10

Chapter 7

Uncovering the Values Driving Organizational, Career and Personal Strategies: The Case for PathFinder Pragmatic Inquiry

6th International Conference
on Social Values in Education and Business
University of Oxford – July, 2002

"The real voyage of discovery consists not in seeking new landscapes, but in having new eyes."

Marcel Proust

7.1 Introduction

Business conduct and strategies are in the headlines today. And we are fascinated.

With so many Americans watching stock portfolios shrink and jobs disappear, we have a lot to get our attention. Collapsing companies, greedy executives bailing out at the top, insider trading, fraudulent accounting practices, failed mergers, huge losses incurred chasing wildly optimistic technology forecasts. What is the real story behind the disastrous business headlines we see every day? What are the lessons to be learned as we examine the evidence of our recent experience? How are we to run our businesses?

7.2   The Premise

The premise of this account of the current state is to ask the oldest question about human behavior: Why?

We see the crime. Just like any good mystery story, we may see the result, but we have to work to understand the motive. All the headlines tell a story of individual and groups of executives making decisions. On what basis were the decisions made?

What values are driving the behavior? Clearly, it isn't the values that are printed on the wall of virtually every corporation mentioned in the headlines.

These are not abstract, theoretical ideas, but flesh and blood people weighing the options and alternatives based on some end in mind, some motivation. Call it beliefs, goals, intent, what-is-important, virtues, purpose. It comes down to values that drive all action.

This chapter will set the context for the argument that values do have a vital role in the conduct of business, not just in compliance, but in the very heart of the business purpose: service to the market and to society. Business may not be driven by "love," but certainly we are coming to the realization that ignoring others and focusing on the enrichment of the few has led to catastrophic results.

Loopholes need to be closed and regulations need to observed as they were in the past when scandals of this dimension have occurred. Consider for a moment all the changes in anti-trust measures enacted at the turn of the century and the government regulations that occurred after the 1929 stock market crash and the onset of the depression. But, in addition to regulatory action, there is a level of focus that cannot be overlooked: the decisions made by the business leaders.

We will make the case for the need to re-evaluate the motives – the values as we will call them – driving business behavior today and offer a way to help executives align their personal values with the values of the corporation, and the marketplace, within the context of society.

The reason why we place such emphasis on the personal motivation of individuals is that this, ultimately, is where change must happen. It offers a rare chance to look at the evidence of the personal motives of leading executives.

This is not an opportunity to be taken lightly; it only comes along once every several generations. The first in American history was the so-called Gilded Age in the late 19th Century with the rise of the "robber barons" and the resultant regulation of the "trust busters". Later there was the "roaring twenties" and the Great Depression hang-over from the party and the New Deal. Post World War II prosperity led to the Great Society development. What will result from our current situation and how will it happen?[1]

7.3   The Decisions Made

When you look at the stories behind the current business headlines, there are three themes:

- Individual ethical breaches

- Company wide cultural values issues

- Disastrous strategic decisions.

Let's take the ethical issues first. Some call this the "few bad apples" theory. Dennis Kozlowski skirts the New York sales tax by shipping paintings to his plant in New Hampshire and then back to avoid $1 million in sales tax. The Rigas family members use Adelphia as a personal bank. Personalities get our attention, but we might ask, on what moral foundation is business based?

Company Culture – Values and Vision

Every one of these fraudulent companies had a mission and values statement. Arthur Andersen was one of the early leaders in establishing ethics programs. Enron's values statement would bring tears to your eyes as you read about the importance of the individual and how they might reach their full potential. In all fraudulent companies, there seems to be an understanding of how things are done at the company which condones broad breaches of behavior. While the attitude clearly begins at the top, these are not cases of just one or two people gone astray, but a culture which understand what is valued above all else. And where breaches occur, they don't stem from the interests of the stockholders, much less the interests of the customers and society.

Strategic Decisions

We began hearing the word *synergy* during the '90s. A classic example is the merger between AOL, at the height of the dot.com bubble, with Time Warner. AOL took the lead. The synergy between the two was loudly touted at the time. Now, with the stock depressed, veteran Time executives are taking over and going back to some of the basics of the business, mainly quality content. In the words of many executives close to the situation, they admit that they got away from serving the customer. Add Vivendi and Bertlesmann's ex-CEOs to the casualty list in moves to bring various media together.

Or look at the so-called Third Generation of telephone service that seized Europe in the bidding for licenses, dramatically over-reaching the market need. Is this an ethical problem? No, just one of over-optimistic market forecasting. The venerable Corning enterprise bet the company on the fiber optic market and made acquisitions funded by the sale of their more traditional and stable long-term Corning businesses. The market responded with great enthusiasm, driving the stock up from under $20 a share in 1998 to over $100 in 2000. When the bubble burst, the stock plummeted to under $2 in August 2002. There was no hint of fraud or overly generous compensation; just a bad bet, based on one view of the core competencies of Corning and a misreading of the market opportunities. But it was a more reasonable bet than the thousands of dot.com smoke dreams where there was no chance of ever making a profit.

7.4   The Purpose of Business

These decisions have raised questions about the American business model making it once again important and useful to ask the perennial question: what is the underlying purpose of business? People forgot to ask that question in the rush for the stock market bubble inflated by dot.com mania, technology convergence and acquisition conquests.

We measure success in business by the valuation of the company. So, not surprisingly, the motive behind these stories of failure was the promise of financial gain through increased stock evaluations. This began as a worthy effort because the market does offer, in the long run, a very efficient way to evaluate companies.

"Pay for performance" grew out of a reaction to the evidence that executives during the '50s and '60s were paid well whether their corporations did well or not. Why not pay them for how well the company did measured by how well the investors in the company did, i.e. by the stock price? The simple and compelling logic went: make the managers shareholders, so their decisions would not be in conflict with the good of the company. Believing it a sensible idea, governing boards implemented stock options programs for executives with a vengeance. As we have now seen, that did little to shift senior executives' focus away from self-interest. All it did was shift the mechanism for fulfilling their measure of success: money.

If we wish to seriously re-examine our purpose in business, we can look at it from the perspective of the three stories behind the headlines: personal values, corporate values and strategy issues.

Investment in Core Competencies – the Essence of Strategy

If business has any purpose in society, it is the function of funneling investments of human, material and financial capital to those projects that are deemed to be in the best interests of the future needs of society. It is about change and innovation. As Peter Drucker has said, "It is the purpose of organization and, therefore, the grounds of management authority: *to make human strength productive.*" He goes on to say: "The principle underlying this is [...]'*personal strengths make social benefits*".[2]

How do individuals as well as companies determine what they are to do? All investment decisions must be considered in the competitive context. Many use the popular SWOT analysis: the Strengths and Weaknesses of the company and the Opportunities and Threats in the marketplace.

Therefore, the discipline of Strategy, which is being more and more driven by marketing considerations, focuses on investment choices which create the points of product differentiation that will give the corporation a "sustainable competitive advantage." One leading strategist has gone so far as to say that the fundamental role and purpose of strategy is to "induce your competitors not to invest in those products, markets, and services where you expect to invest the most [...]"[3]

My forty years experience in advertising has shown that these investments must translate into core competencies which help the organization fill customer's needs better than the competition. The sum total of these features and benefits are well summarized in the meaning in customers' minds as the "brand."

Relationships – the Heart of Marketing

Marketing is, in a nutshell: serving something or someone – the *other*. Behind the ubiquitous presence of the advertising veil, lies the powerful (and some would say seductive) pursuit of meaning. Advertising is designed to define and support a brand – the sum total of the meaning of the product or service; in other words, its philosophy. The activity of *branding* is coming to be seen as the critical component of business strategy, since the purpose of business is to create and serve a customer. In earlier days, marketing was looked on as structuring a one-time exchange between the buyer and the seller. Marketing worked with the Four Ps: product, price, place and promotion – and adjusted these elements to come up with an optimum exchange. Today, marketing's role has been raised to a much higher level. It is responsible for the *relationship* with the customer to determine their needs and then respond with a flow of ideas and products for the long-term benefit of the relationship over time. This change of view stems from our move from the mechanical view of nature, which is highly structured and manipulative, to the organic or biological view of nature as a living entity with a wide range of choices, responses, relationships, and interdependencies. Or, as we have stated, the company must consider the needs of the *other*, whether for love or profit, and then make the necessary choices and investments to deliver what the market needs.

7.5 Marketing Relationships – Three Targets

Elements of strategic relationships in *Pragmatic PathFinder Inquiry* may be shown as in Fig. 7.1:

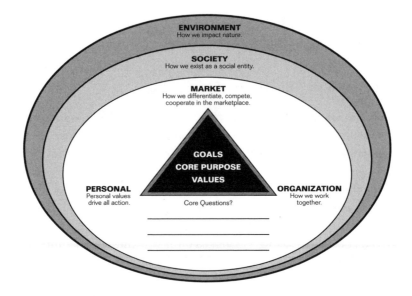

Figure 7.1: Strategic Relationships

Copyright: Corporantes 2002

A successful organization needs to bring into alignment the three key elements of personal, corporate, and market values. All this is done within the context of the broader society and environment which supports the overall effort.

How to reflect on and uncover the values and vision driving these three elements is the subject of the rest of this chapter. The vision of the company grows out of these values and is the basis for making strategic investment decisions.

7.6   How to Think About Values

People have always decided what to do based on their philosophy or belief. Now corporations are very willing to share their philosophies. However, from the evidence, their philosophy's values are not always driving business behavior. How do we connect values to performance? Too often, values, as defined by ethicists, have been constrained by the "don't" more often than the "do"

We all know how easy it is to say what our values are. But the time has come to ask some insightful questions:

- How have the values worked in your life?

- What is the evidence of your experience?

- What decisions have you actually made?

Begin With Your Doubts

The way scientists go about their business is to set up a theory, called an hypothesis, and then design tests to prove, or, more accurately disprove it. We seldom look to prove ourselves wrong, but this element of pragmatic inquiry is invaluable, and leads us to the second feature of Pragmatic Inquiry, learning.

The word, *Pragmatism* needs to be positioned within the three useful ways or categories in which we learn:

1. Know more,

    We are all familiar with this purpose: We don't know much or anything about a topic, so we gain new information.

2. Reformat/re-frame

We think we know something, or have an idea, but then we learn more and realize that we need to put a different meaning on things. This happens often when we challenge our assumptions and realize we need to ask a different question.

3. Transformative

Here is where an the idea takes hold of us. A a quiet "inner voice" or a dramatic event may demand our attention. Pragmatic Inquiry is especially helpful to reflect on this step.

Reflection on Experience

A focus on consequences and action leads naturally to the idea that truth is not told once but is always in the making. This relationship with an *other*, becomes part of your narration – the plot – and tells a great deal about the set of beliefs and assumptions that guide the storyteller as well as the people in the story. Their beliefs drive the action. Only by knowing the underlying beliefs and direction of the story, can we determine such things as success, failure, danger, alliances, and practice of virtues.

This brings us to the central feature of Pragmatic Inquiry. By leading people to reflect on their own experience and see what assumptions and beliefs are behind it, they get clues showing them where the narrative of their lives might go. All of this is based on their vision and beliefs in connection with the "*other.*"

There are many other features and aspects to this rich philosophy, but these three strike me as the most helpful. They offer strong medicine to remedy the traditional narrowness and traps of business thinking characterized before:

The inquiry always begins with a question. In business, this is easy because generally there is some crisis which begins the inquiry. With students, it's a bit more difficult. But after they have stated their preliminary beliefs, assumptions, and answers their minds are free to explore other alternatives.

The exercises are then organized in five steps: *Begin, Explore, Interpret, Hypothesize* and *Act*!

7.7 Conclusion

At the beginning of this chapter we saw how business, through today's headlines, has gotten our attention and that is the first step in the inquiry. You first must have a problem or some issue you want to think about. This is also the time-honored beginning of reflection and what we pay attention to does determine who we are.

Alfred Whitehead in his talk before the Harvard Business School, *On Foresight,* said that business' purpose was to be thinking ahead and making investments in behalf of society. It was in that talk he said:

> " The behavior of the community is largely dominated by the business mind. A great society is one in its men (and women) of business think greatly of their function."

He concluded with this definition of philosophy:

> "Philosophy is an attempt to clarify those fundamental beliefs that finally determine the emphasis of attention that lies at the base of character."[4]

As we reflect on our experience, we begin to see how our fundamental beliefs determine our action. They exhibit, as Whitehead said, our character. When students write their own dramas and learn lessons from their own experience, the Pragmatists would applaud.

Through our stories we awaken to the understanding that something other than one's self is real. That is the key connection between business strategy and the deeper questions of purpose. An *other* is moving and manifesting itself in this world. This movement and manifestation informs our *marketing* endeavors.

Chapter 8

Marketing as Storytelling: Pragmatic Inquiry's Religious Foundations and Practical Applications

7th International Conference
on Social Values in Education and Business[1]
Oxford University – July, 2004

"If we could first know *where* we are, and *whither* we are
tending, we could then better judge *what* to do, and *how*
to do it."

Abraham Lincoln[2]

8.1   Introduction

On March 7, 2000. the Dow Jones Blue Chip stocks plunged 374.47
points on the news of Procter & Gamble's profit decline. When the
day was over, P&G had lost $35 billion of its market value, and the
entire market was down a staggering $322.9 Billion. Then on the heels
of this devastating decline came the Enron, WorldCom, Andersen,
Stewart, et. al. implosions. For many, this dramatically signaled our
passing from the Machine Age to the Information Age. Or, in investor
terms, we moved from the Old Economy to the New Economy and
entered a new playing field for business practice.

Where do we invest? When? How? But more importantly, why?
Certainly we are familiar with the usual analysis of facts, opinions,
trade-offs, and risk/reward. But we also need to make smart investments of our time and talent, as well as our material resources. Perhaps we need, as some brokers suggest, referring to Paine Webber,

a "thematic approach to investing." Do we see the market today as part of the new economy story built on technology or is this a small interlude scene which will be followed by the resumption of the old economy story based again on bricks and mortar earnings? Are there new rules of value? How deeply do these changes affect our assumptions about how the world works? What picture or "story" do we believe? Certainly we know that a case can be made for a movement from the military command-and-control mode, which worked so well in a mechanistic story of business, to a technological mode as we move toward a more flexible, interactive, organic and global model of the new economy. But is there more to the change?

8.2   Challenges Today

What was once familiar and routine no longer feels that way. The issues we probe now seem chaotic, complex, and hopelessly interconnected. But many say that this transition has been underway for a long time and is part of a much larger change. For instance, in a 1930 talk titled "*On Foresight*" for Harvard Business School, Alfred North Whitehead said: "Mankind is now in one of its rare moods of shifting its outlook. The mere compulsion of tradition has lost its force."[3] By "tradition" does he mean traditional religion? Some would say that as we move from the modern period to the postmodern period, the hold of religious tradition has weakened and the swift rise of "spirituality" has come as one voice to fill the vacuum of meaning.

Over the centuries, thinkers have been asking questions similar to ours:

- Why are we investing?

- What are our values?

- What are our goals?

- What is success?

- How do we think about all this?

And one of the more inventive ways religion has helped answer them has been through storytelling. Religion, in this sense, has always been the formulator, propagator, and keeper of the stories and myths which give meaning to the spiritual encounters of a culture. Even the marketing model of relationship which guides today's business investment decisions uses the basic tools. But I propose we add philosophical inquiry to help bridge the gap between spiritual impulse and religious traditions and using storytelling as the way to think about investment decisions. And we have a unique theory of inquiry at hand: American pragmatism.

By using pragmatism as a mind-set for storytelling we are able to discern the meaning of events over time. And with any good story, there is always a dramatic tension when one person or event meets another.

Pragmatism, America's only original contribution to the history of philosophy, was first articulated by Charles Sanders Pierce in the late 1800's. William James, John Dewey, Alfred North Whitehead and others developed it. Pragmatism has come to stand for the worst habits of expediency as in "do whatever works" or "action unguided by principle." Much has been written over the last twenty years to reclaim pragmatism and with some success. Yet, with all the philosophical wrangling about the meaning of pragmatism, few philosophers actually address how to *practice* this most practical philosophy.

I believe pragmatism can help in strategic investment decisions by using pragmatic inquiry to give clarity to the choice of stories in which one might consider investing. The first step is to realize there is a genuine issue or problem to be resolved. These urgent choices will entail investment, as alluded to earlier. Such problems and issues can dynamically be cast in the stories with a past, a present, and a hoped-for-future with all the uncertainty that it holds.

Looking at the story, one can then determine a number of critical issues: What is the meaning of success and failure in the story? Who is friend and who, foe? What is danger? What is one's own personal identification? And then based on that, what action might one take to influence the direction and outcome of the story?

William James asked: "What is the *cash value* of the idea?" I find his question particularly engaging for business people. John Dewey would ask: "If *this* is what we believe, then *that* is the action we should take."

We are all familiar with the general themes of misunderstanding concerning pragmatism which are most easily summed up as: "do whatever works." From this perspective, the pragmatic practitioner is encouraged to look to the results of an action, and if the results are not to one's liking, then take a different action. This flat, one-dimensional focus on results has prevented business practitioners from utilizing pragmatic inquiry in a wide range of strategic issues to determine the best action based on their values, purpose and goals, as well as on financial and market data.[4]

The purpose of this chapter is to outline possible resources for deepening the foundations of pragmatic inquiry and then, based on this deeper understanding, to show how pragmatic inquiry can be introduced into everyday applications. Specifically, we will consider the thoughts of two prominent philosophers of religion: Josiah Royce (1855-1916) and Max Scheler (1874-1923). They both studied extensively the writings of Charles Sanders Peirce (1839-1914), the acknowledged originator of pragmatism. Given that they apparently did not know of each other's work, it seems remarkable how their insights build on the work of Peirce and William James (1842-1910)[5] in such strikingly parallel ways.

The thinking and reflection of these two scholars shows, from two different perspectives, a convergence on the religious foundation of pragmatism. The chapter concludes by outlining a practical application of pragmatic inquiry through the use of the Corporantes *PathFinder* Notebook©.

Pragmatic inquiry gives business practitioners a way to discern more accurately the beliefs we hold and the reality of the world that we live and work in, thereby to develop more appropriate action to fulfill the two fundamental functions of business:[6]

- *Demand:* Define and satisfy customers' needs – the relationship or demand side

- *Supply:* To make human strength productive – the creation or supply side.

The reason a corporation is permitted to exist lies primarily in the first activity, which is to provide some service to society. In order to achieve that purpose, a corporation and its executives must inquire into the deeper role that their company plays in the lives of their consumers as well as in the larger society. This analysis is a far cry from the usual maxim of business purpose stated in almost every proxy statement, proclaimed in every board room, and taught in every business school: the purpose of business is to maximize return to shareholders.

The second purpose of business addresses human potential and how individuals determine which life choices they must make in terms of their career and work in the context of the corporate life. This purpose, also, is reduced to something like: maximize output from every employee to maximize return to shareholders.

From this perspective, is it any wonder that business practitioners find comfort in the usual definition of pragmatism which seems to give a philosophical basis for doing whatever it takes to maximize return to shareholders?

Our goal is to help practitioners who are searching for a better way to understand how their corporation's values, vision and leadership principles can "facilitate a process where personal strengths and resources are turned to serve social benefits."[7] This is what makes a good story, and the foundation of their brand.

To free pragmatism from the yoke of activity unhindered by values, we must first show that pragmatic inquiry can and must be rooted in a more substantial purpose and scope, or what we are calling story, and then show how this larger and deeper understanding of pragmatic inquiry can be put into practice. To establish a base for our task, we will review two of Peirce's major tenants of pragmatism: signs and abduction. We will begin by reviewing Peirce's insights on signs.[8]

8.3   Signs

Peirce realized that what we see as events and facts, so beloved and trusted by business practitioners, are actually signs which must be interpreted. Signs and their interpretation play a large role in our everyday lives. For instance, we plan to go for a walk. We look out the window and see dark clouds and grab for an umbrella. We check the thermometer outside the window and put on a jacket.

But signs can also be more symbolic. We see a hexagonal red sign with the letters STOP. We have seen many of these. We know that these signs were erected by authorities who may or may not cause us to pay a large fine if we fail to stop. We also believe that obedience to the law is a good idea. We interpret the stop sign according to information and values which we possess and make a decision to stop or not.

Signs can be theoretical. As scientists, we observe the motions of the planets. We are aware how celestial bodies move but we consciously choose to entertain the theory as a tentative hypothesis, not a fixed belief. So when we observe a discrepancy between the actual motions of the heavens and the accepted theory, we work to offer a new interpretation of what we have seen.

And lastly, we can reflect from a religious perspective. We observe a beautiful sunset or the face of a laughing child and these reinforce our belief that there must be a higher Being which created these wonders of nature.

These signs – dark clouds, thermometer, stop sign, movement of the heavens, sunset and a child's face – have meaning; but how do we come to understand what they mean? By accepting the need to move from opinion of what the sign means to insight, we will improve our decision making in business. The way we interpret signs leads us to Peirce's second element, that of the interaction between the theory and the reality which he called abduction.[9]

8.4   Abduction

Abduction was Peirce's term for the particular way science pursues "the truth we do not yet know." He regarded this delineation as one of his major contributions to the science of logic. It differed in several ways from deduction and induction, the two epistemological approaches more familiar than abduction.[10]

When deduction is used, we start with the general idea, truth or assumption, and then apply it to the particular. Often this starts with a belief or something we learned from our parents, religion, culture or school and we accept it for the truth. As reality and the experiences in daily life confront us, we adjust the facts to fit our concept or assumptions of reality.

Using induction, we do the opposite. We experiment, experience life and observe facts, holding no prior beliefs or assumptions, and we build a general hypothesis to explain the facts. Conventional

Newtonian science and Cartesian philosophy insists these methods of inquiry follow the inductive method of logic to support its claims to being *objective*.

Peirce realized, however, that science really progresses via abduction, a third way of determining the truth, in which data collected (as in induction) and general assumptions (as in deduction) are *both* held in view. An interior dialogue goes on between past beliefs and the current facts with the future in mind. Finally, a resolution is reached, but this is now treated as a new hypotheses. That is, it is held consciously and tentatively, until repeated testing against reality (á la induction) proves it to be correct, incorrect, or if need by, modified.[11] If correct, it is then elevated to a theory, which must continue to be tested as new facts are gathered.[12]

If a corporation has a general strategy and product line and persists with it despite changes in the market, then it practices deduction. IBM and their attachment to mainframes is a good example. But, if a corporation reacts to every market and competitive blip which does not fit their strategy and product line, then it practices induction. Detroit for decades chased fashion rather than quality in cars. Advertisers search for any message that will attract consumers, often with too little regard for product features. Such companies are stuck in induction and have limited foundational beliefs.

Peircean abduction offers a way to move from strategy to market condition and back to adjust strategy. An example of abduction is what Marshall Loeb, the former editor of *Fortune* magazine, calls "value added journalism." A writer gets an idea for a story (an hypothesis). The writer talks with sixty or seventy people to access what is really going on (fact-collecting/testing of the hypothesis). He then revises his hypothesis for the story in the light of what he has learned through the interviews. The value-added comes from the fact that stories begin with a belief and are developed from more than one person's perspective, which is what Peirce anticipated when he spoke of abduction: beliefs, in the form of hypotheses, are tested in the shared, cooperative endeavor. We call that science.

Peirce's understanding of signs and abduction begins to set the stage for the central realization that the heart of business is not found in the balance sheet and the income statement, and that pragmatic inquiry cannot be to determine "whatever works" to make the numbers. We will now turn to our two philosophers of religion to see how they developed and built on these insights.

Josiah Royce and Max Scheler were contemporaries of Charles Sanders Peirce. Both attempted to understand Peirce and, if their arguments had prevailed at the time, they could have saved pragmatism from its present ignominious state of misunderstanding. Their foundation in philosophy of religion helped them better understand pragmatism as an application and study of the experience of religion in peoples' lives as opposed to the ethical study of the theory of theological concepts. Both believed that religion leads one back to the roots of one's beliefs. (*Religio*: tie fast, tie back.) This belief is important to business practitioners because the case will be made that, by understanding pragmatism through Royce and Scheler, we will be able to help the corporation connect with its deeper values, core purposes and goals as the source of strategic performance.

8.5 Josiah Royce: Peircean Interpreter

We will begin with Josiah Royce because he was in close acquaintance with Peirce and was, at one point, acknowledged by Peirce as his successor. Royce also is very important since, as most of the readers of this chapter will have experienced, Peirce is almost impossible to understand at first reading, and Royce became his admirable interpreter.

Josiah Royce was one of the few people in Peirce's lifetime whom Peirce felt understood what he meant by pragmatism. Indeed, Peirce went so far as to call Royce the only true American pragmatist. While they shared an appreciation of pragmatism, Peirce and Royce were otherwise very different. Unlike Peirce, brought up in erudite privilege in Harvard and Cambridge, Royce was raised in the frontier environment of a mid-nineteenth-century California mining town near Sacramento. Where Peirce found his academic preferment thwarted at every turn, Royce studied in Leipzig and the University of Gottingen under R. H. Lotze. Royce moved easily from Johns Hopkins, where he received his Ph.D. in philosophy and studied with Henry James and Peirce, to the University of California, Berkeley, and then in 1882 to Harvard, as a member of their fabled Philosophy Department, where he spent the rest of his life.

Royce was initially drawn to Peirce through his interest in how ideas get formed. Peirce's logic offered rich insights. Royce admitted years later how difficult he found Peirce's work and how long he had to struggle with Peirce's seminal articles on abduction and the fixation of belief.[13]

Their first personal contact, in fact, was inauspicious. Peirce was blunt in his negative assessment of Royce's skill as a logician. In 1901, Royce recalled the first letter he received from Peirce in response to sending Peirce a copy of his book, *The World and the Individual*. Royce commented that "some twelve years ago, just after I had printed a book on general philosophy, Mr. Charles Peirce wrote to me, in a letter of kindly acknowledgment, the words: 'But when I read you, I do wish that you would study logic. You need it so much.'"[14]

Royce took Peirce's advice to heart, applying himself to Peircean logic to understand how social and religious communities come to their beliefs. Unlike William James, who focused on proving the truth of beliefs by their consequences, Royce stayed true to Peirce's original sense of pragmatism as *action guided by beliefs* that have been *developed through the process of interpretation*. The key issue was not just the consequences which ideas might have, but more importantly the process by which we originally form our ideas. Royce wanted to answer questions about purpose, duty and goals, not just about whether an idea "works." He posed questions such as: "What do we live for? What is our duty? What is the true ideal of life? What is the true difference between right and wrong?" Royce devoted much of his thinking to the virtue of loyalty which he defined as: "The art of discovering what your own rational will is, and of then discovering how to be true to that will, whatever be your tumult, your moods or your life."[15]

Royce acknowledged that he owed to Peirce's "direct and indirect aid" much of the awareness and perspective he eventually reached in his central concern of loyalty. Especially useful in applying Peirce's pragmatism to business is Royce's understanding of the process of interpretation of signs. Royce directed his inquiry into the idea of loyalty to the central question of the Christian community and how the community formed its beliefs through interpretation. He wanted to answer the apparently simple question: How do you come to beliefs to which you can be loyal?[16] He found that the answer started with Peirce's new post-Kantian set of categories[17] but renamed them as categories of knowledge: Perception, Conception and then Interpretation.

Perception, Conception and Interpretation

Royce noted that two categories of knowledge – perception and conception – have dominated "a great part of the history of philosophy."[18] Perceptions are what we see, the signs or evidence around us which we take in through our senses. Conceptions are ideas, especially our beliefs, which filter what we see. Royce took from Peirce the realization that there is a third category of knowledge different from perception and conception – interpretation – that brings perception and conception together and compares them. He states that he is following on Peirce and his ideas of deduction (conception), induction (perception), and abduction (interpretation) and hopes to be accurate.

Royce's conclusion is that, "all philosophy is interpretation [...] it surveys from above. It is an attainment of a larger unity of consciousness."[19]

Interpretation involves a triadic process: 1) an interpreter perceives an object; 2) then filters it through his ideas; and 3) then he interprets it by comparing what is seen with what is known.

This process of interpretation continues, consciously and unconsciously, when we talk with others. Peirce saw thinking as an interior dialogue with ourselves: the mind of the past discussing the issue with the mind of the future. Royce took this idea further by describing interpretation as essentially a social process, applicable as much to the religious realm as to science. That is, both religious communities and scientists are communities of inquirers who seek truth, and who interpret and reinterpret signs in a shared endeavor.

Royce's categories of knowledge and interpretation, practiced as a social process, offer business people a way to think about and develop action (similar to Peirce's abduction). This method of thinking gets people past the pitfalls inherent in our customary way of deciding how to act, based either on perception, leading us to react to the trends of the moment, or on conception, clinging to our beliefs and strategies long after they have ceased to be useful. We can, I firmly believe, create much more successful business organizations if Royce's process of shared interpretation becomes the basis for developing market strategies and corporate goals. And once the interpretation is formulated, then we can determine action not just on "whatever works" but on loyalty.

Royce brought to his ideas of sign and interpretation how one practices the art of loyalty:

> "What one means by loyal conduct can be defined only
> through a continual effort to readjust the problems of
> life to an ideal, which, just because it is always living and
> growing, involves a willingness to reinterpret the situa-
> tions which arise; to reconsider the solutions which we
> have thus far attempted."[20]

How we might undertake this "continual effort" will be better
understood after we consider the ideas of Max Scheler.

8.6 Max Scheler: "Relatively Pragmatic."[21]

Max Scheler developed three major ideas which further deepen the
religious foundation of pragmatic inquiry: functionalization, values
and the sketch.

Scheler had in some ways a career resembling Peirce's experience,
in that, although he was professor of philosophy and sociology at the
University of Cologne for ten years, he failed to find stable academic
employment. The expanse and scope of his writing approaches that
of Peirce's. He was one of the few and certainly the earliest of the Eu-
ropeans to study closely the work of Peirce and James and appreciated
American pragmatism as a "viable philosophy".

Functionalization

Scheler's basic connection to pragmatism came from his idea of functionalization, which is: "a subliminal process of interaction between
spirit and reality". This sounds similar to Peirce's abduction and
Royce's interpretation in that it is an interaction, not some activity
that goes one way or another as in induction and deduction.

He goes on to say: "Functionalization is at work when insight into
a state of affairs occurs while making trials, probes or experiments with

things or states of affairs."[22] Scheler further stated that "the pragmatic methodology of functionalization is a viable alternative to the hitherto unresolved dilemma of whether the human soul possesses ideas prior to entering the body at birth (Plato) or whether they are extracted from the soul's experience with reality (Aristotle)."[23]

This movement of "functionalization" sounds remarkably similar to Peirce's movement of "abduction" and Royce's movement of "interpretation" as practiced in the art of loyalty. Both will serve us well when we arrive at our own methodology of inquiry. What begins the functionalization process is the inquiry led by values in a continuous process,which, according to Manfred Frings, the noted Scheler authority, addresses one of the oldest stories in philosophy:

> "Functionalization, and by implication Pragmatism's major tenet, offer a ground-breaking alternative to the long tradition of the unresolved discrepancies between Plato's idealism and Aristotle's realism. The alternative is to be seen in Scheler's elucidation of human ideas as emerging "sketches" that are 'in-becoming,' not static ideas."[24]

Values

Most ethical philosophies, in Scheler's view, attempted to direct thinking toward what a person "ought" to do in a situation, or a particular situation. All the chaos of different opinions today concerning the seemingly intractable ethical issues raised by technology (e.g. cloning), business (e.g. third world workers and the living wage) and economics (e.g. capital markets and their control) could not be solved, in Scheler's opinion, by rational methods alone. Through his critique of formal ethics, and particularly its inability to foster changes in behavior throughout history, he turned the usual order of thinking/willing/feeling on its head to having feeling be the foundation of ethical action. From these feelings came the awareness and activation of values.

Feelings as the source of action will sound much like Royce's basis of loyalty.[25] But Scheler went further than Royce and ranked values, which he claimed were like colors in that they were independent of the things, such as cloth, that they are on, into five levels of descending order:

- the highest is holiness, as evidenced by feelings of humility, repentance and worship;

- values of the mind such as aesthetic, juridical, and philosophical values;

- life values such as courage and honesty;

- useful values of success and failure; and

- sensible values such as comfort and discomfort.

While these values and their rankings are relatively self-explanatory, consider that, from Scheler's perspective, all are felt in their origin. The simplest case for Scheler's view of values based on feelings can be seen or felt considering Level 5. Certainly, we feel comfort or discomfort such as hot and cold before reason tells us of the condition. Level 4 is not an absolute idea but depends on what one feels is success and failure. Courage at Level 3 is felt in the heart. Level 2 might seem rational, but consider that despite rational legal arguments, one may feel a sense of injustice or ambiguity. (The court scene in the *Merchant of Venice* and the plea for heartfelt mercy comes to mind.) Similarly philosophical ideas might be accepted or not depending on one's temperament and experience, not just on reasons alone. And as for Level 1, Scheler stands with the long German tradition dating back to the medieval mystics who preached their lived experience of the feeling of the Divine Presence as the source of religious values.

Scheler saw clearly that pragmatic values worked at Level 4 where value determines what is useful or not useful. This level of thought lends itself to the quantitative dimension which business loves so much – measuring profit and loss. He felt that pragmatism was limited because it had its origins in work and that the results of pragmatic inquiry had one purpose: To guide processes of work.[26] He also saw that "the ethos of work and profit has settled over humanity."[27]

While identifying pragmatism with the 4th value level, Scheler knew that his own formulation of functionalization is remarkably close to the practice of pragmatic inquiry. We will make the case that his understanding of values and functionalization offers a way for pragmatic inquiry to help discern values at the highest level. And, like Scheler's belief that whenever a person prefers a value of a lower rank to a higher rank, they experience what Scheler called a "disorder of the heart," failing to pragmatically inquire often leads to dysfunction and pain.

Just how are we to decide what we "ought" to do given this foundation of feelings? While we have connected pragmatic inquiry with Scheler's central concept of functionalization, he was well aware of the difficulty that pragmatic inquiry posed, since it was so easy to connect with the Level 4 values of success and failure. Also, he concluded that all action must be seen in terms of the functionalization model: man's relation with the world. He had a remarkable way of seeing just what was working in one's life; he identified it by the engaging metaphor of a sketch.

The Sketch

How are we to go about searching for values and beliefs? Scheler proposes the idea of a sketch – a rough outline of ideas as they emerge.

A growing story. An evolving plan. The image is provocative and offers great ground for inquiry. In effect, the sketch is the process and result of the pragmatic methodology. As we inquire about the relationship between the person and reality, we gain insights. We see emerging not a fixed idea, but a movement. It appears as the outlines of a direction and a meaning of the activities. We can begin to make sense of the relationship that we are inquiring about. We might even get glimpses of what is at the foundation of the relationship – what values might be at the heart of the activity; what is driving it.

We will now turn toward business and begin to apply our exploration into the business decision making context.

8.7   Decision Making in Marketing

Businesspeople realize that they must constantly change, so there is no end to the things which clamor for attention to begin our inquiries. Change affects the interaction between the market and the company. In pragmatism there is a need to explain or interpret in order to determine what is going on, to define some issue and solve it. Explaining some phenomenon is a great deal like both science and detective work. In science the object is to predict and control some process. In detective investigation, it is to figure out "who did it." In drawing a sketch, however, it becomes very clear that there is a "peculiar self-emerging and 'becoming' character of ideas functionalizing themselves with things."[28] The individual appears in this sketch to be living out – through his day-to-day existence – a plan (i.e. a story). The sketch of this emerging "self" is driven by a universal agent of life – or impulse moving through one's life through our construction and filling out the details of the sketch. Pragmatic Inquiry, in Scheler's view, was correct in that belief is neither deductive nor inductive, but is a consequence of activity over time where ideas and puzzles become clear. Many contemporary philosophers have referred to this view of sketch as the "narrative of each human life."[29]

Even this highly selective and brief look at key approaches presented by Royce and Scheler, based on Peirce's ideas of signs and abduction, shows the possibility that pragmatic inquiry can lead to basing business decisions on a deeper value level than simply "doing whatever works." But how can pragmatism actually be practiced to access this deeper level?

Let us take a moment and ground our discussion in the first of the business activities: to define and to satisfy consumer needs. Let's equate the demand side of the business equation with the discipline of marketing.

If we were able to predict and control businesses, then the rational understanding of balance sheets, income statements and market research studies is all that would be necessary to run a business. However, with the uncertainty of the enormous number of interpersonal relationships and shifting contexts, we can never adequately determine the outcome.[30] Businesspeople now realize they cannot ultimately predict or control all aspects of their business. Therefore, forward-looking businesses must rely on something else. The impetus, then, for action comes from feelings put into action as opposed to a mastery of reality. Royce suggested that out feelings come from our hearts, souls, insights and creativity; this is the source of our loyalty. Scheler called these feelings as values.

How does this insight help business people? It means that to find the motivation for action we must look beyond to the balance sheet and the income statement; we have to see past sales figures and market reports. Surely, businesspeople make decisions using these inputs constantly. They adjust their actions based on the results; unfortunately, they follow the usual flat understanding of pragmatism. However, more evidence is accumulating that shows great businesses comes from motivating and focusing people through values and feelings which are found in the hearts and souls and insights and creativity of every individual in the organization. These are the businesses that endure because there are deep beliefs that guide companies through the swings of the market and business conditions. Jay Bragdon calls this *Living Asset Stewardship*: "caring about people and the things people care about." Deep caring, he says, exists when we look beyond the end results of our actions to the processes we use to deliver those results.[31]

In marketing, attempts have been made for decades to establish a quantitative science similar to the physical sciences for predicting consumer behavior while manipulating everything from price points to advertising copy. These attempts have been built on the model of controlling markets by manipulating the variables to produce some optimal result. Marketing from this perspective was seen as an exchange process that is to be structured optimally for the benefit of the buyer in a transaction with the seller as they both came together seeking advantage.

After decades of work on this exchange model hypothesis with less than persuasive results, we see signs that these attempts at manipulation and control of the market are weakening. The evolution of the definition of marketing from the exchange model to a relationship model makes for a compelling story.

In a series of conversations with Philip Kotler, the distinguished marketing professor at Northwestern's Kellogg School of Management, I noted Kotler's observation of the movement in marketing thinking from an exchange model to one based on relationship and one day I asked Kotler just how far one can go in the movement of a close relationship with the customer. After some deepening of the conversation about relationship, Kotler responded by asking if I was thinking at the "I/Thou" relationship model of the great Hasidic mystic, Martin Buber.[32] Kotler observed, with a wry smile, "it might be possible but not much research has been done at that level." Obviously, Professor Kotler himself in his studies of marketing, had begun to develop, and has been applying, the method of pragmatic inquiry.

8.8 *PathFinder* Pragmatic Inquiry®
and Decision Making

We are now ready to turn to *PathFinder* Pragmatic Inquiry® building on the religious foundations and business contexts discussed above. Religious foundations give depth to the pragmatic inquiry practiced today, which so narrowed the original formulation developed by Peirce. This expanded method of interpretation, or inquiry, offers the thoughtful business practitioner a way to:

- Better understand the reality in which they operate;

- Think critically about what they think and what they believe;

- Improve how they think – to think more creatively;

- To think together to make the best use of all our perspectives and talents.

- To therefore make better decisions to guide actions.

How do you persuade business practitioners to observe the outlines of the sketch they may be involved in and listen to their feelings concerning their role in that sketch? We now have a rich background of religiously inspired insights from Royce and Scheler to put our inquiry on very different footing than the usual "whatever works to maximize return to shareholders."

In proceeding to describe the *PathFinder* Pragmatic Inquiry® methodology, we leave the accepted path trod by these giants of pragmatism. If Peirce, Royce and Scheler were reading these pages, I'm not at all sure they would be happy. Peirce thought businesspeople were incapable of getting beyond their narrow thinking toward their own end. Scheler was very concerned that the capitalist ethic of profit and loss was taking over the world. And to my knowledge, Royce said little about business except in his provocative essay on the role of insurance in the fostering of world peace.[33] But, since each one offered some advice on how to engage in inquiry,[34] we believe they would support the effort to apply their work to deepen the inquiries business practitioners take in determining action.

PathFinder Pragmatic Inquiry$^®$ is not just an action/reaction analysis. Nor does it have as its only goal to maximize return to shareholders. (Although if "return" and the time frame are considered from a values perspective, then there can be a maximum result.) Rather, our task is to inquire about a relationship and what might be at the bottom of the relationship. Plato said that ideas are already there ready to be activated. Aristotle said they were formed in response to the stimulus.[35] But Scheler and Royce, following their understanding of Peirce (and James[36]) said that ideas were formed as the inquiry was going on. That forming of ideas is basically what a sketch is. In business terms, we could call it developing a marketing plan. Sacrilege? Not if we remember that Scheler in particular said that all values must come from the lived experience of active people. And remember that Scheler concluded that the formalism in ethics did little good. It was the values of individuals coming from their feelings that led to true ethical action. It was what Royce saw as the cause or belief to which a person was loyal.

This method of inquiry can bring an individual to a different mindset by examining the evidence of their own lives to see what forces, or values, seem to be at work. Then the individual can identify with those forces and feel their importance. The question is, how can people go about practicing the inquiry. That is why the *Corpo-*

rantes PathFinder Notebook© was developed: as a way to conduct a
PathFinder Pragmatic Inquiry®.

The *Corporantes PathFinder Notebook*© has been tested in hundreds of corporate and academic settings including Time Magazine,
3M, Levi-Strauss & Co., Harris Bank, The Quaker Oats Company,
DePaul University, University of Notre Dame, University of South
Florida, St. Mary's College, Kellogg School of Management and Stanford University Graduate School of Business among others.[37] Let's
take a look at how it works in the corporate setting.

Businesspeople are not generally inclined to sustained philosophical reflection. They don't have time. They are people of action. Nor
do they relish uncertainty or doubting themselves, which mark the
necessary stance to begin a genuine inquiry. (Jim Collins, in *Level
5 Leadership* calls for "humility" to challenge their "firm resolve.")[38]
This fact is one of the key reasons why pragmatism has been so little
appreciated (or thought of) by them as an efficient method of helping
them to decide where to invest scarce resources.

Executives cite many reasons for making decisions. From a financial point of view, the company's primary purpose is to make the maximum amount of money in the minimum amount of time. But people
don't buy products to help the company reach this goal. They want
just the opposite: the most product for the least amount of money.
Nor do employees work simply for money. And so the great dance of
commerce goes on, in most cases, without any thought to the values
of customers and employees.

Most business leaders note that before they can make a decision
about direction, they must have all the facts and then a decision can
be made. The advantage of viewing things from Scheler's hierarchy of
values is that the businesspersons can ask what level of facts and activities is important to them. The usual understanding of pragmatism
has always been seen as staying at the useful/not useful level of discernment – or even at the lower value of comfort/discomfort. But, as

Scheler lamented, that brings "heart disorder." How, then, might we bring the present generation to a higher level of values? He felt that we were stuck on the view of the individual – the "I" of the I/Thou relationship. In a familiar theme in philosophy of means vs. ends, the individual is interested only in the usefulness of people and things to maximize the individual's own benefits, comfort and success. Could business strategy, as suggested by the earlier discussion of the change to the relationship marketing orientation in marketing, offer a way out of our individualistic orientation?

If we take the more important idea of a sketch and the power of values and the force that sketch/value has in helping us make decisions beyond the facts, we begin to learn more about the values that are at work internally and externally in a corporation. And we get a deeper interpretation of what needs to be done, or changed, based on the evidence, or what decisions need to be made internally and externally to complete the sketch. This interpretation goes beyond the sense data leading to the intuitive or feeling level. *PathFinder* Pragmatic Inquiry$^{®}$ shows the general direction the individual in any situation is being propelled and called at the same time. The alternative to inquiry is to be robotically moved simply in *reaction* to events.

With this foundation of pragmatic inquiry placed in a business context, we can now turn to its application.

8.9   Practicing *PathFinder* Pragmatic Inquiry$^{®}$

The *PathFinder* process outlined above needs a simple way to practice it. That is the purpose of the *Corporantes PathFinder Notebook*$^{©}$. As we have noted, the inquirer must begin with a question or a doubt, which frames the inquiry. The range of concerns can be considerable:

- Values: beliefs, principles, virtues, "culture" of the organization

- Vision – mission, purpose and goals – of the organization

- Sustainable competitive advantages

- Critical success factors

- Strategy development

- Branding and communications

- Consumer and product relationship

- Competitive response

- Organizational structure

- Personal career direction – values, vision and mission

- Qualities of leadership

- Ethical dilemmas

The next step is to state why that question or concern is important to the individual and the corporation. In other words, what action will the answer enable the individual and the corporation to take; what are the implications of the answer. Then state the preliminary or baseline answer. And finally state what actions are now being considered in light of the baseline answer. The question frames the inquiry and the baseline answers form the hypothesis to be tested.

Before the actual inquiry begins, the inquirer puts the question in the context of the strategic relationships involved. This can be illustrated by the Strategic *PathFinder* Relationships Triangle (see Fig. 8.1)

These relationships can be seen, as we have stated above, as linked together through the discipline of marketing. Philip Kotler referred to in our discussion of the "I/Thou" relationship, has also said : "Marketing serves as the link between society's needs and its patterns of industrial response. (This puts) marketing at the heart of strategy."[39]

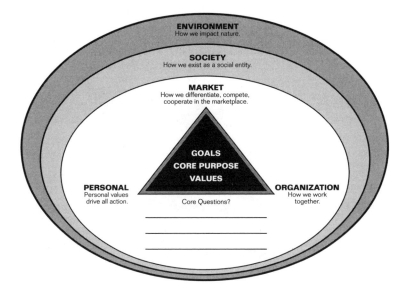

Figure 8.1: Strategic Relationships

Copyright: Corporantes 2002

Finally, marketing can then be rightly seen as a "social activity" since "every product and service that is made and sold performs a social function and every transaction has a social aspect [...]"[40]

The inquiry process has now begun and goes forward with the Steps as shown in Fig. 8.2.

Fig. 8.1 establishes the Strategic *PathFinder* Relationships. Fig. 8.2 illustrates the sequential flow of the inquiry: Question, Explore, Interpret, Hypothesize and Act. The evidence is gained from the perspectives of all three parts of the Strategic Relationship, both what is happening now (bearings) and what has and might happen in the future (path). The data is interpreted through various intuitive exercises. A hypothesis is then formed and action is decided on.

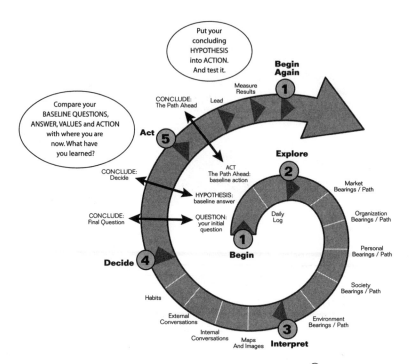

Figure 8.2: Corporantes *PathFinder* Notebook© Steps

As you can see, learning takes place as the inquirers compare their concluding questions, answers and action with their original baseline answers.[41]

The final answer must be considered as a hypothesis, which should be further, tested. At this point the inquirer begins the *PathFinder* Pragmatic Inquiry® again.

8.10 Conclusion

With this brief overview, we have shown a way to deepen the pragmatic inquiry that is based on the writing of three scholars: Josiah Royce, Max Scheler and Charles Sanders Peirce.

Insights of our philosophers of religion, Royce and Scheler, provide the foundation for the inquiry. Data are signs to be interpreted in light of the question. The question is based on an understanding of values and will be tested on that level. Given the relationship model, an inquiry proceeds according to functionalization/abduction – interaction between the inquirer and the market. Central to the *PathFinder* is to treat one's career and the corporation as living entities with values, character, talent, a service to provide and a path to follow – hence the choice of "*PathFinder*" to identify this particular form of pragmatic inquiry. We are inquiring about the sketch of the journey. As with any journey there are questions: What is the destination? What is the best path? How do we prepare? With whom will we travel? When should we go? As in any exploration, the inquirer must be open to surprises, capture vague impressions, feelings, and memories – as well as hard data – and look for patterns and connections. Inquirers must be willing to entertain new explanations and sources of beliefs for action, which contradict what they thought and which they do not now understand. What is the impulsion for action? What values are guiding and driving the journey? They are cautioned to remember that in most cases of discovery involved, there are moments of insight and intuition that do not come through logical methods alone, but involve feelings and values.

The *PathFinder* methodology gives practitioners the way to practice abduction, interpretation, and functionalization. The result is a sketch, which provides an invaluable picture for what the practitioner is experiencing. It shows an impulse of values seated in feeling, which gives attention, impulse and direction to the inquiry. These insights form the way out of the narrowness of pragmatic inquiry intended to control outcomes with little or no attention paid to values. These insights lead to action and practical results based on beliefs – impulses and feelings – which move to the higher levels that Royce in loyalty and Scheler in values refer.[42]

Practicing the flexible framework of exercises in *PathFinder* Pragmatic Inquiry® by using the *Corporantes PathFinder Notebook*© gives corporate executives and others a way to make the decisions which determine the direction they and their organizations will move - a *path* to follow based on the evidence of their own values and vision in action.

Thoughtful business practitioners are coming to realize that feelings are at the heart of values, to which our religious philosophers call our attention and where the real source of success lies, individually and corporately. With pragmatic inquiry now more readily applicable, business practitioners can use it to make better investment of their time, talents and resources in making decisions which further the goal of business: "to facilitate a process where personal strengths and resources are turned to serve social benefits." The challenge is to turn those goals and strategies into "stories" which people will want to be a part of. The anticipated vision is that business will then take its place as the leading force in the world today to help foster a more compassionate and just society in which we, as productive and responsible members, can all thrive and flourish.

What is your story and the story of your organization?

Chapter 9

Where Do Conflicts Begin?
An Inquiry into the Need for Inquiry
in Management Education

8th International Conference
on Social Values in Education and Business
University of Oxford – July, 2006

"The next step forward must come, not from political
agitation or premature experiments but from thought.
We need by an effort of the mind to elucidate our own
feelings. In the field of action reformers will not be successful until they can steadily pursue a clear and definite
object with their intellects and their feelings in tune [...]
We need a new set of convictions, which spring naturally
from a candid examination of our own inner feelings in
relation to the outside facts."

John Maynard Keynes[1]

9.1   Introduction – Purpose

That we live in a world of grave political, social and environmental
conflict, and of too little reflective thinking – as suggested by the title
of this conference – is obvious. The question is: as business educators,
do we need to concern ourselves with this? And if so, what do we do
about it?

If we see our function as preparing management practitioners to
"maximize return to shareholders," then these larger issues are not a

concern. The "invisible hand" of the market will work its magic. But if we want to understand the role of business, its impact in these troubled times, and the role of managers, then we need to look seriously at how we are educating the future business leaders and managers and engaging them to think and act on the pressing issues, the conflicts of our day.

Many agree that business is the dominant force in society, surpassing the traditional forces of religion and government. If that is true, then the education of business leaders becomes a major task in our society.

This is not a new thought.

For instance, in 1926, Wallace Donham, the legendary dean of the Harvard Business School, gave an address in which he discussed the social condition in the country and business's responsibilities. During the question and answer period, a student asked Donham how he reconciled this "social point of view" with the profit motive. "It is a difficult question," Donham admitted. "Intelligent selfishness – the stance of the enlightened capitalist of the early 20th century – was of only limited usefulness."[2] It still is.

Another MBA program opened its doors in the fall of 2003 at Presidio World College (The official name for the program is: Presidio School of Management) to twenty-two full-time students, nearly 100 years after HBS opened its door to twenty-four full-time students. Presidio's is based on offering an MBA in *Sustainable Management*, which is an attempt in a long line of effort to address the question of the social role of business Donham raised.

Our college, while delivering a quality MBA program, addresses the question of how the practice of management can help solve the major social and environmental issues. We can, of course, only superficially deal here with the content of the program and curriculum. But I wish to touch on certain frameworks and features of the curriculum and focus on how we engage our students, emotionally and intellectually to develop *ideas* and the values to drive them, which can change the way we do business – and change the world.[3] One point of interest: we have no ethics course. Why? Because we consider the whole program to be an extended course in the practice of moral reasoning.

Perhaps not surprisingly, we begin the engagement with our students by asking the perennial question concerning our human purpose: "What is the good/worthwhile/flourishing life?" With our management focus, we specifically ask: "What is the work you want to do?" "What are your goals?" "What do you want to do next [...] and why?" Finally, we press the search for meaning and uncover the student's "calling" - where ideas, talents and values meet the world's needs. Students ask, "What's my Big Idea to make the world more sustainable?" vs. "Uh, isn't the purpose of my MBA to help me get a better job?"

These large questions of purpose need to be asked in every changing social circumstance and period, but especially now with the overwhelming and unprecedented environmental and human crises we face. Our program and curriculum are designed to engage our students in disciplines, frameworks, controversies, theories, practices, ideas, cases, mentors, "ways of knowing" and thinking, group and individual work; in sum every way we know to help them challenge and test their ideas.[4]

We use a line of inquiry at Presidio which leads the search for the deep level of a "*calling*." But we begin prosaically with: "What's your big idea?" (Since we are just starting our 4th year, and our 5th class with only two classes graduated, consider this more of a *progress report*.)[5]

Can business education really help business practitioners address the various aspects of conflict in the world? And if so, how?

The common definition of *conflict*, half the title of this conference – "*Ethical Conflict and the 'Sleep of Reason'*" – provides a useful framework for attempting to answer these two questions. Consider the following four definitions of *conflict* from the *Encarta* dictionary, available at the fingertips of every MS Word user:

War *Military*: a continued struggle or battle, especially open warfare between opposing forces.

Difference A disagreement or clash between ideas, principles, or people.

Mental Struggle *Psychology*: a psychological state resulting from the often unconscious opposition between simultaneous but incompatible desires, needs, drives, or impulses.

Plot tension *Literature*: opposition between or among characters or forces in a literary work that shapes or motivates the action of a plot.

There is a progressive connection between these four definitions which is more clearly seen by *reversing* the order. Therefore, we will follow the reverse order in an attempt to show how we pursue our goal of helping students – and by students I mean all of us – find their calling and develop their ideas. We will begin with how all of us are embroiled in a *plot/tension* (def.4). This causes questioning – *mental struggle* (def.3) – which launches an inquiry. We engage in learning through exploring *differences* (def. 2). And then we enter into the serious *battles* (def.1) we face today.

We do have a need to *awaken reason*. And just the thing to do it is to begin with the *conflicts* and the *emotions* that arouse us.

As people move through the Presidio MBA landscape, they focus on the application of recent developments in moral philosophy, particularly as these address the process of Inquiry. The reason for attempting to expose some of these deeper issues driving the Presidio MBA educational philosophy (see Appendix) is again best stated by Keynes:

"The ideas of economists and political philosophers, both when they are right and when they are wrong, are more powerful than is commonly understood. Indeed the world is run by little else. Practical men, who believe themselves to be quite exempt from any influences, are usually the slaves of some defunct economist."[6]

And I would add, business educators and practitioners are equally and unknowingly held captive by educational and moral philosophers as well as by economists.[7]

Because this subject is "difficult" as Dean Donham noted, and given the range of philosophical and psychological as well as business topics covered, this paper might be considered, more accurately, a *sketch*, rather than an in-depth, closely, reasoned argument.

Where does conflict begin? Let's begin with a story.

9.2   Conflict as Story

Conflict definition:

Plot tension *Literature*: opposition between or among characters or forces in a literary work that shapes or motivates the action of a plot.

How do we engage students and executives in moral reasoning? Putting them on the usual treadmill of reading the results of several hundred years worth of work on the theories of Utilitarianism, Deontology, Teleology, Justice, etc. has proven a difficult slog, except for the most gifted teachers and students of business ethics. Instead, we engage them in real life stories – especially *their* story.

Following *conflict* definition 4, here is how an Inquiry starts. We find ourselves at a point in time where something comes along and something is triggered inside of us – call it curiosity, worry, perplexed, awe, depressed, excitement, uncertainty. The important thing to notice is that it begins as an *emotion*, a *feeling* as Keynes called it.

Here is an excerpt from a typical student admissions essay for Presidio School of Management:

"I was depressed when the dot.com bubble burst. It hit our company hard. After a half dozen crazy, work-filled years, our business was imploding and I hadn't been able to 'cash out'. And that's when it hit me – that had been my sole goal. I realized in an instant, as I was cleaning out my desk and packing boxes, what a shallow, empty purpose that was, and what a price I had paid."[8]

This awakening exposes the key elements of any story. It reveals one's motives, what one determines to be success and failure; what characters are involved; what questions are asked and those not asked; who are friends, foes, and allies; what are one's changing goals, purpose and values.[9] The meaning of this jumble of ideas shifts as they are seen more clearly. I call this "learning to read the signs."[10]) Our student then begins –the quest for another story, a connection with something and someone else by asking those great moral questions: "What does all this mean?" "What am I to do next?" And, "What will I base my decision on – what values, core purpose and goals?"[11]

I have long believed in the narrative impulse of reasoning for the simplest of reasons: it is how life is lived.[12] "Life keeps coming at you" as my beloved aunt used to say.

So, what do we do? How do we best engage this life "coming at us?" The American Pragmatists[13] developed a method of inquiry to help. From the mid 19th Century to the mid-20th Century, they looked on and studied the scientific method with great admiration as to its power of focus and analysis. Their followers today, many of them feminist philosophers, are building on their insights.

They recognized that in science, inquiry begins when some fact or observation doesn't fit with the existing hypothesis. The scientist feels a sense of uncertainty. In everyday life, in much the same way but often less rationally, inquiry begins when something doesn't feel right. This emotion begins the inquiry.

The Pragmatists saw the weakness of *deduction* – keep applying the same principle and doing the same thing – and the weakness of *induction*, or constant searching. But in process philosophy, they saw the power, efficiency and effectiveness of continually moving between the two and gave this movement the somewhat ambiguous name of "*abduction*."[14] While the inquiry begins with an emotion, intertwined is also some hunch, idea, or thought. Developing and testing that begins moving the story forward.

The development of a narrative framework from this perspective offers a broad and sturdy bridge between psychology and philosophy by linking stories with moral reasoning.

If you accept the blindingly obvious observation that we are thinking in and with our bodies, how might reason and emotion, body and mind, work more effectively together to understand the meaning of the story which the *plot tension* started?

This brings us to our next "conflict" definition: conflict as *mental struggle*.

9.3   Conflict as Individual Inquiry

Conflict definition:

Mental Struggle *Psychology*: a psychological state resulting from the often unconscious opposition between simultaneous but incompatible desires, needs, drives, or impulses.

In their admissions essays, our students invariably tell the drama which starts the story as we saw above. At the Student Orientation before starting classes, we ask them to take time and reflect on their inner struggle. I assure the students that the struggle can lead to creativity, as John Dewey reminds us:

> "Conflict is the gadfly of thought. It stirs us to observation and memory. It instigates to invention. It shocks us out of sheep-like passivity, and sets us at noting and contriving. Not that it always effects this result; but that conflict is the *sine qua non* of reflection and ingenuity."[15]

They first state their ideas and questions. And secondly, we ask them to look beneath to see what values (deeply felt) are driving their Inquiry. Then they proceed with their Inquiry to challenge their assumptions and gain new insights to come to new understanding of their ideas, goals and values and put them into action to test them.

The inevitable next step is "Begin Again," which is familiar to everyone, and serves as a compelling proof point that Inquiry is something we all have done many times before.

Our students begin in the same manner as the scientist by questioning assumptions (*abduction*), as opposed to proving an idea (*deduction*) or gathering information (*induction*).

To give structure to this process of narrative writing and reflection, we employ a methodology which we call Pragmatic Inquiry, so named as a practice of the pragmatic philosophy. (How to engage in the process of the Inquiry is described in the *Corporantes PathFinder Journal* which each new student receives.)

Its five steps appear simple and straightforward:

1. *Begin:* We begin by getting the assumptions clear as a baseline by asking these questions:

   What is the question, issue, challenge, idea, etc.?

   Why is the question, etc. important? What is at stake? So what? (This sharpens the question.)

What is the preliminary answer, hunch, idea, etc.?

What values, beliefs, purpose, goals etc. are driving the answer (and started the question in the first place?)

What actions are or will be taken.

This establishes the baseline and gets all the assumptions to be tested on the table. We then check in with the students periodically to review their Baseline work. They go through various courses, all of which are designed to give frameworks and disciplines to further their testing and development of their ideas. Then during the last two semesters in their Marketing and Venture Plan courses, they formally go through the rest of the steps in the Inquiry.

The next steps of the Inquiry are straightforward:

2. *Explore*: examine and collect data

3. *Interpret*: what does the data mean?

4. *Decide*: come to some answer of your question

5. *Act*: based on your answer, what action will you take?

Fig. 9.1 is a graphic image of the process of Inquiry.

Our students now compare their final questions and answers with their Baseline. They are often surprised to see just how much their thinking has changed during the course of the inquiry. This exercise fulfills the foundational axiom of learning: "developing" as well as "unlearning" what they thought was true. In this, we are following John Dewey who stated that learning happens only as the "educator views teaching and learning as a continuous process of reconstruction of experience."[16]

This is expressed graphically in the Pragmatic Inquiry Steps in Fig. 9.2.

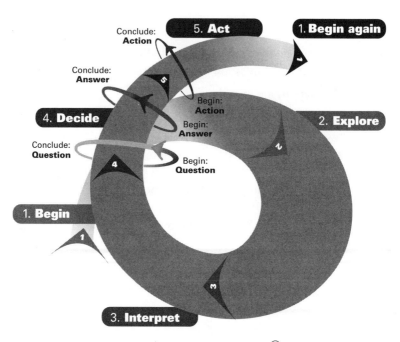

Figure 9.1: The Pragmatic Inquiry® Steps

(From *PathFinder* Lab Journal.)

Emotion and Inquiry

Through twenty-five years working with thousands of executives and students, we hear over and over: "It looks easy, but it's not." The Inquiry is deceptive because it requires "effort of the mind to get intellects and feelings in tune" (as Keynes put it) to challenge assumptions.

If you agree that conflict begins inside each of us, then internal conversations, reflection and inquiry offer the richest areas where conflicts need to be addressed most directly. What are the conflicting

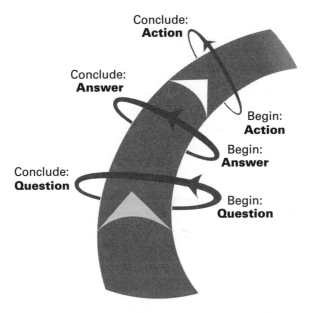

Figure 9.2: "What Have You Learned?"

ideas in each of us? And this is where reason and emotion, philosophy and psychology, have been pitched against each other.

Philosophers too often are rightfully accused of sitting in their
academic armchairs and then floating above us all in the cerebral
world of Metaphysics. They have largely ignored *emotions* during
the long history of moral reasoning because they considered emotions too unstable and only useful in implementation, after *reason*
did the heavy lifting. As a result, philosophy's centuries-old grip on
popular reason has weakened to the point of almost vanishing. Theology hasn't fared much better.[17] Now the practice of psychology, or
dealing with emotions, is on every street corner. But philosophy is
waking up and again might bring its formidable tradition and dis-

cipline to bear on the problems of reasoning and action today. The effort of much moral philosophy, starting in earnest several centuries after Descartes' famous *cogito ergo sum,* has attempted to overcome the dualism between body and mind. Theologians have been arguing over this since St. Paul's writings; as have the ancient philosophers in the East and West, with dramatically different results. The battles are raging over the efficacy and shortcomings of the Enlightenment, Fundamentalism (remember in the last century when people said "God is Dead"?), Modernism, and Postmodernism in philosophy, economics, religion, science, politics, arts, humanities, etc. etc. A few scholars of business management, such Peter Drucker, Willis Harman, Meg Wheatley, Henry Mintzberg and James O'Toole, just to name a few, have engaged from this larger perspective to take seriously the need for dramatically changing our ways of thinking and inquiring, building on and challenging our tradition.

Moral philosophers are catching up by realizing that *emotion* is what kicks off the whole inquiry process, as I have indicated above. One such philosopher says thought begins with a great stirring of emotion, such as falling in love or hate or anger or concern or wonder which leads to "upheavals of thought." The author makes the simple but profound insight that emotions are not to be bridled or ignored, unconnected and only to be controlled by thought. But rather they are a "source of deep awareness and understanding [...] suffused with intelligence and discernment."[18]

Another philosopher observes that these emotions/passions are connected, deeply and inseparably, with thought.[19] This level of awareness can help us greatly and we ignore it at our peril. But what does all this mean for our students? Here's how we bring the two together in the Inquiry.

You will be familiar with, and have probably used or taken, personality profiles. Many of them follow various archetypal categories ranging in sophistication from the Enneagram to the tabloid quickly quiz. The most popular and widely used is Myers-Briggs typology and test, based on the archetypes developed by Carl Jung:

- Introvert – Extrovert

- Sensate – Intuitive

- Perceptive – Judgment

- Thinking – Feeling

Here is just one example of Jung's thinking behind these archetypes. Each of Jung's types has an ancient source. For instance, the Giant predecessors to the Greek gods trusted only what they could touch, what you could hold in your hand. (Sensate = hand).[20]

In preparing for this conference and thinking about the role of emotion in awakening reason, it suddenly became clear to me that each step in the Pragmatic Inquiry of *Begin, Explore, Interpret and Decide and Act* appealed to and utilized different emotional stances that the Inquirer could take.[21] And that helped explain why many students and executives found that, while the process looked simple, in fact it was very demanding. That's because each step requires a different emotional stance. Here's what we have seen:

- The *Begin* phase requires Humility – not knowing the answer and being open to learn.

- The *Explore* phase, where our students take in the facts, impressions, memories, observation, engages the sensate emotion.

- The *Interpret* step is more intuitive where they are "connecting the dots" from the *Explore* phase and using their eyes and ears and gut.

- The *Decide* step is thinking, using the head.

- The next step of of *Action* is ignited and sustained ultimately by the emotion of courage or heart found in the "calling". The two steps of *Explore* and *Interpret* are the ability to Perceive and the second two steps of *Decide* and *Act* are the ability to Judge – thus covering the four basic Jungian types, all of which are essential for an integrated inquiry.

- And the crucial step is now to see the action as a test. Measure and reflect on the results to see what is to be learned. Then, with more wisdom, ask questions and the inquiry goes on...*Begin Again*.

Since many top executives often have hard-wired their reasoning (relying on habits that got them to where they are), certain steps are much more difficult to engage in with others. To point out two obvious examples: the fact-driven operations director may have trouble with imagery and hunches while the creative, spontaneous marketing director will have the opposite problem. And generally, humility is not in overflowing abundance on the executive floor.[22]

While the goal of the inquiry is to bring together emotion and reason to determine an answer to a question, the most important outcome is to uncover the values, core purpose and goals that are driving that answer.[23]

Conflict and Values

Since we have been mentioning values early and often, we need now to define them; "not exactly the easiest definitional question in philosophy."[24]

Here's mine:

Value A value is any belief, principle, or virtue held so deeply (consciously or unconsciously) that it guides your behavior, decisions and actions.

And, reasoning backward, it is from the evidence of behavior, decisions and actions that the values are revealed. After all, pragmatic
philosophy states as its maxim that you will know the meaning of an
idea, value, etc, by its consequences (which is NOT: "whatever works"
"action ungoverned by principle," "only the bottom-line," etc. – but
that is, and has been, another paper [...] and book.[25])

By linking values inextricably to action in a business school, we
give our answer to the time-honored and common sense question:
Can ethics be taught?[26]

The purpose, as we said, is to help our students develop their ideas
and engage, first themselves, and then by leading others, in action.
One great advantage of the Pragmatic Inquiry is that it gives our students a clear story supporting their ideas. A second is that, through
examining the evidence of experience, the values[27] driving our students' inquiry and decisions are clearly revealed – for better or for
worse. All this awareness and data can help in communication and describing the decision and goal to others. This ability to communicate
with others and engage them does not mean they must be charismatic.
Rather, they must be believable, truthful and show evidence in order
to earn trust. Here is how one Student, Terri Passarotti, described her
experience and outcome of the process:

> "I now feel powerful in why I do what I do, where before
> I had only an intuitive sense of it."

Warren Bennis identifies this kind of communication which results from an inquiry as his key assumption of leadership:

> "[...]leaders are people who are able to express themselves fully. The key to full self-expression is understanding one's self and the world, and the key to understanding is learning – from one's own life and experience."[28]

Our students are now ready to test their ideas, assumptions and values. And what better place than in a challenging MBA program in Sustainable Management –where they can experience the clash of ideas and practices, of which the business landscape today is full.

9.4   Conflict in Education and Business

Conflict definition:

Difference A disagreement or clash between ideas, principles, or people.

Why did Harvard establish a business school in the first place? The president, Charles William Eliot, at the start of the 20th Century simply noted that half of its Harvard College graduates went into business. Why did Presidio World College begin offering an MBA? Half of the students being recruited for the College's BA degree completion program in "Sustainable and Ethical Enterprise Design" wanted to go into business, but also wanted a rigorous advanced education and an MBA.

And in a more significant way the parallel goes further. Dean Donham of HBS, whom I mentioned before, felt that a key function of business was to: "control the consequences of scientific development." He went on to say: "We face the necessity of socializing the results of science."[29] Our MBA in Sustainable Management shares a similar view and purpose, but we would add that we equally need to "socialize" the means and results of business.

What is the conflict landscape here? There are literally thousands of problems and differences of opinions, especially in our field of Sustainable Management.

To cover all these different approaches would take a shelf full of books, talks and articles written by leaders in the field, including our distinguished scholar/practitioner faculty. My purpose, here, is to show how we think, and engage our students to think about it within the context of sustainability. Here is a summary.

Integration of the Curriculum

The principles of sustainability Serving the common good by providing a profit (broadly understood) through cultivating, enhancing and restoring human and natural capital is the distinguishing focus and content of our program. A second characteristic is the integrated nature of the program.

Curriculum integration[30], long recognized by most educators as more relevant and effective, and by sustainability professionals as essential, is notoriously difficult to do in most departmental, tenure-driven schools. Simply stated, everything in a global world is connected to everything else, and business programs that fail to recognize this and prepare students to manage accordingly are preparing their students to manage in a world they will not fully understand nor appreciate.

It is well beyond the scope of this report to fully explain the content, power, and elegance of our ever evolving and integrating syllabus. (As I have said, the effort of this report is to position our Program within the specific educational task of fostering moral reasoning.) You are looking at the "core curriculum" – as in "no electives." Paula Thielen, our Finance and Accounting Professor, has aptly described the entire curriculum as an "elective."

PRESIDIO
SCHOOL OF MANAGEMENT

2-Yr Track	People	Numbers	Sustainability	Markets
Semester 1	Effective Management, Communication & Action	Managerial Accounting	Principles of Sustainable Management	Managerial Economics
Semester 2	Evolutionary Leadership, Colloration & Systems Thinking	Operations & Production	Business, Government & Civil Society	Ecological Economics & Macroeconomics
Semester 3	Strategic Management	Managerial Finance	Sustainable Products & Services	Managerial Marketing
Semester 4	Culture: Values & Ethics	Economics, Capitol Markets & the Law	Implementation of Sustainable Business Practices	Integrative Capstone Venture Plan

Figure 9.3: Presidio School of Management Curriculum

Here is an overly simplified list of issues and questions we address within the curriculum which will give you an idea of how we engage our students in practicing and testing their assumptions:

- **Accounting:** Do you achieve better results managing to a single bottom line or an integrated bottom line?

- **Economics:** Do neoclassical economics or ecological economics better prepare a student to allocate resources?

- **Marketing:** Is the goal to encourage consumption to satisfy wants or to deliver satisfaction of needs ("enough")?

- **Governance:** Is a manager responsible for shareholder value or stakeholder responsibility?

- **Communication:** Which better achieves results: dictatorial or conversation?

- **Strategy:** Is this a linear or organic process?

- **Natural resources:** Are they to be exploited or cultivated and renewed?

- **Supply chain:** Can a company optimize one way delivery or must a brand take responsibility for its supply chain as a closed loop?

- **Finance:** Is the appropriate time horizon short-term or long-term?

- **Management:** Do you use command and control or self-organizing?

- **Product Design:** Do we learn from machines or from nature?

Sometimes there is a direct conflict between the two views. At other times, students experience competition as well as a blend or synthesis of the opposing views. Presidio has practically eliminated conflict between disciplines, freeing faculty to bring their collective talents to solve the challenges facing each discipline. Our faculty face the main challenge of sorting all that out along with the implications for action. What we do acknowledge, as Hunter Lovins who heads our Sustainability Strand and helped craft the list above likes to say, is: "This is an emergent field. We are literally making it up as we go along." Our work is proceeding pragmatically, as we test ideas to develop and implement the best.

Practice –Project-oriented Learning

The theme of our communication and recruiting is to ask students: "What's your big idea?" As you have seen, the first thing we do when they arrive is to have them state their ideas, then we challenge them through the various courses and projects to test, develop and invariably change their idea in some, often significant, way. Our students work on projects dealing with questions of sustainable practices in a broad range of companies – over 100 to date – including Wal-Mart, Mattel, PG&E, and Williams-Sonoma as well as community based service organizations such as Goodwill Industries; their work runs the spectrum from small start ups to high-tech to spas.

Our students bring together both education and training in the process of learning, thus bridging one of the enduring conflicts in education, as Richard Pring noted in his Prologue.

Our students' educational experience culminates in their Venture Plan which exhibits their competence in all the disciplines of the program.

Each course prepares our students for this final goal. They experience what we call "living cases" as opposed to the more familiar "closed" cases. They work on real projects, following the ancient tradition of "learning by doing," "practice," and "apprenticeship" through what Whitehead has referred to as "first-hand knowledge."[31] This is sometimes called "problem-based learning" as opposed to "discipline-based learning." (See the Appendix for our Educational Philosophy.) During this time they are also trying out various ideas which might lead to their Venture Plan.

We are focused on helping our students develop their ideas, test them and implement them. We are often asked if we help in job placement. We have a simple answer and formula that:

- A *job* is what somebody else wants you to do. (Result: *security*.)

- A *career* is what you want to do. (Result: *loyalty* to the organization.)

- A *calling* is something that you need, must, are compelled – cannot *not* – do. (Result: finding *meaning* in your work.)

One way to think about this is to put these steps on a "hierarchy of needs" following Maslow.[32]

And if, at the end of the program, their Venture Plan does not lead to an actual next step, we work with them to see where their ideas and passion might lead. In any case, our students now are able to develop actionable sustainable plans. They are ready to practice Sustainable Management, whatever field or ideas (or calling) they pursue.

9.5   Sustainable Management

Organizing ourselves to serve the needs of the community.

Ever since Adam Smith's opening paragraphs of *Wealth of Nations*, describing the famous pin factory,[33] we have argued the merits of orga-

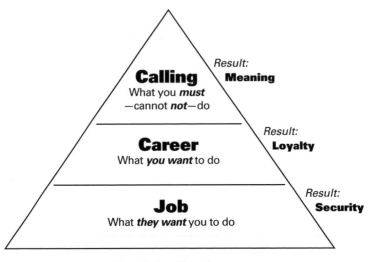

Figure 9.4: Hierarchy of Job/Career/Calling

nizing ourselves in various ways to produce the products and services people need.

On the supply side we need to consider where the materials come from. It is no secret that we are using up our resources at an alarming rate to feed our consumerist society.

The present business model is based on neoclassical economics which has been reduced to continuous growth to maximize return to shareholders. This has led to the pre-eminence of Finance as a discipline for wealth creation.

But what is the real source of wealth of nations? Smith turned our attention away from wealth in the ground to the wealth contained in the energies of its citizens.

Business captures the moral energy to harness the sources of material and energy to produce the vast quantities which society needs. And therein lies the problem: how do we fill the *perceived* needs of society? Philip Kotler, professor at Kellogg School of Management has defined and redefined marketing many times over his distinguished career. Here is a recent one:

> "Marketing serves as the link between society's needs and its patterns of industrial response.
>
> It must be put at the heart of strategy."[34]

What caught my attention is this definition considerably broadened the scope of marketing beyond just *consumer* needs, but *society's* need and the way we go about filling these needs. That got me thinking about sustainability. To point out the obvious, we are consuming so much oil, water, food, energy, shelter, medicine, entertainment, and material of all types and fashions because we think we *need* it. If we took Kotler's definition and more broadly defined the needs, the resources, the time horizon (using the Bruntland Commission definition to include the needs of future generations, the key constraint), and expanded beyond just the industrial sector, we might have something like this:

> **Sustainable Management** is the practice of cultivating, linking and renewing our resources – human, social, natural, manufactured, financial – to serve the needs of present and future generations.
>
> It guides every successful community's civic, cultural and commercial strategies.[35]

In a word, all aspects of society are joined together to serve the needs as each society comes to identify what these are in order to answer our now-familiar moral reasoning question: "What is the good life?"

One advantage of this simple definition is that it stretches the meaning of sustainability in business management. One friend, when asked: "What does Sustainable Management mean?" responded quickly and heartily: "Get your friends on your board of directors!!" Obviously, this is an extreme case of the more broadly and commonly understood idea: "the continuation of the business and succession planning." The answer can then evolve easily and more broadly to include "continuation of the society and world in which the business operates." And since this isn't an impossible stretch for business people to realize, I have found it an easy way to begin to weaken the strangle hold of the myopic "maximize return to shareholders" mantra has today on management and business educators. But does this line of inquiry lead our students to another path of management practice altogether?

We are now at the point of developing one way to guide the core of energy we have been referring to as a "calling." We will now more closely link it to the familiar business concept of serving the needs of others.

Moral philosophers have long noted the two poles of either egoistic or altruistic motives. The usual middle position is to link the two into an "enlightened self-interest" position. This is the "I do this for the good of the whole because it would, in the long run, be good for me," position. But Donham, as previously noted, has found this of "limited usefulness."

Others claim that the basis on which we make decisions needs to be understood in the social context of the society in which decisions are being made, and also the tradition from which the circumstances spring.[36]

Here is a third position between either egoism or altruism: we do our work because we *must* given what it is we see. We are compelled by the "outside facts" to which Keynes referred. We are drawn to the work because we see it must be done, and we can do it.

I have approached the question of big ideas and calling from a business and marketing perspective. But a more demanding test is the lessons we must learn from Nature.

9.6   Nature and Our Place In It

Business and much of humanity in recent history has seen itself as apart from and over Nature. It is a very long and difficult path to summarize how we came to this increasingly untenable position except to say that in the West we have had a view of Nature that it was there to be exploited and manipulated. This has to do with the Christian anthropocentric view which posited that Nature was created to serve us. We haven't recognized ourselves as stewards and part of an evolving nature.[37]

Therefore, one of the major tasks of Sustainable Management in reconstructing our economic and business practices is to reconfigure our place and role in Nature. We do this by showing the context within which the individual, the organization and the market work, compete and exist. You'll notice the core questions, issues and concerns lie at the center of it all.

If you wanted to mention leading environmental lights who have helped develop this view, where would you begin? With Henry David Thoreau, John Muir, David Brower, Aldo Leopold, James Lovelock, or Rachael Carson? And where would you stop? Or do you focus just on the literally hundreds of experts developing and leading the sustainability movement today, many of whom are on our faculty, visiting lecturers, advisors and speakers. I will mention just five ground-breaking books here (not to mention the increasing flood of stories that pour out of the media hourly). These immediately struck

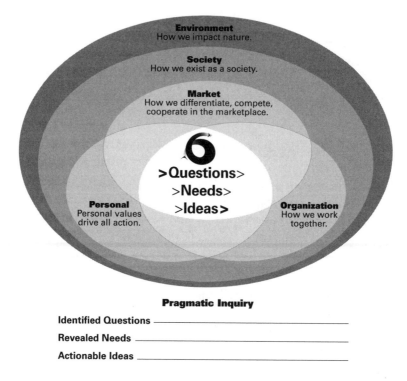

Figure 9.5: Strategic Relationships

me, when I joined the Presidio community two years ago and started to become familiar with some of the literature, as offering incredibly strong, immediate and direct applications for business: *Natural Capitalism, The Ecology of Commerce, Biomimicry, Cradle to Cradle, For the Common Good,* and *Crimes against Nature.*[38] There are dozens of other worthy ones, especially those focusing more exclusively on ecology and the spiritual and physical beauty and meaning of Nature and our responsibilities.

Moral philosophy offers one approach to support the contemporary debate. It recognizes our relationship with Nature as central, as opposed to just life of the mind; we rely on it for the just distribution of our food, air, and water. And if we don't take care of that, in the famous words of David Brower: "There's no business to be done on a dead planet."

These moral philosophers today are reclaiming a much older tradition (Psalms, Aristotle, St. Augustine, St. Francis in the West and the Native traditions everywhere) from which to view Nature. After centuries of reasoning about what to do as rational beings, they are coming to a different starting place: We are not a separate, nor just a higher species, but are an integral part of creation and share the emotions and the thoughts and actions this arouses, similar to many other species. One moral philosopher, attempting to bring back Aristotle's Biology, observes that we are "dependent rational animals," meaning that, at the least, we have to acknowledge that at various times in our lives such as when we are young, old, infirmed, injured, unemployed, etc., we need the support of others for longer or shorter periods of time. This further gives reason to conclude that our single-minded focus on individualism and "what's in it for me" is a badly overdeveloped human characteristic. Further, this insight lifts the process of work and exchange from the pedestrian, secular and individual task it has long held (the work of slaves in ancient times and beneath the role of aristocracy later) to the centerpiece of our purpose as humans. This is a fate we share with other species. Science, and especially the Systems Sciences, have long realized the interconnectedness of all elements of Nature, but seen from a place of exchange puts this insight directly into the realm of Sustainable Management. As such, we are dependent on each other for the things we need. And we need to organize ourselves to fill these needs along with the other species and earth on which we depend.[39] The way we humans go about filling these needs lies at the heart of business.

This focus on dependence corrects a second great misplaced focus or misunderstanding of Nature. We have for too long and too often focused on "survival of the fittest," "red in tooth and claw," etc. But, following up on our "dependent" Nature, there is another point of view. If it is our nature to serve and be served, then through the process of business supplying the demand, we must *compete* to serve because the customer whom we serve has a choice. A third element now challenges us. Sustainable Management as a practice turns our sole attention from the opponent we wish to destroy in conflict to a focus on a customer to be served. Sustainable Management, then, as we have defined it, is no longer just one activity of many in society; it becomes the center of what we as humans are to do. In its practice lies the answer to the question that has driven this Inquiry: "What is the good life?" (And in this sense, you might consider our definition of Sustainable Management a form of "biomimicry.")

Is there really a difference in moving from conflict to competition? Isn't that just playing with words? If words are important, then the difference is huge. In looking at all the definitions of "conflict", never once was "competition" mentioned, not even as a synonym. Competition means to "strive together." Strategy includes competition at its foundation: "competitive positioning", "competitive advantage" "competitive leverage" – for customers on the demand side, and for funds, employees and resources on the supply side.

But we have witnessed how competition can and does escalate to conflict. How do we *decide* what is worth fighting over and what we wish to dedicate our time, effort and lives to? Can we shift the focus from not being winners and losers, but on the "striving with" by testing, making us all better?[40] .

Our students, now with their Venture Plans in hand, go into the world to compete, and undermine the need for war through the practice of Sustainable Management.

9.7 Conflict as War

Conflict definition:

War *Military*: a continued struggle or battle, especially open warfare between opposing forces.

"Ethical conflict," the first part of the conference title, brought to my mind, and perhaps to yours as well, the massive, horrendous wars plaguing much of our world which fill the headlines daily. I dismissed the idea of even addressing these larger issues as beyond the scope of business education. But when I thought about the four Encarta definitions, I saw a way that we in business and in educating our Students can have a profound role. Here's how it might work.

What can our students do in the face of the political, social and environmental challenges? We have graduated fifty-six students to date. So we certainly can't claim great results …yet. They are working in the broadest range of areas of society. A director of sustainability for a major university, an owner of an eco-friendly home improvement store, a consumer products brand manager, CFO of an upstart electric motorcycle company, head of operations for a community resource group, host of a "green" consumer lifestyles TV show, engineering, health care, venture capital, investment planning, just to name a few. And because of the growing concern about sustainability, the demand by organizations for our students is rising.

Our graduates may be involved in small beginnings in helping to run their organizations more sustainably, at the same time they are participating in the building of a more peaceful society.

Along with many others, we believe business is the major force for change in the world, by as Alfred North Whitehead has said," linking together knowledge, labour and moral energy." He goes on to say:

"In the contest of races which in its final issues will be decided in the workshops, and not on the battlefield, the victory will belong to those who are masters of stores of trained nervous energy, working under conditions favorable to growth."[41]

9.8   Culture's Role in Conflict Today

One of the major conflicts today is over the Middle East and the chasm between liberal and conservative. Huge topics to be sure, but there is something to be learned as our students inquire about their business ideas as citizen of a country and indeed of today's world.

That is not to ignore the larger theme, but in fact, I will make the case that a better educated and motivated business community occupied with guiding our organizations in the practice of Sustainable Management can provide a strong modulating effect on the extremists who are driving the larger conflict.

I will take it as a given that the development of a stabilizing middle class – the often maligned merchant/bourgeoisie class – has proven durable as the foundation of every strong democracy in history. Consider that the growth of the middle/merchant/bourgeois class weakened and finally ended Feudalism in the West, and quickly ended it in Japan centuries later. No mean accomplishments.

By offering the opportunities for growth of the individual, business can provide better career paths for disaffected persons who see no way out of their difficulties than war, and the response of those attacked to respond in kind – a conflict-formula we seem to be mired in

To show the possibilities of business as a foundation for peace, take the example of the winner of this year's Nobel Peace Prize, Muhammad Yunus, the 66 year old Bangladeshi economist and banker behind the Grameen Microcredit Movement, which has the goal to create a "poverty-free world". Their micro-loans to small groups of poor people without collateral – 98% of which are to women with a 99% loan-repayment rate – have to date benefited some 100 million families with the goal by 2015 to benefit 175 million. The average loan is $130 for everything from cows to raise, to cell-phone time to sell, and cookies to resell. The award, announced on October 13 of this year stated: "Lasting peace cannot be achieved unless large population groups find ways in which to break out of poverty."[42] By the fact that the loans are overwhelmingly to women, this is giving financial clout and independence to women challenging fundamentalist Islamic culture. And it is a long-known fact that one factor in stable societies is the level of women's literacy and education.

Here is another example involving credit from the *Financial Times*, reporting on the access to credit on a larger scale, but with the same hoped-for stabilizing effects of commerce and the moderation of Islamic fundamentalism. The article is aptly named for our purposes: *"Make money, not war."* It would be no secret that the bankers of the world would like to service the credit requirements of the vastly rich Islamic CFOworld. We in the West know a great deal about all kinds of debt instruments and have elaborate products, laws and procedures for their distribution and use. The trouble with credit for a devout Muslim business person is that credit instruments all involve, in some way, interest, or *"riba"* in the Koran, which is unlawful. In the Islamic tradition, money is supposed to be used as a store of value for business activities, not as a commodity in itself. Money may be used for trade, but it should not be used by itself simply to create more money. Therefore, money cannot be exchanged between a lender and a borrower, but invested between two investors. They enter into an agreement to share the risks and rewards. Imagine what this availability of "credit" would do to unleashing the energy and resources of the Islamic world enabling it to enter the global economy. It could help build a stabilizing middle class based on meritocracy: best ideas win. And imagine the impact in the US and Las Vegas (our fastest growing city) in particular, not to mention much of our financial markets, if we adopted the Islamic belief that money cannot to be used for gambling.[43]

China and India also wrestle with the process of modernization. Imagine, if you will, how the roles as customer/supplier might promote peace by forming corporations, relationships and developing a middle class.

If we anchored our relations on competition, rather than conflict, individuals and communities would be free to buy, engage, and trade. While history shows this is not the panacea for our problems, it at least moves people one step closer to what might be called a relationship. The model is not two opponents facing each other, but two competitors facing a market. It might promote peace such as we see through the European Union, ending centuries of wars. (As one Frenchman told me years ago: "Of course the EU will promote peace. You don't go around bombing your best customers and suppliers.")

9.9   Conclusion

This linking of moral energy and material and human resource development is not a new idea. The rise of monasteries after the fall of Rome, for instance, preserved and developed knowledge during the Medieval (the misnamed "Dark") Ages; and the role of religion and the rise of technology beginning in the ninth century led to the Renaissance and the Enlightenment. Later came the well known drive of Weber's "Protestant Work Ethic."

I offer these concluding thoughts because it might give at least a plausible interpretation of evidence that a moral impulse to serve can actually be the source of what binds people together through developing goods and services leading, inevitably, to transactions and exchanges. This means that ethical thought – moral reasoning – is not a constraint, but can actually be a source of creativity and energy.

Yes, of course there is the profit motive. That's not the case to be made. The effort is the opposite: to show the role and power of moral choice. We must remember that, before writing *Wealth of Nations* and coining the most memorable line in all economics: "[...] the invisible hand [...]" Adam Smith was basing his economic analysis on the moral philosophy (the chair he held in Glasgow) set forth in the far lesser known, understood or appreciated *Theory of Moral Sentiment* and *Lectures on Jurisprudence*.

It is in our nature, ultimately to share our home, the earth, which gives us physically, psychically and spiritually literally the ground we stand on. And because of the beauty and the mystery of the Divine – however understood – which breathes through Her, Nature offers a pathway to meaning and significance of our brief existence.

I have attempted to bring together and develop the ideas of inquiry concerning the best way to engage business students to prepare them for the practice of Sustainable Management. We link emotion and reason, and then use both to help our students inquire into their "calling." This unique management education helps them discover their individual ways of making our world and all lives more sustainable. These ideas were organized around a progression of thought using *all* the dictionary definitions of *conflicts*. I hope following the reverse order of the definitions aided my effort to show how our Presidio MBA in Sustainable Management works by taking into account the broadest context of the social and environmental issues and conflicts facing us today.

At Presidio, we believe the path to making our world and all lives more sustainable lies through Sustainable Management.

In a talk on philosophy and its application for business Dean Donham asked Alfred North Whitehead to give at HBS, Whitehead said:

"The behavior of the community is largely dominated by
the business mind. A great society is a society in which
their men (Sic.) of business think greatly of their function.[44]

If everyone were so occupied in the constructive activity of developing ideas for products and services and then competing to serve
the genuine needs of others, I believe the evidence shows the world
would move to be a more cooperative, thriving world. Each person
would develop their gifts to the greatest of their potential. The ancient
Greeks called this "flourishing." As each one of us, each culture, and
each generation comes to understand more fully just what it means
to be fully human, we will happily depend on others and Nature for
the things we need and can offer. We will, as Keynes put it, pursue
"clear objectives with our feelings and intellect in tune." In the end,
we want our students to find the reasons – *values, core purpose and
goals* – for making choices leading to their calling.

In this life, we are all students who can and need to test our as-
sumptions and inquire constantly: "What must I do to flourish?"
"What is my calling?" "What can/must I do next?" "Whom do
I serve?"

When our students submit their Venture Plans as the demonstra-
tion of their competence, they also submit a companion paper to state
the "calling" driving their business plan. ("[…] where your deep gladness meets the world's deep needs.")[45]

It is fitting that one of students, Jeni Rogers, should have the last
word in this collection of essays. Her journey, prior to enrollment, led
her through the desert of New Mexico as a metal sculptor in which
she dealt with themes of conflict: gender vs. power, voice vs. social silence, and finally business vs. the environment. She began to
think that business + environment was not only possible, but also vi-

able. After completing her Presidio MBA and continuing her career in marketing, she concluded:

> "I do believe that some organized fashion of exchanging the things people need and value is quite noble."

It is to this noble calling we all find ourselves, in one way or another, engaged.

Epilogue

The Path Ahead:
What's *Really* Going on…
and What Can I Do about It?

Every good story begins with a question, point of tension, challenge or a problem. These nine essays are no different in that they have been written from a management perspective as the story of the search for a way to make better business decisions. If these journeys have a point, it can be summarized in Pragmatic Inquiry's promise:

> to help guide us to reflect on our experience, ask better questions, make better decisions, test our ideas and learn from our actions…and *begin again*.

In fact, the arc of inquiry is like the writing and telling of a story. (In sustainability terms, a story can be seen as a system – where all parts are connected.)

Therefore, by way of briefly concluding this series of journeys and looking at the path ahead, I want to highlight three key characteristics of Pragmatism which provide the structure for creating and telling a story: context, continuity and fallibilism. (There are others, of course; most importantly, the "hero." And we will conclude with that.)

The Importance of Balance

Every story also has a theme – what it's about. As the journeys to Oxford and the search for the values driving our decisions and actions continue, the title of the ninth OXSVEB conference – "Beatitude beyond Utterance – Balancing Life, Career, Values and Ethics" – provided a provocative theme for our moving forward: "Balance." While it can be applied to the areas suggested in the title, the graphic image of a balance scale, or better, the Yin and Yang symbol, quickly brought to mind the overwhelming social and environmental evidence which shows us to be *radically* out of balance. You probably have your favorite examples or statistics. Three of mine are:

1. If the Chinese consume at the US per capita rate, and they are moving quickly in that direction, we will need at least four more planet earths to sustain our lifestyle choices.

2. According to the Intergovernmental Panel on Climate Change (who shared the Nobel Peace Prize with Al Gore), we have passed the global warming "tipping point" of 455 parts per million of CO_2 in the atmosphere. While causing increasing rises in temperature and water levels, it is a threat to every ecosystem.

3. Water will be the scarce and valuable natural resource of the future.

There is no greater need today than to make the business case for management in all kinds and sizes of organizations to engage in better investment decisions in serving the needs of society in a sustainable way. One way to make the case is to be better at interpreting the evidence of the times and then telling a compelling story, told in the language of business: a problem, a need, an idea, a strategy and specific plan of implementation.

The three characteristics of Pragmatism to guide us in making a business case are:

- **Context:** Where we are now – what's the situation, the problem?

- **Continuity** How we got here and where we are going?

- **Fallibilism** How to think about what to do – what is the learning?

So as you read on, think of these three practices as the elements of creating a good story. And management education, as you saw in Chapter 9, is a great place for creating one to address the imbalance we are experiencing.

The Purpose of Management Education

Of course, at its foundation, all education aims to develop the potential and focus the energy of individuals to be worthy citizens of a democracy. Management education goes further to focus that energy and bring it together within organizations to serve society's needs. This requires fostering ideas and acquiring the skills, but more importantly gaining the conviction and courage, the *firm persuasion*[1] – the energy – to create and implement their ideas.

Peter Drucker said, in his Magnus opus on management, that "the purpose of business is to make human energy productive" in serving the needs of society.[2] The practice of Pragmatism, above all, offers a logical theory of inquiry that helps people reflect on the evidence of their experience in order to make better decisions regarding where to invest their time and talent. And in the process, they find meaning in their work to answer such fundamental questions as: *What is my mission, purpose, goals, values, "calling." What's driving me?* In that sense, business schools can rightfully be called "vocational."

We are always giving meaning to our experiences, determining what is important and useful. And how we interpret or "read" the signs – which change over time and in different contexts – determines our actions. As we make sense of our experiences and see our individual values, purpose and goals driving our actions, we are making sense of the larger story – with its own goals and purpose, characters, plot lines, adventures – of which we seem to be a part.

So, while much attention has been focused on the global warming crisis, caused by our reliance on carbon-based fossil fuel for our *industrial* energy, it is important to also focus on the sources of our *human* energy. The case can be made that this point of individual motivation and action offers the best place of leverage to help people realize the need to search for and move toward balance.[3]

Think of these three frameworks – context, continuity and fallibilism – as the energy for generating values and vision as told through stories.

Context – Out of Balance

More than in any other time in history, the drastic evidence of declining quality and quantity of our natural resources and life-support systems is focusing the attention of thoughtful executives and business students everywhere. These concerns, now coupled with the perennial corporate social responsibility agenda, are forcing engagement with questions about the purpose of business and the role of values and goals in driving business performance with an unprecedented sense of urgency.

The purpose of a pragmatic inquiry is to address a strategic issue, idea, challenge, opportunity, or problem that you and your organization face. We now need to consider the larger context of the dramatic evidence of climate change, energy issues, and the increasing scarcity of resources all societies face in our efforts to build a sustainable world for us and for future generations. Every part of our carbon-constrained, consumer economy – how we live together and exchange the things we need and value – has to be re-thought, re-designed and re-marketed. And the process of facing these enormous challenges starts with each of us.

There's good news and bad news. First, the bad: We are confronting the dark side of technology and the consequences of "domination and exploitation "of human and natural resources, as seen by all the environmental and social imbalances – catastrophes is a more accurate assessment – surrounding us.

The good news is that we can re-think and re-design our way of serving the needs of society. Since that is the role of business and organizations of all kinds, these are times of great opportunities.

Continuity – Moving In and Out of Balance

The Pragmatists (notably Peirce, Royce, James, Holmes, Whitehead, Addams and Dewey[4]) gave us a clue: All inquiry is an ongoing process, like a story. Therefore, the best we can aim for is the continuing growth and learning of a community in the pursuit for better understanding, decisions and action to make sense and an approximation of truth within a chaotic, evolving world. (That's why the dynamic Yin Yang symbol for balance is more realistic of the movement toward truth than the static balance scale.)

It appears that we must come back to some movement of balance based on a respect for nature after our several hundred year quest to dominate and exploit natural resources. And of course, the framework of sustainability forces us to consider the impact of our decisions on future generations.

So it is well to step back and consider the movement of our economy, and our social and natural environment. The signs of the present time suggest that we are in the midst of a great transition, a hinge

point in history, which has long been predicted, and for many, anticipated with great hope. This transition promises to be at least as great
as the Industrial Revolution fueled by the scientific mindset of the
Enlightenment. The short story is a simple one: since the industrial
revolution began, we have consumed resources and released tremen-
dous amounts of carbon that have been created over billions of years,
far beyond the capacity of the eco-systems to renew.

As a result, we can now see the compelling need to enter a new,
rapidly developing *age of sustainability*, which can also been called an
age of *justice* or *balance*.

Contrary to popular belief, there is not the need for a technological revolution, although new electronic and biological technolo-
gies are certainly relevant to our future. We have enough technology
now to dramatically reduce the impact our methods of production
are causing. The great transition is a philosophical revolution, a revolution in thinking about the nature of reality, about how the world
works and our place within it. Ways of thinking that seemed adequate
in the past are incapable of meeting the challenges of the future. We
must rethink virtually every aspect of our lives. In effect, we must
create a new narrative or story for our time.

Business and Organization as the Means to Balance

Why has business been so successful as a model for organizing ourselves to deliver goods and services we need? It is because we share the
optimistic belief that with a good idea, we can bring people and resources together and launch a business. That's the reason the business
exists. Business balances the interests of the individual and society
as mediating organization structures by structuring supply and demand. This simple but profound connection of supply and demand
is where our collective visions and values as a society - producers and

consumers - are captured and expressed. And at the center is the marketplace: the point of exchange/sale (see Fig. 1).

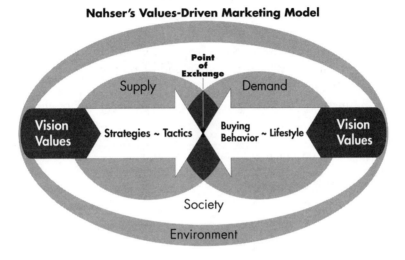

Figure 1: Values-driven Model of Supply and Demand

And, seen from this perspective, business puts the individual in the context of serving the needs of another which has always been a place of meaning and significance. We can even refer to this Supply/Demand equation at a poetic level as: "where your great passion meets the world's great needs (Frederick Buechner) and "to feel that what we do is right for ourselves and good for the world at exactly the same time." (David Whyte).

Consumers – Demand

Serving the needs of customers, as pointed out, is the reason for business's existence. But what, exactly do we *need*? This is the significant point of leverage often overlooked.

That's because there is rightfully a great deal of focus on the *supply* side in the search for addressing the sustainability crisis: redesign products, lean manufacturing, reduce waste, and renew resources. The more fundamental *demand* question is: what and why do we buy the goods and services in the first place? This quickly comes down to differentiating between "wants" and "needs" and finally facing the ancient question: "What is a good life and what do we need to live it and flourish?"

Business model and language is very helpful here to ask producers and consumers alike:

- Where do I plan to invest my time and talents – to what end?

- What is driving me?

- What do I decide is a worthwhile life?

- Why am I on this particular path in life?

- What job do I have to do – whom do I serve and fill what needs?

Our business plans and strategies set the path for organizations to render the things and services people want and need to experience what they determine is a worthwhile, fulfilling, flourishing, thriving, meaningful, purposeful, satisfying, etc. life. How do people make sense of their lives; how do they feel important, attractive, exciting? What provides a sense of identity and belonging? How do they sense the story of which their lives are a part, with its values, purpose and goals? It is a great irony that in our consumer society, we have been so successful by offering material things to meet these non-material needs[5] And in the process, we have dramatically overshot our economy's ability to deliver on these needs on a sustainable basis. As a result, our U.S. private-sector debt is estimated to be over $6.5 trillion beyond the economy's capacity to handle that debt. (One source of the debt: The increasing value of "home equity" allowed us to purchase more; now we are mired in a subprime debacle.[6] The answer? We will have to consume less. And since we are talking about sources of energy, we might start by consuming less meat, a favorite source of our human energy and as wasteful as oil is for our industrial energy.

To generate and deliver one calorie of available energy from meat, it takes an estimated 56 calories of production and transportation.[7] Now imagine the decimated rainforests needed to raise the grain to feed the cattle. Imagine the animal rights issues. And the pollution from manure which, along with the production of other food, causes, by some estimates, 75% of all water-quality problems in the nation's rivers and streams. As a result, meat-eaters have increased heart problems and more and more people are starving because their resources are being diverted in order to raise the meat in the first place. And just consider that about ten times more grain is required to produce a single calorie of energy through livestock than if we ate the grain ourselves and skipped the "middle-meat."[8] We replicate this scenario throughout our patterns of consumption.

Production – Supply

Business, because of its central role in structuring supply of resources to meet demands, can restore a balance when things get out of balance better and faster than other institutions. Why? Because business thrives on change so as a system it moves quicker and more creatively. It also has the power of marketing and advertising, mentioned often in these essays, to shape demand.

Every part of our society will have to be re-thought as we remove fossil fuel as the base of our industrial energy. Every business needs to re-think their "carbon footprint." We will need to alter the design of every product or service as we consider how to renew all the resources we use.

Fallibilism – The Way to Learn

I have mentioned *context and continuity* as the first two key features of Pragmatism. Together, they give us the points of leverage we need to help think about meeting the needs of society – to re-think our story which gives purpose and meaning. But there is a crucial third key. Charles Sander Peirce called it *Fallibilism*. It can cause us to change, in our minds and hearts, what we believe to be true.

At the simplest level, this concept merely states the obvious: when we are confronted by new contexts, our learning must continue. In order for that to happen, we must be open to test our ideas, realizing that we are "fallible." So, in the practice of Pragmatism, we learn by always testing our assumptions. Pragmatic Inquiry and its practice with The *PathFinder* Lab Journal, the subject and result of these many journeys to Oxford, offers a disciplined and organized way of testing the assumptions to keep track of "ideas, activities and observed consequences." Dewey goes on to say:

> "Keeping track is a matter of reflective review and summarizing, in which there is both discrimination and record of significant features of a developing experience. To reflect is to look back over what has been done so as to extract the net meanings which are the capital stock for intelligent dealing with further experiences. It is the heart of intellectual organization and of a disciplined mind."[9]

Putting this reflection into practice has been the purpose of these essays, engaging us in the process of *learning*, echoing Dewey's words, "teaching and learning is a continuous process of reconstruction of experience."[10]

If we have learned one thing about nature, it is that we don't fully understand all of its mysteries. In fact, as time goes on, we discover we know far less than we thought we did. Therefore, this stance of *Fallibilism* or humility is the inevitable and reasonable one for us to take. Each of us, as we confront the issues that hit us daily in our lives and read and hear about in the media, need to read the signs and be open to new interpretations.

Begin Again – The Search for Balance

It is fitting to conclude with the final step of pragmatic inquiry, which originally was not formally part of the 5-step method of *Begin, Explore, Interpret, Decide and Act*. But, after working with thousands of business executives and business students over these past twenty-five years, I now believe it may be the most important. Practitioners tell us it is the living, learning lesson of the inquiry: *Begin Again*.

It goes something like this:

> "I thought this […] but now after inquiring I think this
> – based on my disciplined reflection on my experience.
> Therefore, I now have a new question, a problem to be
> solved, a need to fill, this idea to meet the need and I will
> now undertake this action to test it."

This step shows us our new and different path on our journey.

Each of us is called to make the best decisions in our time and place for a sustainable, just and flourishing life for us all. That has always been our task. But now, given the mysteries of nature and the context and continuity in which we live, our challenge, whether we are rich or poor, young or old, regardless of the creeds or philosophies or jobs we hold, is to find a sustainable balance. How we respond to this call, with its multiple challenges and multiple constituencies, will determine our success or failure in creating a just and sustainable world for ourselves and for future generations.

It is in this time of great crisis and opportunity, with increased humility and a little more wisdom after each experience, that we *Begin Again* in our elusive, never-ending pragmatic journey toward a just, sustainable society. As we journey together, in business and education, we sense a larger purpose; a bigger and better story with the on-going glimpse of a theme of what life and its challenges is about which we share with others. A story in which we act a part and in which each of us can be a hero.

Appendix

Presidio World College
Educational Philosophy – Our Values

Our educational philosophy, developed to enable students to engage in the world sustainably as managers, leaders, entrepreneurs and professionals in business, nonprofit and government organizations, is based on three tenets.

1. Learning from Interactive Experience and Reflection   The first tenet is that learning is an *interactive experience* whose quality depends in large measure on the learner's engaged participation – intellectually, physically, intuitively and ethically. Presidio School of Management believes that goal-directed action, mutually agreed upon, is more motivating and more potent than random or scattered action. The same is true of self-directed action, as opposed to authority-directed action.

We place primary emphasis on Project Oriented Learning referred to by Alfred North Whitehead as "first-hand knowledge," who noted that: "The second-handedness of the learned world is the secret of its mediocrity."

It follows, then, that a positive, transformative education cannot be "delivered" to the student. It is, instead, an experience of co-creation by student and mentors, a stream of encounters and interactions and feedback, some carefully designed, some true adventures. John Dewey expressed this focus: "The aim of education is not to put theory into practice, but to make practice understandable."

Therefore, the School believes that *pragmatic inquiry* and learning – the process of disciplined reflection and action based on experience – is far more effective and lasting than learning from experience alone (inductive reasoning) or reflection in the abstract (deductive reasoning). It is this continuous, testing movement between experience and assumptions (called "abductive reasoning"), which leads to genuine understanding, education and authentic action.

2. Systems Thinking and Practice   The second tenet – *systems thinking and practice* – involves looking at issues or problems as a whole and designing solutions and practices that take into account the interrelationships among human, organizational and ecological systems. The systems perspective is often omitted from and even discouraged by the highly specialized, discipline-centered model of higher education we have known for the past 150 years.

While this specialization model has given the Western world a high state of technological advancement, its narrow focus has operated on the principle of separation (This was the concern of the Fribourg Union for a more systemic/organic view of business and society. Chap. 1). The approach has been to separate the goal to be reached and then to focus on reaching that goal – without respect to other goals or impacts – whether the challenge was growing uniform apples or putting a person on the moon.

The result of this approach is that yesterday's solutions have a way of becoming today's problems. In the words of the 1999 State of the World Report, education has increasingly taught "disconnection."

But the earth is telling us today that it operates (in both the personal, social and natural spheres) on the principle of integration and wholeness. Each part of each system is related to every other part, and all systems are related, in turn, to one another.

So the need is not so much for specialists who can isolate issues as it is for "connectionalists" who can think creatively about the way those things, numbers and people, relate to one another. Jerome Bruner of Harvard has defined creativity as "the capacity to make unexpected connections." The ability to recognize and articulate those connections – human and material – in tangible, narrative language as commitments and promises in the world, leads to action. These are the principal capacities for which future leaders must be prepared. Which leads to the 3rd tenet.

3. Integration and Communication of Knowledge   The two tenets described above, in combination, lead to the third tenet, which is the *integration and communication of knowledge.* Since we learn from active participation and seeing interconnections, the Presidio curriculum culminates in the Integrative Capstone course. In this course students develop a Venture Plan – also known as an "AdVenture" Plan – that captures the narrative quality of their work. This plan draws on all their studies, engages the marketplace through the creation of a business plan and demonstrates their mastery of the Program's Core Competencies.

For Presidio students, creating and developing their Venture Plan also provides the opportunity to uncover, define, articulate and test their calling – the work they sense they are called to do – engaging others and leading toward their goals, and the School's goal, of furthering sustainability in the world.

Competencies Expected of Presidio MBA Graduates

Communication Skills   The ability to effectively communicate through oral and written mediums as demonstrated by coursework, online engagement, papers, and presentations.

Sustainability   The ability to apply the principles of whole systems thinking to the leadership decisions of a public, private or non-profit organization, as demonstrated through coursework and the development of an effective implementation plan of a sustainable management taxonomy.

Numbers Demonstrated understanding and mastery of the practical skills needed to run an organization, such as accounting, finance, operations, statistical analysis, budgeting and strategic planning, as demonstrated through coursework, papers, cases, exams, and the successful development of a sustainable venture plan. Graduates are expected to have confidence in their ability to understand the financial realm of business and the wisdom to know how to get the information they need to lead effectively and sustainably.

Markets The capacity and commitment to develop and communicate a vision for a successful organization that values not only financial profit, but also human development and ecological sustainability. Demonstrated understanding of markets, economic paradigms, the development of products and services, selling one's ideas, and communication within a market environment will be assessed through successful completion of coursework, papers, exams, case analysis, and the successful development of a sustainable venture plan.

People The ability to work and learn collaboratively and effectively toward a common goal as demonstrated by the successful completion of group projects and measured by faculty and peer evaluation. Graduates will know how to give and receive feedback, with personal development in the areas of authenticity, networking, community engagement/support, and mentorship of others as evaluated by their peers and faculty in coursework and final written reflections.

Leadership   The wisdom and courage to function as an effective change agent toward sustainability and renewal in whatever organization or field one works or plans to enter. This capacity will be assessed in the final semester of the program, through successful completion of the venture plan course.

Sustainable Management – Definition

Sustainable Management   is the practice of cultivating, linking and renewing our resources – human, social, natural, manufactured, financial – to serve the needs of present and future generations.

It guides every successful community's commercial, cultural and civic strategies.

> Ron Nahser, PhD
>
> Provost Emeritus,
> Presidio School of Management
> With the Presidio faculty,
> staff and students

Inspired by Philip Kotler, Kellogg School of Management:

> "Marketing serves as the link between society's needs and its patterns of industrial response. It must be put at the heart of strategy."

For more information about Presidio School of Management, visit: www.presidiomba.org

Notes

Preface

1. John B. Wilson and Samuel M. Natale, *Education in Religious Understanding*, (Lanham, MD:University Press of America, 1987), 65.

Prologue

1. Newman, John Henry, Discourse V, 1893.
2. Oakeshott, Michael, "Learning in Teaching," T. Fuller (ed.), *Michael Oakeshott and Education*, (New Haven: Yale University Press, 1972) 32 (author's italics).
3. Oakeshott, Michael, "Education: It's Engagement and Its Frustrations", *Op.cit.*, 69.
4. Mill, J.S. "Inaugural Lecture at the University of St. Andrews, Cavanagh", 1867,133.
5. *Ibid.*, 133.
6. *Ibid*, 134.
7. Ruskin, J. "The Nature of the Gothic" published by William Morris, 1892, para. 12.
8. Roger Slee, 1986,11.
9. John Dewey, *Democracy and Education*, (New York: The Free Press, 1918), Chapter X.

Introduction

1. Harman, Willis, "The Shortcomings of Western Science", *Qualitative Inquiry*, Vol. 2 No. 1, March 1996, 35.

1. Pouring Old Wine Into New Wineskins…Again!

1. Minutes from the meetings of the Fribourg Union, unedited documents 1884 to 1891.188.2. Extracted from "Social Catholicism and the Fribourg Union" given by Normand J. Paulhus at the 21st annual meeting of The Society of Christian Ethics, 1980. Dr. Paulhus' remarkable paper and personal conversation I had with him

proved invaluable in clarifying my thinking. I wish to thank him for preserving and disseminating the work of the Fribourg Union.

2. *Ibid.* 1886: 15.

3. *Ibid.* 1886: 14.

4. *Ibid.* 1885: 4.

5. *Webster's Dictionary*, (New York: Lexicon Publications, Inc., 1989).

6. *Ibid.* 1891: 9.

7. Leo XIII, "On the Condition of the Working Classes" (Boston: St. Paul Editions, N.C.W.C. Translation, 1942), 18

8. John Paul II, *Laborem Exercens* (Boston: St. Paul Editions, 1981), 10.

9. *Economic Justice for All* (Washington D.C.: National Conference of Catholic Bishops, 1986), VI and VII.

10. *The Great Encyclical Letters of Pope Leo XIII* "Condition of the Working Classes" (New York: Benziger Brothers1903), 218.

11. Altgeld, John, *Live Questions* (Chicago: Donohue and Henneberry, 1890), 74.

12. Ginger, Ray, *Altgeld's America* (Chicago: Quadrangle Paper Books, 1958), 29.

13. Minutes of the meetings of the Fribourg Union (1887: 6).

14. Addams, Jane, *Democracy and Social Ethics.* (London: The MacMillan Company, 1911), 176-177.

15. John Paul II, *Centesimus Annus.* (Washington D.C.: United States Catholic Conference, 1991), 70.

16. Motorola Presentation ("The Information Age" published report 1991).

17. Hudiburg, John J., "Harris Bank: Conversations for the 90s." (Harris Bank Reprint: Fourth Conversation moderated by R. Hudiburg. November, 1990).

18. Senge, Peter M., *The Fifth Discipline* (New York: Doubleday, 1990), 13.

19. Kotler, Philip, *Marketing Science Institute Review* (Cambridge, MA: Spring, 1991), 1.
20. Piper, Thomas R., *Creation of the Ethics Module* Delivered in a Speech (1990).
21. Keynes, John Maynard, *Essays in Persuasion* (London: Macmillan & Co., 1939), 339.
22. On the Condition of the Working Classes. (St. Paul Edition), 26.
23. *Ibid*, 30.

2. Peircean Pragmatism and the Social Values of American Business

1. Alfred North Whitehead, *Adventures of Ideas.* (New York: Mentor Books, 1955), 104.
2. *The Encyclopedia of Philosophy,* (New York: Macmillan Publishing Co., 1967), Vol. 6, 435.
3. William James, "Philosophical Conceptions and Practical Results," *University Chronicle* (September, 1898), 291.
4. *Ibid.,* 304.
5. *Ibid.,* 308.
6. Alexis de Tocqueville, *Democracy in America* (Garden City, N.Y.: Anchor Press, 1969), 429.
7. *Ibid,*.
8. Ibid., 506.
9. William James, *The Will to Believe* (Cambridge, Mass: Harvard University Press, 1979), 1.
10. Charles Sanders Peirce, *Philosophical Writings of Peirce* (New York: Dover Publications, 1955.), 1.
11. Ibid.,162
12. John Dewey, *A Common Faith* (New Haven: Yale University Press, 1955).

13. Jeffrey L. Cruikshank, *A Delicate Experiment*(Boston: Harvard Business School Press, 1987), 75.

14. Robert N. Bellah, *Habits of the Heart* (Berkeley: University of California Press, 1985), 47.

15. *The Economist*(17 July 1993), 16.

16. Robert Bellah, Foreword, F. Byron Nahser, *Learning to Read the Signs* (Boston:Butterworth-Heinemann, 1997), xiii.

17. Alasdair MacIntyre, *After Virtue* (Notre Dame, Ind.: University of Notre Dame Press, 1981), 135.

18. In my view, the first time was with Benedict, bringing together work and prayer in the monastery. The second time was with Luther and vocation. The third time was with Weber and the Protestant Work Ethic.

19. Whitehead, *Adventures of Ideas*, op. cit., 104.

3. Learning to Read the Signs: Reclaiming Pragmatism for American Business and Education

1. *The Encyclopedia of Philosophy* (New York: Macmillan Publishing Co., 1967) Vol. 6. 435.

2. For a more complete explanation of the theoretical basis of pragmatism, see: F. Byron Nahser. "Peircean Pragmatism and the Social Values of American Business," *Values, Work, Education: The Meanings of Work*, VIBS-22, 1993, Chapter 16.

3. Josiah Royce, *The Problem of Christianity* (Chicago: The University of Chicago Press, 1968), 297.

4. Peter Senge, *The Fifth Discipline*. (New York: Doubleday Currency, 1990), 238-249.

5. William James, of whom we have been critical at times, does share the same spirit as Peirce in terms of the role of philosophy. He said: "No particular results then so far, but only in attitude of orientation is what the pragmatic method means. The attitude of looking away from first things principles, categories, supposed necessity and

looking toward last things. Fruits, consequences, facts." *Abbott's Familiar Quotations.*

6. Charles Sanders Peirce, "Man's Glassy Essence," *The Essential Peirce*, Ed. Nathan Houser and Christian Kloesel (Bloomington, IN: Indiana University Press, 1992) Vol. 1, 350.

7. F. Byron Nahser, *The Corporantes PathFinder Notebook* (Chicago: Corporantes, Inc., 1995 Study Guide, 4.

8. Alasdair MacIntyre, *After Virtue* (Notre Dame, IN: University of Notre Dame Press, 1981), 135.

9. I take this to mean that we define ourselves by what we have. Acquisition becomes the end in itself.

10. Alfred North Whitehead, *Adventures of Ideas*(New York: Mentor Books, 1955), 98. The Harvard Business School, in a preliminary confidential discussion draft, has begun their MBA Program vision with this statement: "We aspire to develop outstanding business leaders who contribute to the well-being of society." I am happy to see that the FCN statement of purpose, written a dozen years earlier, paraphrases the same idea:

"Our purpose is to create and implement outstanding ideas to help our clients' businesses grow, benefit the user, and contribute to the well-being of society."

11. Of course we aren't the only ones searching. You know the question has reached critical mass (or "tipping point") when it makes the cover of *Newsweek,* Nov. 28, 1994: "The Search for the Sacred. America's Quest for Spiritual Meaning." See particularly. "On the Road Again," by Kenneth L. Woodward who concludes: "In the traditions of the West, every serious sojourner arrives at the still point of an abiding Presence, who sustains the seeker and justifies the search." 62.

12. In such a view, products and services take on a meaning far beyond their utility and importance in how they relate to personal being. This criticism may explain why advertising practitioners are always

ranked second-to-last (just above car salesmen) when asked: How would you rate the honesty and ethical standards of people in these different professions? (Out of two dozen occupations.) July 19-21, 1993, *Gallup Poll Monthly*, July 1993.

13. Mark Crispin Miller, *interview* with Christopher Lasch, "Advertising and our Discontents." *Adweek* (December, l984), 36.

14. Our employee, after hearing this, said that Phase II should be "Putting Down Your Sword."

15. Robert Coles, the Harvard psychiatrist interested in storytelling has used literature as a way to teach an ethical stance to life for several decades. We have lost something valuable as we have shifted in recent times away from the study of literature which reveals values and vice in human life, to an emphasis on entertainment in our books, movies and television.

16. Charles Sanders Peirce, *Peirce on Signs*, ed. James Hoopes (Chapel Hill, NC: University of North Carolina Press, 1982), 264.

17. Plato says much the same thing in the *Phaedrus*, Number 270, as Socrates says, Every great art must be supplemented by leisurely discussion, by stargazing, if you will, about the nature of things."

18. MacIntyre, *After Virtue*, 244.

19. *Ibid.*, 245.

20. *Ora et Labora* actually was coined in the nineteenth century by a German Abbot, Maurus Wolter. One Benedictine monk has called it "our trademark," another parallel with the modern corporation near and dear to my advertising heart. I thank Fr. Terrence Kardong, O.S.B., for sharing his unpublished paper, "Work is Prayer: Not!" and leading me to the article by M.D. Meeuws, "*Ora et Labora*: *devise Benedictine?*", *Collectanea Cisterciensia* 54 (1992), 193-214.

21. The word *conversation* was dropped from copies of the *Rule of St. Benedict* early on and never appears in the other most widely used rule, *The Rule of the Master*, which was written just before Benedict's

Rule. The word *conversion* was used instead to mean conversation. Many modern scholars conclude that much was lost by this substitution. The actual phrase, *conversation morum*, the nominative and genitive cases, indicates a close intertwining of conversation and way of life to suggest conversation of, or as a way of life that is difficult to capture in English. See Louis (Thomas) Merton, "*Conversation Morum*," *Cistertian Studies* (1966) 130-144.

22. Alfred North Whitehead, *The Aims of Education* (New York: Mentor Books, 1961), 68.

4. What's *Really* Going On: Creating the Need for Philosophical Inquiry, and How to Do It

1. Iris Murdoch, *Existentialists and Mystics* (London: Chatto & Windus, 1997), 337.

2. John Wilson, *Thinking with Concepts*(Cambridge: Cambridge University Press, 1995), 126. If this is true, then how much greater must the gap be between philosophy and business life.

3. "Valuing Companies", *The Economist*(August 2, 1997), 53.

4. Wilson, *op.cit.*, 132.

5. James Collins and William Lazier, *Beyond Entrepreneurship* (Englewood Cliffs, NJ.:Prentice Hall, 1995), 48.

6. "Your Brand is Your Future", (American Association of Advertising Agencies, 1996), 12.

7. David Aaker, *Building Strong Brands* (New York: The Free Press, 1996), 190.

8. *Ibid.*, 87.

9. Murdoch, *op.cit.* , 337.

10. F. Byron Nahser, "Learning to Read the Signs", from the Proceedings of the Fourth International Conference on Social Values, *Learning To Read The Signs* (Boston: Butterworth-Heineman, 1997). Indeed the two preceding papers delivered at the first and second conferences show a development of thought leading to the

present position of showing ways to engage executives and business students in philosophical reflection.

5. Pragmatism: Putting Philosophy to Work in Business

1. Philosophy could even be called hot as indicated by a recent article in *Elle* magazine one of the most sophisticated women's fashion publications. In an opening section of their Fall Fashion issue, they had an article entitled "The Philosopher" which described philosophy as the new way to get in touch with your life and the choices you might make using Socratic dialogue, logic, and reason. (September, 1999), 170.

2. Bruce Henderson, *Strategy*Boston: BAT Press, 1985), 10.

3. I first got the clear sense of the connection between business and personal inquiry from Br. Paul of Gethsemini Monastery in Kentucky. As the advisor to the young men contemplating commitment to monastic life, he asks them: "Where do you wish to invest your life and talents?" He asked me, with a gentle smile, if I thought this question might be helpful in business school discussions.

4. Max Fisch, (ed.), *Classic American Philosophy* (New York: Fordham Press, 1996).

5. Christopher Hookway. *Peirce* (London: Routledge, Inc., 1992). Cover

6. William James said: "The ultimate test for us of what a truth means is, indeed, the conduct it dictates or inspires."

7. Josiah Royce. *The Problem of Christianity* (Chicago: University of Chicago Press,. 1968), 273-300.

8. *Oxford: Companion to the Mind,* (Oxford: Oxford University Press, 1987).

9. William James, *William James Writings 1902-1910* (The Library of America), 745,746.

10. Charles S. Peirce, *The Philosophical Writings of Peirce* Justus Buchler, (New York: Dover Publications, Inc., 1955), 5.

11. *Ibid.*, 4.

12. John Dewey, *Experience and Education*(Old Tappan, N.J.:Macmillan Publishing Co., Inc., 1963), 89.

13. So truth appears to always be in movement or may even be considered as a verb as in the Hebrew definition of truth which means something like "a consciousness sitting in a great and loving lap learning about the world." Truth, then, really exists. Pragmatic truth is not things made, but things in the making.

14. Alfred North Whitehead, *Adventures of Ideas* (New York: The Free Press, 1967), 98.

15. Oliver F. Williams, John W. Houck, *Full Value*(San Francisco: Harper & Row, 1978), xvie.

16. This portrays only the levels of "economic" life. The other two parts, following Weber, are the personal relationship with family and the cultural relationships through civic, art, lifestyle activities.

17. In a long-standing conversation with my old Marketing Professor, Philip Kotler, at the Kellogg Graduate School of Management, Northwestern University, I asked him just how far we can stretch that marketing relationship concept. After some discussion, he looked at me and queried: "You mean to the level of I – Thou?" We were referencing the reflections of Martin Buber. We both feel that as marketing continues to evolve, it must reflect authentic relationships and not the manipulative models that often rule today. Professor Kotler suggests, as an example, that we move from the "hunter" model of markets to the "farming" model.

6. Business as a Calling; The Calling of Business: A Pedagogical Model and Practice

1. 2nd paper delivered at the 6th Conference. This is an update of the July 1999 Oxford talk, then delivered at the St. Thomas University Conference on "Business as a Calling" in Bilbao, Spain, 2003. It

was also published in the Journal of Business Ethics, Vol. 34, Nos. 3-4.

2. Buechner, Frederick, *Wishful Thinking: A Seeker's ABC* (San Francisco: HarperSanFrancisco, 1993), 119.

3. Bronson, Po, What Should I do with My life? The True Story of People who Answered the Ultimate Question (New York: Ballantine Books, 2005).

4. Bolles, Richard Nelson, *What Color is Your Parachute?* (Berkeley: Ten Speed Press), 2007.

5. Seligman, Martin , Authentic Happiness: Using the New Positive Psychology to Realize Your Potential for Lasting Fulfillment (New York: Free Press, 2004).

6. Sanders, Tim, "Love is the Most Powerful Force in Business" Fast Company, February, 2002, 66-70.

7. Whitehead, Alfred North, *Adventures of Ideas* (New York: Free Press, 1967).

8. Lonergan, Bernard, *Method in Theology* (Toronto: University of Toronto Press, 1990).

9. Morrill, R.L., *Teaching Values in College* (San Francisco: Jossey-Bass, 1980).

10. A Program for Renewed Partnership: The Report of the Sloan Commission on Government and Higher Education by Sloan Commission on Gov. and Higher Ed., 1980.

11. Pascarella, Ernest T. and Patrick T. Terenzini, *How College Affects Students*, (San Francisco: Jossey-Bass, 1991).

12. Maccoby, Michael, *The Gamesman: The New Corporate Leaders* (New York: Simon & Schuster, 1977).

13. Kochunny, C.M and H. Rogers, "Head-heart Disparity Among Future Managers: Implications for Ethical Conduct," *Journal of Business Ethics*, 1994 13:718-729.

14. Ruhe, J. and Drevs, R., "Character Development in Management Education," Proceedings of the Midwest Society for Human Resources (Chicago: Industrial Relations Association, 1989).

15. Stevens, G.E., "Ethical Inclinations of Tomorrow's Managers: One More time," *Journal of Business Education*, 1985, 60 (7):291-296.

16. Kreitner, R. and W.E. Reif, "Ethical Inclinations of Tomorrow's Managers: Cause for Alarm?", *Journal of Business Education*, October, 1980: 25-29.

17. Allen, W.R. Davis et al, "Character Trait Importance and Reinforcement for Future Business Leaders: A Longitudinal Assessment," *Journal of Contemporary Business Issues*, 6, 1998 (1):5-22.

18. Ruhe, J.W. et al, "Value Traits Reinforcement and Perceived Important: Does Context Matter?", *International Journal of Value-Based Management*, 11, 1998: 103-124.

19. Progoff, Ira, The Dynamics of Hope: Perspectives of Process in Anxiety and Creativity, Imagery and Dreams (New York: Dialogue House Library, 1985).

20. Dash, E.L. Muñoz and J. Sung, "You Bought. They Sold," *Fortune*, September 2, 2002, 64-74.

21. *Fortune*, June 24, 2002.

22. Frederick, William C, *Research in Corporate Social Performance and Policy* (Greenwich, CT:JAI Press, 1987).

23. *Time*, 2002; Swartz & Watkins, 2003.

24. Witzel, Morgan, "Guru Guide Phil Kotler: First Among Marketers," *Financial Times*, August, 2003, 6.

25. Scott, Elizabeth, "Organizational Moral Values," *Business Ethics Quarterly*, 2002, 12 (1):33-55.

26. Niehoff, B.C.A. Enz, and R.A. Grover, "The Impact of Top Management Actions on Employee Attitudes and Perceptions," *Group & Organizational Studies*, 1994, 15 (3):337-354; Jehn, K.A., "Enhancing Effectiveness: An Investigation of Advantages and Dis-

advantages of Value-based Intragroup Conflict," *The International Journal of Conflict Management*, 1994, 5 (3):223-238.

27.   Bretz, R.D. and T.A. Judge, "Person-organizational Fit an the Theory of Work Admustment: Implications for Satisfaction, Tenure and Career Success," *Journal of Vocational Behavior*, 1994, 44:32-54.

28. Vancouver, J.B. and N.W. Schmitt, "An Exploratory Examination Person-organizational Fit: Organizational Goal Congruence," *Personnel Psychology*, 1991, 44:333-354; Finegan, J.E., "The Impact of Personal and Organizational Values on Organizational Commitment," *Journal of Occupational and Organizational Psychology*, 2000, 73 (2): 149-169.

29. Bretz, R.D. and T.A. Judge, "Person-organizational Fit and the Theory of Work Adjustment: Implications for Satisfaction, Tenue and Career Success," *Journal of Vocational Behavior*, 1994, 44: 32-54.

30. Scott, Elizabeth, "Organizational Moral Values," *Business Ethics Quarterly*, 2002, 12 (1):33-55; Cable, D.M. and T.A. Judge, "Person-organizational Fit, Job Choice Decisions and Organizational Entry," *Organizational Behavior and Human Decision Processes*, 1997, 67 (3):294-311; Cable, D.M. and T.A. Judge, "Interviewers' Perceptions of Person-organization Fit and Organizational Selection Decisions," *Journal of Applied Psychology*, 1996, 82 (4): 546-561.

31. Williams, Oliver R. and John W. Houck, *Full Value: Cases in Christian Ethics* (San Francisco:Harper& Row, 1978).

32. Anne Colby, "Whose Values Anyway" in M. Damon, (ed.) *Bringing in a New Era in Character Development* (Stanford, CA: Hoover Institutional Press, 2002).

33. Ibid.

34. Morrill, R.L., *Teaching Values in College* (San Francisco: Jossey Bass, 1980).

35. Pattilo, M.M. Jr. and D.W. Mackenzie, *Church Sponsored Higher Education in United States* (Washington D.C.: American Council on Education, 1966).

36. Hauerwas, Stanley, "How Universities Contribute to the Corruption of Youth," *Christian Existence Today* (Chapel Hill: University of North Carolina, 1988).

37. Leatherman, C., "Catholic College to Step up Efforts to Teach Values," *The Chronicle of Higher Education*, May, 1990: A 16+.

38. Naughton, Michael, J. and Thomas Bausch, "Catholic Identity of an Undergraduate Management Education: Survey Summary and Conclusions," Paper presented at the Conference of the Association of Catholic Colleges and Universities, St. Paul, MN., Aug.3, 1995.

39. Palmer, Parker, *The Active Life* (San Francisco: Jossey-Bass, 2000).

40. Buechner, Frederick, *The Sacred Journey* (New York: Harper & Row, 1982), 72.

41. McGee, James J. and André L. Delbecq, "Vocation as a Critical Factor in a Spirituality for Executive Leadership in Business," in Oliver F. Williams (ed.) *Business, Religion and Spirituality* (Notre Dame, IN,:University of Notre Dame Press, 2003).

42. Damon, W. H. Gardner, and M. Csikszentmihalyi, *The Moral Underpinnings of Enduring Success: How are the Laws of life Learned and Used* (West Conshohocken, PA.:John Templeton Foundation Press, in press).

43. McGee and Delbecq, *op. cit.*

44. Hutcheon, Pat Duffy, *Building Character and Culture* (Westport, CT: Praeger, 1999).

45. TeSelle, Sallie McFague, *Speaking in Parables: A Study in Metaphor and Theology* (Philadelphia: Fortress Press, 1975).

46. Elwood, J. Murray, *Discovering Life's Directions* (Notre Dame, IN.: Ave Maria Press, 1995).

47. Grabner, Kenneth E., *Focus Your Day* (Notre Dame, IN.: Ave Maria Press, 1992).

48. McCann, Dennis P., "The Business of Storytelling and Story-telling in Business," in Oliver Williams and John Houck (eds) *A Virtuous Life in Business: Stories of Courage and Integrity in the Corporate World* (Lanham, MD.: Rowman and Littlefield, 1992). With a similar intent but from a different starting point, Michael Ray and Lorna Catford demonstrate the importance and act of sto-rytelling in their *Path of the Everyday Hero.* Forestville, CA: Creative Quest Publications, 1991.

49. MacIntyre, A., *After Virtue: A Study in Moral Theory* (London: Duckworth, 1985).

50. Downs, Jonathan and Jonathan King, "Towards a Science of Sto-ries: Implications for Management Education," Academy of Man-agement Proceedings, August, 1999: MED B1-6.

51. Ready, D., "How Storytelling Builds Next Generation's Leaders," *MIT Sloan Management Journal,* Summer, 2002: 63-69.

52. Pascal, Roy, *Design and Truth in Autobiography* (Cambridge: Har-vard University Press, 1960).

53. TeSelle, *op.cit.*

54. Pascal, *op.cit.*

55. TeSelle, *op.cit.*

56. Nash, Laura, "Intensive Care for Everyone's Least Favorite Oxy-moron: Narrative in Buseinss Ethics," *Business Ethics Quarterly,* 10, 2000, (1):277-290.

57. Meyer, John C., "Tell Me a Story: Eliciting Organizational Values from Narratives," *Communications Quarterly,* 43, 1985 (2): 210-224.

58. TeSelle, *op.cit.*

59. Wilder, Amos N., *Early Christian Rhetoric: The Language of Gospel* (Cambridge: Harvard University Press, 1971).

60. Grabner, Kenneth E., *Focus Your Day* (Notre Dame, IN.: Ave Maria Press, 1992).

61. Dewey, John, *Experience and Education* (Old Tappan, N.J.:Macmillan Publishing Co., Inc., 1963), 89.
62. Stark, A., "What's the Matter with Business Ethics?", *Harvard Business Review*, 1993, 71:38-48.
63. Scott, Elizabeth, "Organizational Moral Values," *Business Ethics Quarterly*, 2002, 12 (1):33-35.
64. Peck, Scott, A World Waiting to be Born: Civility Rediscovered (New York: Bantam Books, 1994).
65. Ruhe, J.W., Allen, R. Davis, J.H. Geurin, V. and Longnecker, J., "Value Traits Reinforcement and Perceived Importance: Does Context Matter?", *International Journal of Value-Based Management,* 1998, 11: 103-104.

7. Uncovering the Values Driving Organizational, Career and Personal Strategies: The Case for PathFinder Pragmatic Inquiry

1. Fogel Robert William, *The Fourth Great Awakening*(Chicago: University of Chicago Press, , 2000).
2. Consider the words of John Paul II concerning corporate purpose from a spiritual development perspective stated in *Centesimus annus*: "The purpose of a business is not simply to make a profit, but is to be found in its very existence as a community of persons who in various ways are endeavoring to satisfy their basic needs, and who form a particular group at the service of the whole of society."
3. Bruce Henderson, *Strategy* (Boston: BAT Press, 1985), 10.
4. Alfred North Whitehead, *Adventures of Ideas* (New York: The Free Press, 1967), 98.

8. Marketing as Storytelling: Pragmatic Inquiry's Religious Foundations and Practical Applications

1. Based on a paper of the same title delivered earlier: *Praxiology and Pragmatism. Vol. 10* (2002).

2. Abraham Lincoln captured the essence of *PathFinder* Pragmatic Inquiry® in the opening sentence of his June 16, 1858 pivotal speech, "A House Divided," his first speech which began his path to national office (*ital.* are his).

3. At the request of Dean W. B. Donham of the Harvard Business School, Whitehead's talk was the Introduction to his book, *Business Adrift* (New York: Whittlesey House, 1931), xxix) a title that could be used today.

4. The "street" conversation goes something like this: "Don't get me wrong, Ron. Values are very important. But when things get bad, and they will at some point, you have to take the necessary steps to survive." But, of course, this situation is exactly the test point when values must guide behaviors, decisions and actions.

5. To begin to comment on James's insights into religion, pragmatism and psychology would take another paper. Suffice to say, Scheler was much impressed with James's *Pragmatism* and, of course, Royce and James were colleagues. . At the beginning of this chapter, however, it might be useful to note the importance James places on "selective attention" which gives another reason for the importance of values and inquiry: they focus our attention. *The Principles of Psychology* (Chicago: Encyclopedia Britannica, Inc., 1952), 260-298 and cf. Dennis McCann Chapter in this volume: "Assessing Willliam James' Potential Contribution to Business Ethics".

6. Nahser, F. Byron, *Learning To Read the Signs: Reclaiming Pragmatism in Business* (Boston: Butterworth-Heinemann,1997), 9. Much of this chapter is adapted from the writings of the author from this book and the *Corporantes PathFinder Notebook – Practicing PathFinder Pragmatic Inquiry* (Chicago: Corporantes, Inc., 2000). Additional information can be obtained by contacting Corporantes, Inc., 308 W. Erie Street, Chicago, IL 60610.

7. Drucker, Peter, *Management* (New York: Harper Books, 1985), 809-811.

8. Peirce's comments on signs are spread throughout his writings. Check the index in *The Essential Peirce*, Vols. 1 and 2. (Bloomington: Indiana University Press, 1991). This idea of signs, or semiotics, which Peirce preferred, has captured much attention. See the bibliography for specific references.

9. Peirce's comments on abduction are also spread throughout his writings. Check the index in *The Essential Peirce* Vols. 1 and 2 (Bloomington: Indiana University Press, 1992). Also cf. "Pragmatism as the Logic of Abduction" Vol. 2, 208-225.

10. Religion is often considered a deductive inquiry beginning with certain truths and science as inductive inquiry starting with the facts. Peirce's abduction bridges this gap.

11. Peirce said that an hypothesis can be stated this way: "If thus and so were true all along, then it would not be surprising that thus and so happened." Peirce often referred to mathematical equation as examples of hypotheses. For his description of abduction cf. Christopher Hookway, *Peirce* (London: Routledge. 1985), 223-228.

12. John Dewey noted this example as an outstanding contribution of Peirce. Dewey called it the "principle of the continuum of inquiry" in his *Logic: The Theory of Inquiry* (Carbondale: Southern Illinois University Press, 1991), 3. This "continuum of inquiry" will be considered later in the chapter as the story, narrative or path of an inquiry.

13. This expression was Peirce's term for the need to come to an end to a question. But a person had to be aware that the end point – "the fixation of belief" – was really a hypothesis. Peirce developed the idea of "fallibilism" as the best state of mind for the inquirer to have. Cf. "The Fixation of Belief", *The Essential Peirce*, Vol. 1. (Bloomington: Indiana University Press, 1992), 109-123.

14. Royce, Josiah, *The Problem of Christianity* (Chicago: University of Chicago Press, 1968), 276-277.

15. Royce, Josiah, Second Pittsburgh Lecture, "The Art of Loyalty" (HARP 78, NO. 2), 58.

16. Further, Royce helps us with questions he poses in *The Philosophy of Loyalty* with his definition of philosophy. "It (philosophy) does desire to add its thoughtfulness to the intensity of life's great concerns and to enlighten us regarding what aims life has always really intended to pursue [...] the religiously disposed man begins by learning that the chief end of his existence is to come into harmony with God's will." John J. McDermott (ed.), *The Basic Writings of Josiah Royce*, Vol. 2 (Chicago: University of Chicago Press, 1969), 865 ff.

17. The Essential Peirce, op.cit., 2-10.

18. Royce, op.cit., 277.

19. *Ibid.*, 306.

20. Oppenheim, Frank M., *Royce's Mature Ethics* (Notre Dame, IN.: University of Notre Dame Press, 1993), 134.

21. Frings, Manfred. S., *The Mind of Max Scheler* (Milwaukee: Marquette University Press, 1997), 227. I owe an enormous debt to Dr. Frings who helped me understand Scheler and his connection to pragmatism, which has been essential to the argument of this paper.

22. *Ibid.*, 61.

23. *Ibid.*, 60.

24. Frings, Manfred "A Novel Look at the Structure of the Pragmatic View of the World: Max Scheler", *Praxiology and Pragmatism, Vol 10.* (New Brunswick NJ: Transaction Publishers, 2002), 118.

25. James said much the same thing about feelings at the base of action. *William James Writings 1902-1910* (New York: Library of America, 1987), 741-744.

26. Frings, op. cit., 214.

27. *Ibid.*, 140.

28. *Ibid.*, 61.

29. The *sketch* is like the narrative, which has become so popular recently as a base for understanding ethical issues. Particularly persuasive in this matter is Alasdair MacIntyre's question: "Of What Larger Story am I a Part?" Cf. *After Virtue* (Notre Dame, IN: University of Notre Dame Press, 1981), 201.

30. Frings, Manfred, *Philosophy of Prediction and Capitalism* (Dordrecht: Martinus Nijhoff Publishers, 1987), 13-62. The argument proceeds to cover the *sketch* and to show how ideas and plans might turn out differently.

31. Joseph H. Bragdon, *Profit for Life: How Capitalism Excels* (Cambridge, MA:Society for Organizational Learning, 2006), xi.

32. Buber, Martin *I and Thou* (New York: A Touchstone Book, 1970), 62. Such an encounter in Buber's terms requires a complete fusion, (probably not called for in marketing relationships) as in Scheler's functionalization. In Buber's words: "All actual life is encounter." This model equates to Scheler's Level 1 values.

33. Royce, Josiah "The Possibility of International Insurance", *The Basic Writings of Josiah Royce* (Chicago: University of Chicago Press. 1969), 1135-1144. He suggested a plan to prevent war by having countries take out insurance policies to cover the cost of a war.

34. Peirce spoke of the importance of "musement" for reflection. *Essential Writings, Vol. 2.* 436-440. Royce wrote about practicing the "art of loyalty". Scheler developed a technique to accomplish a "phenomenological attitude" and "Dionysian reduction" cf. Frings, *The Mind of Max Scheler*, 192. William James suggested we "dive back into the flux itself" in *William James Writings 1902-1910, 745.* John Dewey spoke directly about this situation for teachers *in Logic: The Theory of Inquiry*, 415-436. Also cf. John Dewey, *How We Think* (Amherst NY: Prometheus Books, 1991), 68-78.

35. It is popular in this age of neuroscience to update this ancient argument by referring to the brain as either a blank film to be exposed by experience or a negative to be developed through experience.

36. James, William, op. cit., 574, in which he said essentially the same thing: "Truth *happens* to an idea. It *becomes* true."
37. For more complete cases see Nahser op.cit., 99-132.
38. Collins, Jim. "*Level 5 Leadership.*" Harvard Business Review, July August, 2005.
39. Wetzel, Morgen, "First Among Marketers", *Financial Times*, (Aug. 6, 2003), 9.
40. *Ibid.* 9.
41. To learn more about the steps and how the *Corporantes PathFinder Notebook©* was developed, see Nahser, op. cit., 85-95.
42. Sidney Hook, *The Metaphysics of Pragmatism* (Amherst: Prometheus Books, 1996), 70. Peirce, in answer to the question: "What then is the general defining character of the phrase 'to exist'?" responded: "Existence means precisely the exercise of compulsion." I have Philip and Susan Marineau to thank for leading me to this insight. As CEO of Levi Strauss & Co., Marineau has adopted this concept that values drive business performance as his principle of corporate leadership.

9. Where Do Conflicts Begin? An Inquiry into the Need for Inquiry in Management Education

1. Keynes, John Maynard, *Essays in Persuasion "The End of Laissez-Faire"* (New York: W.W. Norton & Co. 1972), 321-322. This quote is also in Chap. 1. Many years later, I now better understand why Keynes stressed the central importance the link between reason and emotion plays in inquiry.
2. Harvard Business School President and Fellows, *A Delicate Experiment : Harvard Business School 1908-1945*, (Boston: Harvard Business Press, 1987), 155.
3. Presidio World College's founder, Richard M. Gray has pointed out this difference in educational purpose between "information transfer vs. concept development."

4. While many schools offer a "Venture Plan" course, we are unusual in devoting the entire curriculum to the effort. I must also mention two outstanding examples of courses that address creativity and innovation: Michael Ray's course at Stanford Business School called "Creativity in Business" and Srikumar Rao's course in "Creativity and Personal Mastery" at Columbia Business School.

5. The experience of Harvard Business School over the years is instructive how difficult it is to keep this focus. As an example, in the early '90s, Thomas R. Piper remarked: "MBA education seems to have failed in its most important responsibility: to generate excitement about careers and the opportunity for making a difference [...]" He cites the emphasis on analytics and finance demanded by employers.

6. Keynes, John Maynard, *The General Theory of Employment, Interest and Money* (New York: Harcourt Press, 1972), 383.

7. If you think this is too trivial, subtle or lofty idea, try to think what ideas are driving the seemingly intractable conflicts between Liberals and Conservatives – Blue vs. Red states – in the U.S., and the similar conflicts in countries around the world, not to mention the Middle East.

8. The President of Presidio World College, Steven Swig, tells the story of his own awakening when, as a mergers and acquisitions lawyer, he handed a multimillion dollar check to a client after the merger of two companies. The check nearly equaled the savings from firing now-redundant workers. The moral of the transaction became immediately and painfully clear to both Steven and the executive. Steven's career then began to move in a considerably different, and sustainable, direction.

9. Alasdair MacIntyre puts it this way: "[...] to adopt a stance on the virtues will be to adopt a stance on the narrative quality of human life [...]" *After Virtue* (Notre Dame IN: Notre Dame Press, 1984.). See esp. p 144.

10. Nahser, F. Byron. *Learning to Read the Signs.* (Boston: Butterworth-Heinemann, 1977.) This book explains in more detail the development and use of pragmatic inquiry. The subtitle is: *"Reclaiming pragmatism for business"* which is our attempt at Presidio.

11. You will see "values, core purpose and goals" repeatedly in this report. I am following the remarkable work of Jim Collins who first presented this framework with William Lazier in *Beyond Entrepreneurship* (Englewood Cliffs, NJ: 1992), 48ff.

12. In the introduction I said this paper would not be complete by any means. Already I have moved through many hopelessly truncated statements in philosophy. But this is a really big one, I must acknowledge: *Narrative and process philosophy move in a different way in the pursuit of truth than do the classical disciplines of metaphysics and epistemology and ethics that searched for a static, immutable Truth.*

13. Charles Peirce, Josiah Royce, William James, John Dewey, George Herbert Mead, Jane Addams, George Santayana, and Alfred North Whitehead are considered the "Classic American Philosophers." They are now joined by Feminist Pragmatists such as Charlene Seigfried and Susan Haack.

14. This unusual term does not, as people often ask, have anything to do with extra-terrestrial visitors.

15. Dewey, John, "Morals Are Human," *Dewey: Middle Works, Vol.14,* 207.

16. Dewey, John. *Experience and Education,* (New York: Touchstone Book, 1997), 87.

17. Religion and Spirituality, on the other hand, have flourished, often with unintended consequences.

18. Nussbaum, Martha, , *Upheavals of Thought* (Cambridge, UK: Cambridge University Press, 2001), 30. "If emotions are suffused with intelligence and discernment, and if they contain in themselves an awareness of value or importance, they cannot, for exam-

ple, easily be sidelined in accounts of ethical judgment, as so often then have been in the history of philosophy." I am also reminded of the work of Daniel Goleman and Howard Gardner who approach the issue of emotions from different starting points but end up with similar conclusions.

19. MacIntyre, Alasdair, *Revision: Changing Perspectives in Moral Philosophy* (Notre Dame, IN.: University of Notre Dame Press,1983), 9. Here is the actual quote. "The virtues, however conceived, always must stand in some determinate relationship to the passions, and any cogent account of the virtues requires at its foundation a cogent account of the passions and their relationship to reason."

20. King, Thomas J. S.J., *Jung's Four and Some Philosophers* (Notre Dame IN: University of Notre Dame Press, 1999). King points out how various leading philosophers' works are affected by their Jungian type.

21. I owe Don Parker, former Dean of the business school at Oregon State University, credit for bringing this insight forward. For the past several years, Don has been administering the Myers-Briggs typology prior to the *PathFinder Pragmatic Inquiry* during the Beta Gamma Sigma (the honor society for AACSB member schools) Student Leadership Forums. It was a short but important step to see that students of different typologies would have difficulty with different steps in the Inquiry.

22. One CEO has said the doors on the executive floor should have bigger doors so the egos can get through.

23. We have shown the value of adopting different psychological states of mind during an inquiry. This brings to mind the work of Jim Collins as presented in "Level 5 Leadership" article in the *Harvard Business Review* —"The High Performance Organization," July-August 2005, 1ff. He concludes that he doesn't know the exercises to develop Level 5 leadership which he characterizes as "Humility and Firm Resolve". You will note that these are the begin-

ning and ending values/virtues/psychological states of the steps in Pragmatic Inquiry. In our experience we have found that Collins' Level 5 leaders are thoughtful, reflective and action-oriented which follows the spirit and practice of Pragmatic Inquiry.

24. Nussbaum, op.cit., 30. I have to credit this exact phrase to Martha Nussbaum since it expresses so accurately the task and allows me to add my definition with some degree of confidence and considerable humility.

25. Nahser, op.cit.

26. Here is a typical view: Gloria Scoby, Group Publisher of Crain Publications, recounted recently, when I told her about our effort at Presidio School of Management to base a program on moral reasoning, that she was asked several years ago to teach a business ethics class in a business school. She declined, saying that it was too late in life by that time for the students. After Enron and the other spate of ethical crises, she is rethinking her position. She is not alone. In fact, based on the evidence, we might say that in business schools, ethics is too often being *un*-taught.

27. Since we talk often of values, let me cite another reason why they are so important. They answer, based on evidence of experience, the "central problem of the epistemological tradition: What counts as good, strong, supportive evidence of belief?" Susan Haack, *Evidence and Inquiry: Toward Reconstruction in Epistemology* (Oxford, UK: Blackwell Ltd., 1994), 5.

28. Bennis, Warren, *On Becoming a Leader* (Cambridge MA: Perseus Books, 2003), xxvii.

29. President and Fellows of Harvard, op.cit.,155.

30. This opportunity to develop and integrate a core curriculum is one of the major reasons I took the position of Provost at Presidio World College. Before I took the job, I sought advice from several deans of business schools whom I had met through our Inquiry work with Beta Gamma Sigma. They would ask various questions

about the college, students, etc., and then invariably they would ask: "Do you have tenured faculty?" When I would say "No," they would immediately say, with wry humor, "Take the job." However, a leading moral philosopher told me not to take the job. I asked why. He responded, scowling: "I never met a Provost I didn't *detest.*"

31. Whitehead, Alfred North, *The Aims of Education* (New York: Mentor Books, 1961), 61. He goes on to say "the second-handedness of the learned world is the secret of its mediocrity."

32. I have Chip Conley, CEO of Joie de Vivre, Inc., to thank for ordering our "job/career/calling" in the Maslow Hierarchy of Needs format which he did at a class in Marketing at Presidio School of Management.

33. .Smith, Adam, *Wealth of Nations* (New York: Random House, 1937). The famous opening: p. 4. But to his credit, he also saw that this would lead to the most degrading state of human condition from the repetitive nature of the job.

34. Witzel, Morgten "First Among Marketers" *Financial Times,* Aug. 6, 2003, p. 9.

35. We acknowledge the truncated nature of this definition, particularly when we focus just on three types of resources – human, natural and financial, or the more familiar statement of "People, Planet, Profit." There are many more specific designations for wealth, such as infrastructure, cultural, social, manufactured, etc. Also, I thank the students, faculty, and staff at Presidio School of Management for their help.

36. T.S. Eliot in his essay "Tradition and the Individual Artist" offers the perspective that each society has its own turn of the creative mind. Pragmatists claim that this process of abduction is universal. One philosopher, Manfred Frings, has noted that Pragmatism brings together the idealism of Plato with the realism of Aristotle by putting the pursuit of truth into the mode of abduction.

37. While the subject of the relationship has been often studied from Toynbee, the Durants, Christopher Dawson, to name just a few, there is a particular view of how Christianity has formed an arrogance toward nature. One view of interest is by Lynn White in *Medieval Religion and Technology* and in *Medieval Technology and Social Change.* Another recent book in this effort is by Rodney Stark, *The Victory of Reason.* I follow Whitehead, however, on the best combination of religion and commerce was the Benedictine model, Whitehead, *The Aims of Education*, op.cit.

38. Hawken, Paul, Amory Lovins, L.Hunter Lovins, *Natural Capitalism,* (New York: Little, Brown and Co., 1999.). Hawken, Paul, *The Ecology of Commerce,* (New York: HarperCollins, 1993.) Leopold, Aldo, *Sand County Almanac* (Oxford: Oxford University Press, 1966). Brower, David, *Let the Mountains Talk, Let the Rivers Run.* (New York: HarperCollins Publishers, 1995). Benyus, Janine M. (*Biomimicry: Innovation Inspired by Nature* (New York: HarperCollins Publishers, Inc., 1998). McDonough William, and Michael Bramguart, *Cradle to Cradle,* (New York: North Point Press: 2002). Daly, Herman and John Cobb, Jr. *For The Common Good,* (Boston: Beacon Press, 1989). Kennedy, Robert F. Jr. *Crimes Against Nature* (New York: HarperCollins Publishers Inc. 2004. Hunter Lovins is on our faculty and I owe her much in introducing me to the literature and leading members of the sustainability movement. Benyus's insight into the concept of working as and with nature is a landmark breakthrough. And Bobby Kennedy, who gave our Presidio World College 2006 commencement address, brings the economic dimension as well as the religions: "Nature is not God, but it shows us the face of God."

39. MacIntyre, Alasdair, *Dependent Rational Animals,* (Peru, IL: Open Court Press, 1999), x. "[…] no account of the goods, rules, and virtues that are definitive of our moral life can be adequate that does not explain – or at lest point us toward an explanation

– how that form of life is possible for beings who are biologically constituted as we are, by providing an account of our development toward and into that form of life."

40. Even Matthew Fox, no great friend of business, has kind words to say about competition – ending his book on *One River, Many Wells*, (New York: Tarcher Publishing, 2000), 425, stating that there should be a "gentle competition between the world's religions to serve the needs of the young." A good description of defining a need as the basis for a marketing strategy. The book is his study of religions and how we need to recognize the wisdom of them all – "wells" – as ways to get to the Divine, which he characterizes as a "river."

41. Whitehead, op.cit., 68. Keynes says much the same thing. "Nevertheless, I may do well to remind you [...] that the fiercest contest and the most deeply felt divisions of opinion are likely to be waged in the coming years [...] round questions which are psychological or, perhaps, moral."Op. cit., 319.

42. Dugger, Celia W., "Peace Prize to Pioneer of Loans to Poor No Bank Would Touch" *New York Times*Oct. 14, 2006,1 And combining this 2006 award with the 2004 Nobel Peace Prize to Wangari Maathi for her work in sustainable development, is another landmark example broadening the definition of peace beyond conflict resolution, showing the potential power of sustainable management to be the foundation for peace. Amartya Sen, another Bengali economist and Nobel laureate, has said that for the first time in history the interests of the rich and the needs of the poor are in alignment, by which he means that the needs of the poor represent market opportunities. This is the "bottom of the pyramid" which C.K. Prahalad and others have noted. It also has been good business. Some including the *Economist* have complained it doesn't deserve the Peace Prize, especially since Grameen's return

on equity reached 21%, up from 9% in 2004. Johnson, Jo, "Give the Man Credit" (*Financial Times*, Dec 9-10, 2006), W3.

43. Tett, Gillian, "Make money, not war" (*Financial Times*, September 23, 2006), W1.

44. Whitehead, Alfred North, *Adventures of Ideas* (New York: The Free Press, 1967), 98. This was from a talk he gave at HBS in 1931. Whitehead's insights have helped spur my inquiry as to the purpose of business since I first read them in undergraduate school. The insights, in the nature of a "calling," wouldn't let me go and have led/urged me on a life-long pursuit in search for the spiritual foundation and drive of business. I found the working answer in the pursuit – the journey/inquiry is the message.

45. Palmer, Parker, *Let Your Life Speak* (San Francisco: Jossey Bass, 2000). The full quote is: "Vocation is the place where your deep gladness meets the world's deep need." This famous quote is actually by Frederick Buechner, but often quoted by Palmer and others. Palmer goes on to say: "Today I understand vocation quite differently – not as a goal to be achieved but as a gift to be received." I believe this, but we are careful in working with students to steer clear of too religious or mystical concept of "vocation." They find for themselves the real nature of calling as something that won't seem to let them go, something they are drawn to, "something they cannot *not* do." (Hunter Lovins.)

Epilogue – The Path Ahead: What's *Really* Going on…and What Can I Do about It?

1. Whyte, David. *Crossing the Unknown Sea.* New York: Riverhead Books, 2001. P. 3. This is a quote from William Blake.

2. Drucker, op.cit. p. 810.

3. Meadows, Donella, *Thinking in Systems, Draft.* Hartland VT: The Sustainability Institute. P. 178.

4. As an example, "Greatness is not where we stand, but in what direction we are moving." Oliver Wendell Holmes, Jr. "[…] attention is called particularly to the principle of the continuum of inquiry, a principle whose importance, as far as I am aware, only Peirce had previously noted." Dewey, John, *Logic: The Theory of Inquiry*, Carbondale, IL. Southern Illinois University Press: 1991. P. 3. Later, Mary Parker Follett applied this perspective to business, noted in her *Dynamics of Administration*.

5. Meadows, Donella, et. al. *Beyond the Limits*. White River Junction VT. Chelsea Green Publishing Co.1992. This is Meadow's succinct insight stated poetically and memorably.

6. Nocera, Joseph, "Hate to spoil your weekend." New York Times, Jan.6, 2008. P. B1.

7. Calculations done by Presidio School of Management, Sidney Mitchell, for Managerial Marketing class, Fall, 2007. His project is to develop a fish hatchery which would require 1.5 calories to deliver 1 calorie. Still not a sustainable model, but way ahead of meat.

8. Bittman, Mark. *"Rethinking the Meat-Guzzler."* New York Times, Jan. 27, 2008. Week in Review, p. 1.

9. Dewey, John, *Experience and Education*, p. 87.

10. Dewey, John, *ibid.*

Bibliography

Aaker, David. *Building Strong Brands*. New York: The Free Press, 1996.

Addams, Jane. *Democracy and Social Ethics*. London: The MacMillan Company, 1911.

Altgeld, John. *Live Questions*. Chicago: Donohue and Henneberry, 1890.

Angle, Paul M., (ed.). *Created Equal? The Complete Lincoln-Douglas Debates of 1858*. Chicago: University of Chicago Press, 1958.

Robert N. Bellah, et.al. *Habits of the Heart*. Berkeley: University of California Press, 1985.

Bennis, Warren. *On Becoming a Leader*. Cambridge MA: Perseus Books, 2003.

Benyus, Janine M. *Biomimicry: Innovation Inspired by Nature*. New York: HarperCollins Publishers, Inc., 1998.

Bolles, R. N. *What Color is Your Parachute?* Berkley: Ten Speed Press, 2001.

Bragdon, Joseph H. *Profit for Life: How Capitalism Excels*. Cambridge, Mass. Society for Organizational Learning, 2006.

Brower, David, *Let the Mountains Talk, Let the Rivers Run*. (New York: HarperCollins Publishers, 1995).

Bronson, Po. *What Should I do with My Life? ? The True Story of People Who Answered the Ultimate Question* New York: Ballantine Books, 2005.

Buber, Martin. *I and Thou*. New York: A Touchstone Book, 1970.

Buechner, Frederick. *The Sacred Journey*. New York: Harper & Row, 1982.

————. *Wishful Thinking: A Seeker's ABC*. San Francisco: HarperSanFrancisco, 1993.

Carson, Rachael. *Silent Spring*. New York: Houghton Mifflin, 1962.

Cavanagh, F.A. *James & John Stuart Mill on Education*. New York: Harper, 1969.

Cavanagh, G. F. *American Business Values with International Perspectives*. Upper Saddle River, New Jersey: Prentice Hall, 1998.

Colby, Anne, M. Damon, ed., *Bringing in a New Era in Character Development*. Stanford: Hoover Institutional Press, 2002.

Colby, Anne, Jacquelyn James, and Daniel Hart. *Competence and Character Through Life*. Chicago: University of Chicago Press, 1998.

Collins, Jim and William Lazier. *Beyond Entrepreneurship*. Englewood Cliffs, New Jersey:Prentice Hall, 1995.

Collins, Jim and Jerry Porras. *Built to Last*. New York: HarperCollins, 1994.

————. *"Organizational Vision and Visionary Organizations."* California Management Review, Fall 91, Vol 34, Issue 1.

Collins, Jim. *Good to Great*. New York: HarperCollins, 2001.

————. *"Level 5 Leadership."* Harvard Business Review. July 2005.

Cruikshank, Jeffrey L. *A Delicate Experiment: The Harvard Business School 1908-1945*, Boston: Harvard Business School Press, 1987.

Daly, Herman and John Cobb, Jr. *For The Common Good*. Boston: Beacon Press, 1989.

de Tocqueville, Alexis. *Democracy in America*. Garden City, New York: Anchor Press, 1969.

Dewey, John. *Democracy and Education*. New York: The Free Press, 1916.

———. *A Common Faith*. New Haven: Yale University Press, 1955.

———. *Experience and Education*. Old Tappen, New Jersey: Macmillan Publishing Co., Inc., 1963.

———. *How We Think*. Amherst, New York: Prometheus Books, 1991.

———. *Logic: The Theory of Inquiry*. Carbondale, Ill.: Southern Illinois University Press, 1991.

———. *The Middle Works of John Dewey, Volume 14, 1899-1924*. Carbondale Ill.: Southern Illinois University, 1988.

Drucker, Peter. *Management*. New York: Harper Books, 1985.

Eco, Umberto and Thomas A. Sebeok. *The Sign of Three*. Bloomington, Ind: University of Indiana Press, 1983.

Elwood, J. Murray. *Discovering Life's Directions*. Notre Dame, Ind.: Ave Maria Press, 1995.

Fisch, Max H. *Peirce, Semiotic, and Pragmatism*. Bloomington, Ind.: University of Indiana Press, 1986.

———. *Classic American Philosophy*. New York: Fordham Press, 1996.

Fogel, Robert William. *The Fourth Great Awakening*. Chicago: University of Chicago Press, 200.

Fox, Matthew. *One River, Many Wells*. New York: Tarcher Publishing, 2000.

Frederick, William C. *Research in Corporate Social Performance and Policy*. Greenwich, Conn: JAI Press, 1987.

Frings, Manfred S. *The Mind of Max Scheler*. Milwaukee: Marquette University Press, 1997.

————. *Philosophy of Predictions and Capitalism*. Dordrecht: Martinus Nijhoff Publishers, 1987.

Ginger, Ray, *Altgeld's America*. Chicago: Quadrangle Paper Books, 1958.

Grabner, Kenneth E. *Focus Your Day*. Notre Dame, Ind.: Ave Maria Press, 1992.

Gregory, Richard L., ed. *Oxford Companion to the Mind*. Oxford: Oxford University Press, 2004.

Haack, Susan. *Evidence and Inquiry*. Malden, MA: Blackwell Publishers, Inc., 1998.

Haack, Susan and Robert Lane. *Pragmatism, Old and New: Selected Writings*. Amherst, New York: Prometheus Books, 2006.

Hauerwas, Stanley. *Christian Existence Today*. Chapel Hill: University of North Carolina Press, 1988.

————. Alasdair MacIntyre. Ed. *Revisions: Changing Perspectives in Moral Philosophy*. Notre Dame: University of Notre Dame Press, 1983.

Hawken, Paul, Amory Lovins, L. Hunter Lovins. *Natural Capitalism*. New York: Little, Brown and Co., 1999.

Hawken, Paul, *The Ecology of Commerce,* New York: HarperCollins, 1993.

Henderson, Bruce. *Strategy*. Boston: BAT Press, 1985.

Hook, Sidney. *The Metaphysics of Pragmatism*. Amherst, New York: Prometheus Books, 1996.

Hookway, Christopher. *Peirce*. London: Routledge, Inc. 1992.

Hoopes, James, ed. *Peirce on Signs*. Chapel Hill: University of North Carolina Press, 1982.

Hutcheon, Pat Duffy. *Building Character and Culture*. Westport, Conn: Praeger, 1999.

James, William. *The Will to Believe*. Cambridge, Mass: Harvard University Press, 1979.

———. *Writings 1902-1910*. New York: Literary Classics of the United States, Library of America, 1987.

John Paul II. *Centesimus Annus*. Washington D.C.: United States Catholic Conference, 1991.

———. *Laborem Exercens*. Boston: St. Paul Editions, 1981.

Kennedy, Robert F. Jr. *Crimes Against Nature*. New York: HarperCollins Publishers Inc. 2004.

Keynes, John Maynard. *Essays in Persuasion*. London: Macmillan & Co., 1939.

———. *The General Theory of Employment, Interest and Money*. New York: Harcourt Press, 1972.

King, Thomas J. S. J. *Jung's Four and Some Philosophers*. Notre Dame Ind: University of Notre Dame Press, 1999.

Lazier, William. *Beyond Entrepreneurship*. Englewood Cliffs, New Jersey, 1992.

Leo XIII. *The Great Encyclical Letters of Pope Leo XIII* "Condition of the Working Classes." New York: Benziger Brothers, 1903.

Leopold, Aldo. *A Sand County Almanac*. Oxford: Oxford University Press, 1966.

Lonergan, Bernard. *Method in Theology*. Toronto: University of Toronto Press, 1990.

Maccoby, Michael. *The Gamesman: The New Corporate Leaders*. New York: Simon and Schuster, 1977.

MacIntyre, Alasdair. *After Virtue: A Study in Moral Theory*. London: Duckworth, 1985.

———. *Dependent Rational Animals*. Peru, Ill.: Open Court Press, 1999.

McCann, Dennis P. *A Virtuous Life in Business: Stories of Courage and Integrity in the Corporate World*. Lanham, MD: Rowman & Littlefield, 1992.

McDermott, John. J. (ed.). *The Basic Writings of Josiah Royce* Vol. 2. Chicago: University of Chicago Press, 1969.

McDonough William, and Michael Bramguart. *Cradle to Cradle*. New York: North Point Press: 2002.

Meadows, Donella, et. al. *Beyond the Limits*. White River Junction VT. Chelsea Green Publishing Co.1992.

Meadows, Donella. *Thinking in Systems – a primer*. Hartland Vt. Sustainability Institute. Draft. V. 13, 11.9.07.

McGee James J. and André L. Delbecq, Oliver F. Williams, ed. *Business, Religion, & Spirituality,* Notre Dame, Ind.: University of Notre Dame Press, 2003.

Morrill, R. L. *Teaching Values in College*. San Francisco: Jossey-Bass, 1980.

Murdoch, Iris. *Existentialists and Mystics*. London: Chatto & Windus, 1997.

Murray, Elwood J. *Discovering Life's Directions*. Notre Dame, Ind.: Ave Maria Press, 1995.

Nahser, F. Byron. *Learning to Read the Signs*. Boston, Mass.: Butterworth-Heinemann, 1997.

———. *PathFinder Lab Journal: Pragmatic Inquiry*. Chicago, Corporantes, Inc., 2000.

Newman, John Henry. *The Idea of the University*. New York: Longmans, Green & Co., 1893.

Nussbaum, Martha. *Upheavals of Thought*. Cambridge, England: Cambridge University Press, 2001.

Oakeshott, M, T. Fuller (ed). *Michael Oakeshott and Education*. New Haven: Yale University Press, 1972.

Ogilvy, James. *Living Without a Goal*. New York: Currency, Doubleday, 1995.

———. *Many Dimensional Man*. New York: Oxford University Press, 1977.

Oppenheim, Frank M. *Royce's Mature Ethics*. Notre Dame, Ind.: University of Notre Dame Press, 1993,

Orr, David. *Earth in Mind*. Washington, D.C. Island Press, 1994

O'Toole, James. *Creating the Good Life*. Rodale, 2005.

———. *The Executive Compass*. New York: Oxford University Press, 1993.

Palmer, Parker. *The Active Life*. San Francisco: Jossey-Bass, 2000.

———. *Let Your Life Speak*. San Francisco: Jossey Bass, 2000.

Pascal, Roy. *Design and Truth in Autobiography*. Cambridge: Harvard University Press, 1960.

Pascarella, Ernest T. and Patrick T. Terenzini. *How College Affects Students*. San Francisco: Jossey-Bass, 1991.

Pattillo, M. M. Jr. and D. W. Mackenzie. *Church-Sponsored Higher Education in United States.* Washington, D.C.: American Council on Education, 1966.

Peck, Scott. *A World Waiting to be Born: Civility Rediscovered*. New York: Bantam Books, 1994.

Peirce, Charles Sanders. *The Philosophical Writings of Peirce*. Justus
    Buchler. Reprint, New York: Dover Publications, Inc., 1955.

————. James Hoopes, ed. *Peirce on Signs*. Chapel Hill: University
    of North Carolina Press, 1982.

————. *The Essential Peirce*. Vols. 1 and 2. Bloomington, Ind.:
    Indiana University Press, 1992

————. *Pragmatism as a Principle and Method of Right Thinking*.
    Albany: SUNY Press, 1997.

Pfeiffer, Raymond S. and Ralph P. Forsberg. *Ethics on the Job: Cases
    & Strategies*. Belmont, Calif.: Wadsworth Press, 1993.

Progoff, Ira. *The Dynamics of Hope: Perspectives of Process in Anxiety
    and Creativity, Imagery and Dreams*. New York: Dialogue
    House, 1985.

Ray, Michael. *The Highest Goal*. San Francisco: Berrett-Koehler,
    2005.

Ray, Michael and Lorna Catford. *The Path of the Everyday Hero*.
    Forestville, CA: Creative Quest Publications, 1991.

Royce, Josiah. *The Philosophy of Loyalty*. New York: Macmillan Co.,
    1908.

————. *The Problem of Christianity*. Chicago: The University of
    Chicago Press, Ltd., 1968.

————. *The Basic Writings of Josiah Royce*. Chicago: University of
    Chicago Press, 1969.

Ruskin, John. *The Nature of the Gothic*. William Morris, 1892.
    Reprint, Whitefish, Mont.:Kessinger, 2007.

Ryan, Leo V. CSV., F. Byron Nahser, Wojciech W. Gasparski.
    Praxiology and Pragmatism. New Brunswick: Transaction
    Publishers, 2002.

Seigfried, Charlene Haddock. *Pragmatism and Feminism*: Re-weaving the Social Fabric. Chicago: The University of Chicago Press: 1996

————. *Feminist Interpretations of John Dewey.* University Park, PA: The Pennsylvania State University Press: 2002.

Seligman, E. P. *Authentic Happiness: Using the New Positive Psychology to Realize Your Potential for Lasting Fulfillment.* New York: Free Press, 2004.

Senge, Peter M. *The Fifth Discipline.* New York: Doubleday, 1990.

Senge, Peter M., et.al. *The Dance of Change.* New York: A Currency Book, Doubleday, 1999

Slee, Roger. School *Effectiveness for Whom? (Student Outcomes & the Reform of Education).* London: Routledge, 1998.

Smith, Adam, *Wealth of Nations.* New York: Random House, 1937.

————. *Theory of Moral Sentiments.* New York: Prometheus Books, 2000.

TeSelle, Sallie McFague. *Speaking in Parables: A Study in Metaphor and Theology.* Philadelphia: Fortress Press, 1975.

Weber, C. E. *Stories of Virtue in Business.* New York: University Press of America, 1995.

Werhane, Patricia. *Adam Smith and His Legacy for Modern Capitalism.* Oxford, Oxford University Press, 1991.

————. *Moral Imagination and Management Decision-Making.* New York: Oxford University Press, 1999.

West, Cornell. *The American Evasion of Philosophy.* Madison: University of Wisconsin Press, 1989.

Whitehead, Alfred North. *The Aims of Education.* New York: Mentor Books, 1961.

————. *Adventures of Ideas.* New York: Free Press, 1967.

Whyte, David. *Crossing the Unknown Sea.* New York: Riverhead Books, 2001.

Wilder, Amos N. *Early Christian Rhetoric: The Language of Gospel.* Cambridge: Harvard University Press, 1971.

Williams, Oliver R. and John W. Houck. *Full Value: Cases in Christian Ethics.* San Francisco: Harper & Row, Publishers, 1978.

Williams, Oliver R. *Moral Imagination.* South Bend IN: University of Notre Dame Press, 1998.

Wilson, John B., Natale, Samuel M. *Education in Religious Understanding: A Report from the Foundation for Education in Religion and Morality.* New York: University Press of America, 1987.

Wilson, John. *Thinking with Concepts.* Cambridge: Cambridge University Press, 1995.